## Praise for *Too Close to the Falls*

"Richly detailed and absorbing. *Too Close to the Falls* has only one fault. It ends too soon." — *Toronto Life*

"Catherine Gildiner's *Too Close to the Falls* supplies no end of mischief and delight. . . . *Too Close to the Falls* shimmies and shakes with Gildiner's hilarious antics as an inquisitive, competitive school girl. . . . Like a good comedian, Gildiner has a split-second sense of timing. Her writing sparkles on the page and the episodes she recounts have the clarity of ice after a winter storm in Lewiston. This is a memoir that makes the world seem fresh again, and worthwhile." — *Literary Review of Canada*

"Hilarious and moving . . . Gildiner tells her tales with a sharp humour that rarely misses a beat and underscores the dark side of what at first seems a Norman Rockwell existence." — *Publishers Weekly*

"Memorable and skillfully told. . . . Anyone who ever was, or has, a child considered different will enjoy this book." — *Globe and Mail*

"Often dangerous, [Gildiner's] experiences, as related here, are also amusing, charming, and relevant. Highly recommended."
— *Library Journal*

"Gildiner's writing is punctuated by both an eye for the absurd as well as her gentle appreciation of human frailty. Her vivid descriptions and quiet pacing carry the reader along without calling attention to her careful style, a fine example of creative nonfiction at its best." — *Coast Reporter*

"Anyone who appreciates a good story, well told, will find it in *Too Close to the Falls*." — *St. Louis Post-Dispatch*

# Praise for *After the Falls*

"*After the Falls* is a darker book than its predecessor, and a sadder one, but it too contains an abundance of humour and humanity."

— *The Wall Street Journal*

"Downright irresistible . . . Gildiner delves into the bonds of family and love, all in a voice so infectious I'd follow it anywhere." — *Boston Globe*

"Entertaining portrait of a resourceful, smart, offbeat girl and the decade of upheaval in which she came of age." — *Kirkus Reviews*

"On the page as in life, comedy, tragedy, and elegy live right on top of each other, and as with most remarkable memoirs, the straightforward, honest voice and perspective are steady even in the most painful moments." — *Publishers Weekly*

"The author's offbeat attitude, born of her unusual upbringing and wide-ranging experiences, proves to be charming, amusing, and even inspirational." — *Booklist*

"Hard to put down. . . . One quickly feels an empathy and fascination with this frank girl whose radically changing life plunges her back and forth between child and adult several times. It's no surprise she became a clinical psychologist." — *Winnipeg Free Press*

"Gildiner . . . is a born raconteur. Her writing style is lively and conversational; dialogue, which figures strongly, comes easily to her."

— *The Gazette*

# coming ashore

# coming ashore

CATHERINE GILDINER

ECW PRESS

Published by ECW Press
2120 Queen Street East, Suite 200, Toronto, Ontario, Canada M4E 1E2
416-694-3348 / info@ecwpress.com

To the best of her abilities, the author has related experiences, places, people, and organizations from her memories of them. In order to protect the privacy of others, she has, in some instances, changed the names of certain people and details of events and places.

Library and Archives Canada Cataloguing in Publication

Gildiner, Catherine, 1948–, author
Coming ashore: a memoir / Catherine Gildiner.

ISBN 978-1-77041-225-5
Also issued as: 978-1-77090-632-7 (PDF); 978-1-77090-633-4 (epub)

1. Gildiner, Catherine, 1948–. 2. Women psychologists—Ontario—Toronto—Biography.
3. College students—Great Britain—Biography. 4. Teachers—Ohio—Cleveland—Biography.
I. Title.

BF109.G552A3 2014     150.92     C2014-902529-7
C2014-902530-0

Editor for the press: Jennifer Knoch
Cover and text design: Tania Craan
Cover and interior images: Courtesy Catherine Gildiner
Author photo: M.K. Lynde
Printed and bound by Edwards Brothers–Malloy in the United States  5  4  3  2  1

The publication of *Coming Ashore* has been generously supported by the Canada Council for the Arts, which last year invested $157 million to bring the arts to Canadians throughout the country. We acknowledge the support of the Ontario Arts Council (OAC), an agency of the Government of Ontario, which last year funded 1,793 individual artists and 1,076 organizations in 232 communities across Ontario, for a total of $52.1 million. We also acknowledge the financial support of the Government of Canada through the Canada Book Fund for our publishing activities, and the contribution of the Government of Ontario through the Ontario Book Publishing Tax Credit and the Ontario Media Development Corporation.

Canada Council for the Arts / Conseil des Arts du Canada

Canadä

ONTARIO ARTS COUNCIL
CONSEIL DES ARTS DE L'ONTARIO
an Ontario government agency
un organisme du gouvernement de l'Ontario

Ontario
Ontario Media Development Corporation

*To Michael*

*All life is an experiment. The more experiments you make the better.*
*What if they are a little coarse, and you may get your coat soiled or torn?*
*What if you do fail, and get fairly rolled in the dirt once or twice?*
*Up again, you shall never be so afraid of a tumble.*

— Ralph Waldo Emerson

AUTHOR'S NOTE

Thirteen years have passed since I wrote my first memoir, *Too Close to the Falls,* which covered my life from the age of four to thirteen. I grew up in the small town of Lewiston, New York, in the Eisenhower conformist years of the 1950s. I was the only child of older parents and was, as my mother said, "not the child they expected." At age of two I began climbing trees, and by age three I was going solo to the general store and doing imitations of Ed Sullivan for money.

Fortunately in 1948, the year I was born, there were no psychological labels for such singular and on occasion wild behaviour, so I was simply called "busy, bossy and Irish." By the time I was four, my mother appealed to the pediatrician for help, saying that I was "born eccentric." He said I needed to work full-time. Thus, before I went to kindergarten, I began my job in my father's drugstore in Niagara Falls, working from 5:30 in the morning until 10:00 in the evening. I worked with a black delivery car driver named Roy. He drove and I read the map, and together we delivered drugs throughout the Niagara Frontier. It was a wonderful and secure childhood. After all, when you deliver narcotics, people are happy to see you. No one had more fun than Roy and me as we trudged through the snow, dining in taverns and delivering our prescriptions to the rich and poor alike, since illness does not discriminate.

The second volume of my memoirs, *After the Falls*, covers the 1960s. It begins after my life took an abrupt turn at the age of thirteen. Roy left and the drugstore in Niagara Falls was sold because urban planner Robert Moses rerouted traffic out of the downtown core and the inner city died a quick death. My family moved to a Buffalo suburb where I would never again know everyone in town, nor would they know me. Our lives were rerouted again when I was fifteen, when my father was diagnosed with a brain tumour.

While my family was falling apart, the '60s were in full swing and America was also undergoing its own struggles. I was enmeshed in what was then called "heavy" political activity, and eventually the FBI investigated me for my role in "the movement" and my possible (but unfounded) involvement in a murder. Fortunately, I managed to procure a place at Oxford, which not only got me out of Ohio, but also out of the country.

This volume, *Coming Ashore*, focuses on the late '60s and early '70s, chronicling my journey through three countries and from age twenty to twenty-seven. It saddens me to say that this is my last volume because as time goes on, other people enter my life and through no choice of their own get pulled into the narrative. (In this volume, I have used pseudonyms for most of the characters; however, for those who will eventually become my family, and I theirs, I have used their real names.) It is one thing to give an account of my *own* life in the subjective terms that a memoir necessitates, but it is quite another to describe the thoughts and feelings of those who travel with me. I feel I can only report on or interpret my own journey.

Memory is such a tricky phenomenon that I want to take responsibility only for myself. I've accepted that memory is not reality. It does not give an accurate picture of the past, for no one can do that; every memory gets shifted through our unconscious needs. After running family therapy sessions for twenty-five years in my career as a psychologist, I learned that family members do not share *memories*; they share *events*. They have all taken the shards of the past and put them together into either a slightly skewed or drastically different picture. They see and interpret them through their own lens of need. When I did court work as a psychologist, it was interesting to me that people with drastically different interpretations or memories of the same event could all pass a lie-detector test. We all believe our own realities. As Walter

Lippmann said, "We are all captives of the picture in our head — our belief that the world we have experienced is the world that really exists."

I will miss writing my memoirs. I have thoroughly enjoyed sharing my stories with you. I have thousands of letters and emails from readers telling me how much they liked the books. What was more important to me, however, was that so many people said that they shared my experiences, from thinking that the TV was talking to me at age four, to getting expelled from school, to beating up a bully and then paying the price. I was amazed by how many readers also swung on vines over a river. When I admitted to having been a poor judge of character, I received hundreds of letters reminding me that at least I got involved in social change and tried to make a difference. I will miss your support, and thanks for sharing your feelings. I guess we all think that the way we interpret the world is weird, or that we have made mistakes that no one else could ever have made, yet your comments have helped me to see that no matter what I have done or thought, I was never alone.

*Catherine McClure Gildiner*
*January 2014*

# coming ashore

PART 1

# England

CHAPTER 1

# hoisting the sails

*When we get out of the glass bottle of our ego and when we escape
like the squirrels in the cage of our personality and get into the forest
again, we shall shiver with cold and fright. But things will happen to
us so that we don't know ourselves. Cool, unlying life will rush in.*
— D.H. Lawrence

You can get into a bad situation and have no idea how you got
there. I'd done it many times, and I was barely out of my teenage
years. One second you can think you're helping humanity and the
next you have to get out of the country.

I'd been kicked out of grade schools, arrested at age thirteen, caused a three-alarm fire — all the normal things for an American girl. However, when the FBI turned up on my doorstep, flashing their identity cards and letting me know I was implicated in insurrection, drugs and murder, I realized this episode had trumped my other escapades by a long shot.

The FBI coming knocking was just the last in a series of several shocks. The civil rights organization I had been in for years no longer wanted white people in the rank and file, so I was summarily kicked out. Laurie, the black poet I had been involved with, turned out to be married with children. Splits, our mutual friend in the movement, turned out to be a drug dealer and was killed behind a building at the University of Buffalo in what remained an unsolved crime.

On Thanksgiving weekend in 1968, I was home visiting from Ohio University when the two agents arrived at my home in Buffalo, New York. Fortunately my mother was at a master bridge lesson, and my father, who was in his sixth year of a brain tumour, thought that the FBI men were selling Hoover vacuums.

One FBI agent, who had a red flushed face, a houndstooth jacket and must have bathed in English Leather, carried legal-size boxes, which he plopped onto the kitchen table, then began leafing through their contents. Each letter I'd written to the poet was individually wrapped and sealed in a plastic cover. There were also mementos of our time together that Laurie must have kept such as playbills, which were carefully inscribed with the date and notes like *cool spring evening — magical*. I saw the beer coasters on which I'd written rhyming couplets when we were in bars. There was the tiny felt zebra I'd bought him when I was eighteen — I'd written *interracial dating* on its tag. I was surprised he'd saved it all.

Each of these bags contained a cherished memory for me. There was a pile of bagged, broken dreams on my table. I looked at them bewildered. I wanted to light them as kindling and have a bonfire in honour of my spectacular bad judgment. The profoundly sad part of it was I never saw the bad side of him so I couldn't use it to hate him. All I could do was sit down beside the mountain of delusion in my kitchen and watch the FBI set up a recording machine that would chronicle my idiocy on a kelly-green record for posterity.

The perspiring FBI man said in a befuddled tone, "All these letters are about books or poems or details of voters' registration. Did you have any idea what these guys were up to?" The FBI side-kick had a good line that pretty well summed up my life to date: "You can either see the best in everyone or else you can miss the elephant in the room." I hoped for the former but suspected it was the latter.

When I told Leora, my best friend since junior high school, that the FBI had just turned up on my doorstep, she suggested that I get out of town, pointing out that when there are murders and drugs there are trials. I wouldn't be leaving much behind: I was an English major along with thousands of the other hapless hayseeds planted at Ohio University and longing to be harvested. I had no idea how I'd become marooned in the breadbasket of America surrounded by people who had the linguistic parlance of Gomer Pyle. Leora reminded me that in my political zeal, or more likely my years of attachment to the wrong male, I had turned down a great opportunity. The previous year I had been offered a spot at Oxford. I wonder how many women turn down stellar offers for a man? Probably more than there are hayseeds in Ohio.

This Oxford opportunity was, appropriately for the '60s, drug related. I had too many essays to write in too short a time, so I did something I'd never done before — I bought a green pill for five dollars from a girl in my dormitory who had majored in fashion merchandising. She, in turn, had bought the pills from a clerk who worked in accessories at May Department Store in Cleveland. The pill, a shimmering accessory, was guaranteed to keep me awake to write a paper on Milton's *Paradise Lost*.

After ingesting this kick-ass army-green pellet of inspiration, I locked myself in my room for two days. During that time I began to believe that I was the serpent in *Paradise Lost* and that I had been unfairly demonized for merely delivering a message from God to Adam and Eve in the Garden of Eden. (I got my five dollars' worth on that one.) Instead of writing the paper, in a fit of hallucinatory self-righteousness I wrote a lengthy poem that answered God in the same rhyme that Milton used in his twelve books of *Paradise Lost*. I called it "Book Thirteen." Once the pill wore off, I shed my serpentine skin, realizing it had been a psycho-pharmaceutically induced delusion. However, I handed in the paper anyway since I was going home for spring break.

Ohio had buckets of football money and could afford to pluck big-name academics from the top schools, and my professor was a famous poetry critic who was on leave from Oxford. He was beguiled by "Book Thirteen," the only poem I'd ever written before or since, and sponsored me to go to Oxford as a "promising poetry student." I had declined his offer at the time, thinking that I was involved with the love of my life and in changing the world, both of which were far more delusional than believing I was a snake in the Garden of Eden.

The FBI visit forced me to hoist my sails, and Leora set my direction. I was hoping to catch the trade winds for England. It was time to leave the country quickly and I needed to revisit the Oxford offer. This time I'd grab the apple, call the professor and tell him I'd changed my mind.

CHAPTER 2

# special delivery

*'Twas Mulga Bill, from Eaglehawk, that caught the cycling craze;*
*He turned away the good old horse that served him many days;*
*He dressed himself in cycling clothes, resplendent to be seen;*
*He hurried off to town and bought a shining new machine;*
*And as he wheeled it through the door, with air of lordly pride,*
*The grinning shop assistant said, "Excuse me, can you ride?"*
— Banjo Paterson, "Mulga Bill's Bicycle"

The following January, as my London-bound plane prepared to taxi

out of one of the Buffalo airport's two icy runways, I caught a last

glimpse of my parents standing at the fence, waving to their only

child as she was about to leave them. My father waved his denuded

head and his purple, I.V.-ravaged hand in my direction. When

I watched him more carefully, I realized he was waving to all the planes, wishing all the departures a good flight. Even as his brain was eaten away by cancer and he slowly lost his mind, he never lost his cheerfulness, his cordiality or his egalitarianism.

Next to him stood my pretty mother, holding his hand as if he were a child who might run onto the icy tarmac at any second. As always, she dressed for the airport as though she were travelling or being met by foreign dignitaries when she disembarked. In fact, she was being met by no one. She had to return to her dreary Buffalo bungalow, with a man who would die soon, leaving her a penniless widow. (His six years of illness had devoured their savings faster than the cancer had ravaged his brain.) She had to manage a six-foot-tall man who had lost his mind but not his ability to walk and talk. He forgot everything that was said to him within seconds of it being uttered. Once the cancer had chewed up his short-term memory, it started on his long-term. When I left for England, he knew who I was; but when I returned home, he thought I was a nurse. He did retain a memory that he'd had a daughter at one time and he told me about her when I went to see him. He said, "You never met Cathy? She was a real pip." *A real pip.* His mind was now stuck in the '50s, our family's heyday, the Eisenhower years when he owned the drugstore in Niagara Falls.

The plane took off, and I turned my attention to Professor Clifford Beech's note on white stationery with royal blue lettering that said *Trinity College, Oxford*:

*Dear Miss McClure,*
    *I would find it most rewarding to act as your tutor and*
    *would be gratified if you would join me at high table the*

*night of your arrival. You may have some difficulty locating
me upon the dais. I could tell you that I am desiccated and
doddering; however, I fear that would not distinguish me
from the other members of our humble establishment. Please
inform the Barson, our earthy gatekeeper, who hopefully has
not barred our paradise with flaming swords, to ring me when
you've arrived. Although we are far from a classless society,
I fear the Barson may have trouble detecting the accent of a
Sauropsida. However, I am sure he will have no trouble with
your forked tongue and undulating gait.*

*The Son of Morn in weary Night's decline,*
*Clifford Beech*

Leora thought it was hilarious that I could transfer to Oxford based on a one-paragraph letter. We figured when a guy was famous and he took you on, no one would say boo. Of course, little did Professor Beech know that I would never again write one more word of poetry in my life — not even a couplet. I lost my poetic licence when my green pill wore off.

Hours later, as the plane flew over England, I began to feel lighter. I hadn't realized how much I'd been shouldering. Out of the plane's small window, I saw the orderly fields with their straight furrows. I longed for the stability that their tidy rows promised. The countryside lay like a quilt made of myriad shades of taupe in different fabrics and textures. Occasionally there was a row of evergreens standing like soldiers on the march guarding their furrowed fields. I was soothed by the order and I felt the nascent anglophile that lived within me kicking to get out.

While we circled for a landing at Heathrow, it was slowly

sinking in that I no longer had to endure the stigma of having an interracial relationship, which would have been hard enough in New York City but was even more ostracizing on the border of West Virginia in Ohio, where I'd been marooned for two years. I wouldn't be shunned anymore, nor would I have to live with the constant fear of reprisal. I was no longer in charge of political change. I no longer had to worry about the grinding details of the American civil rights fight; I no longer had to organize the voter lists, nor canvass to get new signatures while still getting my schoolwork done and maintaining an A average. I could take my first break from the harried home front, where I'd been in charge of my father's illness from my early teenage years. It was no longer my job to make sure my father did not drive or try to with-draw funds from an already empty bank account. I didn't have to wrestle the car keys away from him; I could take a breather. When family, relationship and sanity crumble, you need to hold onto something even if it's the image of straight rows of evergreens.

Now all I had to worry about was that Oxford thought they were getting an inspired poet. They were really getting a rather ordinary, uninspired tall blond from Buffalo who'd taken a pill from the clerk at May's accessory counter and been creative for a day.

—

On my way to Oxford, the train porter shook his head and told me to prepare for cold weather and a big snow when I got there. I didn't find it cold, snowy or windy by Buffalo standards; in fact it was downright balmy. In terms of snow, there was only a slight dusting of what looked like icing sugar on some of the roofs.

The beauty of the town bowled me over. I immediately fell in love with not only the spires of the university but the small town that was packed with Dickensian characters, old bookshops and tobacconists. It reminded me of simpler times in historic Lewiston. There were the High and the Broad Streets and a few other narrow, winding roads and that was it. I had never seen a bookstore before other than one for university textbooks, but England was full of new and used bookshops with real lit fireplaces and stationery shops with rows of fountain pens where I could poke around for hours.

Trinity College, or "Trins" as even I would come to call it, was surrounded by a high stone wall, and an immense iron gate that had a guardhouse manned by a white-haired man. He had red spidery veins on his plump face and, as they say in England, "high colour." I had no idea, and still don't know, if all men who manned the guardhouses of all the thirty-eight colleges were called "Barsons" or if this particular man's name was Barson. If the latter was true, then I never understood why he was called *the* Barson in the letter from Professor Beech. I was never called *the* McClure. When I said I was looking for the Barson, he took his pipe out of his mouth and I noticed his teeth, which were the yellow-orange of a Tibetan monk's robe. They had become moulded around his pipe, leaving a pipe-gap when he took it out to speak. Looking over the top of his half spectacles, he said, "I am he."

I explained that I needed a key. He looked at me as though I were asking for keys to the Crown Jewels in the Tower of London and said whatever gentleman I was visiting could be called to the gate, "presuming we had a prior arrangement." I said I wasn't visiting anyone. Before I could explain myself, he said with the same tone you would use to inquire if I was carrying the bubonic plague, "So, you are a tourist?"

"No. I am going to be a student here."

"We have only men's rooms here at the moment, my dear."

"A professor has left a key for me and I believe you should have a letter about my room assignment. I was told you would escort me to my new room."

"Rooms," he corrected me. "*I* would escort you? My dear, my dear, what a plethora of misinformation."

"Okay," I said, "*rooms* and *keys*. How's that?"

"A key left by whom?" He asked "by whom" with the intonation of the caterpillar who blew smoke rings in *Alice's Adventures in Wonderland.*

"Professor Beech."

"Oh. I see," he said, as if I'd mentioned God.

"My name is Catherine McClure."

He began bustling around until he found an envelope. "Ah, C. McClure," he said, and then he called someone and told them to come and help with the trunk I'd left on the sidewalk. He immediately changed his tune and said, "Yes, yes, Miss McClure. I'm afraid we thought you were Mr. McClure, an error I would not have made in person."

"No problem, my dear," I said.

"Your scout will be with you momentarily."

*My scout?* How far away was this place? Did I need a scout to get there? I mean, wasn't Deerslayer or Davy Crockett a scout? It didn't look all that perilous on the Trinity green to me. Maybe they were giving me a cabin in the woods or something. Maybe all Americans got paired with scouts and the English got footmen.

A tall, gaunt man with a Hapsburg chin who was about my age appeared in a white starched linen coat, black trousers and plastic

pointed shoes. Looking flustered as he rushed into the little gatehouse, he said, "Yes, Barson?"

"Reggie, this young lady is to have the rooms of the recently
departed Mr. Hampshire. I presume you have prepared them for
her."

"Ye' sir," he said through teeth that were green and black along
the edges. "Only I thought that she was . . ."

"You needn't share your every thought with us, Reggie."

The flushed scout said, "Well? What about the —"

"Reggie, surely you have seen a young lady before. The details
will fall into place. So without further ado . . ." He flicked his wrist
twice toward the door.

There was very little point in asking Reggie anything because I
couldn't understand a word he said.

I was led to a beautiful courtyard surrounded by ancient stone
buildings. On the east wing of the quadrangle was my staircase.
Everyone lived off a staircase — I mean literally. There was a winding staircase with doors that opened right off the edge of a riser.
The stairs were painted a dull green and each step was concave in
the middle. You could see how many thousands of scholars over
centuries had trod those stairs and shared those rooms. The stairs
sagged with the weight of history and the greater weight of the
expectations of all who had sent them there. The droop was less
pronounced at the top of my staircase where I was housed, as it
was a dead end.

My rooms were baronial. I entered a large wood-panelled sitting room, which contained a monumental Ben Franklin desk, a
divan and two large sitting chairs. A blood-red oriental carpet was
laid in the middle of the wide plank floor. There were two huge

leaded casement windows that shared a detachable iron crank you screwed in whenever you wanted to wind them open. Each had deep window wells with seats done in petit point to match the antique chair coverings. Both windows looked over the assorted snow-dusted roofs and spires of Balliol, the next college over. The ceilings were sixteen feet high and the gilt-framed paintings were original oils in desperate need of restoration. They had darkened over the years as disintegrating scholars had left an oily dust.

My adjoining bedroom had what Reggie told me was a six-teenth-century sleigh bed and small table and sink. It also had a great reading chair and ottoman in ancient cracked black leather with horsehair stuffing.

Reggie said that washing facilities were a bit difficult since there was only one other woman at the college, a visiting scholar like myself. She had been at Oxford for over a year already. He said she was from *New England*. He then smiled, finding the phrase terribly amusing.

"Oh, where in New England?" I asked.

"In America," he said as though that were sufficient information. "Miss Mitchell lives four doors down the staircase. The washing facility for women, the only one at the college, is on the ground floor across the quadrangle in a back building that is still under construction."

"I've just wound up five flights. Now I have to wind down and cross the long quadrangle and find some building behind the spires every time I want to go to the bathroom?"

"I'm afraid it is frightfully cold in the stairwells this time of year, so you will need your woolies to make the trek." In truth there was not much difference between the temperature outside and the temperature in my room. I'd need "my woolies" just to sit at my desk. In all the time I was there, I never figured out what was with the English and the heat. They just didn't get that there was supposed to be a temperature difference between the outside and the inside. (They *never* got it. In 2013, 31,000 people froze to death in England.) My most vivid memory of England is of being cold and not being able to warm up.

Reggie looked at my foldout map and showed me how to get to my classes. He advised me to rent a bike to get to Magdalen College as it was a bit of a hike. He said he'd ring the bike rental and tell them I would be coming. I couldn't help but note that Reggie was taking special attention to orient me. "Wow, you've been a great help. It's awfully kind of you."

He looked embarrassed and confused as he stammered, "I'm just doing me job."

"Do you get a lot of Americans here?"

"No. We get the occasional scholar." He didn't volunteer any information but later, when I asked him about his role as scout, he told me he brought in the morning tea, the mail and then a high tea in the afternoon. He tidied the room and made the bed. In between those times, he worked as a waiter in the dining hall at all three meals. He said, "The entire southeast stairway is mine. I'm a third-generation scout. Me brother and father both work at Balliol."

I was surprised that Reggie was so proud of maintaining a family position that was actually quite menial. In America, it would be strange for someone to say they had the same job as their father unless they had somehow risen up the ladder. He took a great deal of pride in his work and was quite discrete since he brought my tea and mail to me in the morning when I was in bed. Once I began to understand his dialect, I engaged him in conversation to get the lay of the land. One of the things I learned was that Brits tell you very little. They are quite perfunctory. I noticed when Reggie began to explain certain things, the Barson shut him up, saying it was unnecessary. Chat was "too familiar." Yet the scout really knew everything that went on. Reggie, like almost everyone else I met at the college, described people in some way through their social rank. When I asked who lived in my staircase, he said, "Your closest neighbour to the south off the stairway is Mr. Aaronson."

"What's he like?" I asked, as Reggie unlocked my cupboards for me.

"Scholarship student. Jew from Birmingham." I was shocked to hear someone's religion described in their introduction. "Actually he's quite a taciturn chap — always reading about some lugubrious topic if you ask me." Reggie's vocabulary, like that of other working class people in England that I encountered, was far above that of most Ph.D.'s in America.

"So tell me about everyone in my stairwell. I need the scoop, being the new girl on the block." As he walked about throwing open the curtains and laying the day's paper on my desk he said, "There is Mr. Hunter-Parsons. He's most agreeable. Got a first in sixteenth century, I believe. Most well liked by everyone and very commanding in his speech. He is sixth generation in the same rooms at Trinity."

"You're kidding."

"No. His family has bequeathed most of the furnishings for the southeast quadrangle over time. They donated a pew to the chapel in the 1600s."

"God. What does his father do, own a furniture store?"

"Oh, I have no idea. I've never thought to ask," he said as though I'd asked about his sex life. That was the second lesson I was to learn. Never ask what anyone does. You can ask who they *are* but never what they *do*. It is terribly bad form and so dreadfully American. (I was shocked to learn that the term *bad form* and *American* could be synonyms in certain circles.)

If you are upper class, it is assumed you don't have to do too much. To even ask the question is nosy, terribly middle class and, most importantly, just not done. Yet these details dribble out over time, because when I left I knew the family histories of everyone. I learned them through the English method of osmosis. Accent reveals everything and I was initially unable to detect the differences. I assumed the dialects were regional, but they were far more than that to the trained British ear. The way someone said "how do you do" told anyone present his station in life and whether he was from old or new wealth and, as an adjunct, where he was from. After the Englishman says "hello," he knows all he needs to peg you in the elaborate social hierarchy.

"Then there is Margaret-Ann Mitchell, our other American." After much inquiry on my part he continued. "She is a true scholar. She rarely ventures out and studies so much the pro-vice-chancellor had to tell her she must go to meals."

"She is going to be my only female company. What is she like?"

"Oh she is very lady-like, isn't she? Keeps to herself — never a spectacle or any kind of trouble."

I guessed that was what lady-like meant.

"Then there is Mr. Andover. He went to Eton with Mr. Hunter-Parsons. They've been mates since grammar." As he took the curtains that reeked of cigar smoke down to clean them, he asked me, "Have you ever heard of the singer Donovan?"

"Mellow yellow," I sang off-tune.

"Yes. He was here a few weeks ago playing his guitar in Mr. Hunter-Parsons' room with some friends. We have quite the block," he added proudly.

"It's rather common for the staircase to dine together at one long table. I understand you're to meet Professor Beech this evening at high table."

"Right."

"Have you anything in need of immediate pressing for the occasion?"

"I only brought one dress. Am I supposed to wear it?"

"I believe he is getting an award and you are his student. People wear their gowns to class and to meals; however, high table usually requires a wee bit more."

A gown like the kind you wear for the senior prom? Did he mean wear an evening gown — to class? "I didn't bring any gowns," I said. "Is there a formal dress shop in town?"

"I have taken the liberty of stocking some for you." Gowns were bad enough, but if I had to wear them I sure as hell didn't want Reggie picking them. He opened the wormwood closet and there hung a row of black robes. It looked like a church vestry on funeral day. I pulled one out. It was floor length with huge wing-like sleeves — the kind of thing Scrooge McDuck would wear to bed. As I slid the hangers back and forth, I noticed one gown had a phone number written on the inner sleeve while another had a whole set of tiny mathematical equations written on the inside of the hem in a pale grey ink.

I also had to wear a strange little flat hat with a tassel. I eventually found that the tassel came in different colours to denote your college, year and whether you got a first or something so degrading that you would never want to wear on your hat. I'd rather wear Hester Prynne's scarlet A than that thing. Believe it or not, the side on which you wore your tassel gave some vital information about where you stood in the labyrinthine pecking order of English society. Leave it to the English to fit all that social stratification on a cap.

"Don't you just wear this kind of thing for graduation?" I asked, holding up the gown.

He pointed out the window and I saw men trooping across the quad in flowing, floor-length black robes with pleated drop sleeves. I was reminded of one of my favourite fairytales, *The Twelve Brothers*. The only sister in the family picks a flower and the brothers turn into ravens. Of course, it was the sister's fault for picking the flower. (The authors weren't called Grimm for nothing.) There was one illustration that always fascinated me, where the brothers were transforming from men into ravens. Although they had developed large ebony wings and back feathers, they still had human heads and feet. These men below in the quadrangle looked ominously mid-raven to me, especially when their capes and sleeves billowed in the wind. This was my first hint of how frightening these men could become.

—⁀—

That evening as I got ready for my first social outing in England, I wondered what a high table dinner was — a table on stilts? I wore my only dress, a tie-dyed orange, red and turquoise mini with a halter top that tied at the back of my neck. It wasn't right for January at Oxford (or actually anytime at Oxford) but how was I supposed to know how cold it was *inside*? I figured it was no big deal to wear a dress that left me overexposed since I had to wear the black gown on top anyway. I also wore red patent-leather shoes with red, white and blue-checkered laces. They looked like old-fashioned tap shoes from *42nd Street* except they had enormous platform heels.

Teetering in my heels, I clomped down the narrow winding stairs in my mini-dress and much-too-large robe that dragged on the ground like a wedding train in mourning. Because the stairwell was more like an educational silo than a normal staircase, the sound of my slapping shoes was magnified by the echo.

I walked down the stairs and doors swung open as I passed them. The first guy to pop his head out was Marcus Aaronson. He was short, slight and had brown curly hair that fell in unruly corkscrews on either side of his centre part. He wore a maroon sweater and a Trinity tie. He scowled, saying, "Oh I thought I heard a blacksmith's hammer," and then abruptly closed his door.

As I wound down to another floor, a guy confidently strolled out of his rooms into the narrow staircase. He looked quite dapper, in a calculatedly casual sort of way, in a crumpled wool sports jacket and Oxford cloth white shirt, baggy black khakis, and black leather boots. I later learned this was the consciously dishevelled look that so many English graduate students affect while still technically following the dress code called *subfusc*. (*Subfusc* is Latin for dark/dusky colour. I had to go out and buy all black skirts and black tights. With my yellow hair, I looked like a pencil in mourning.) He was slightly built but tall and had fashionably shaggy blond wavy hair, royal blue eyes and an aquiline nose. He looked a bit like Virginia Woolf on steroids, but then again so did many of the men I'd seen from my window. He screamed landed-gentry-with-edge. I was sure that he was the man called Clive Hunter-Parsons who Reggie said was so universally admired.

"Hark," he said, cupping his hand to his mouth and addressing the man who lived on the floor, "time's horses gallop down the lessening hill." I was indeed clomping along, and as the shoes flipped off my narrow heel when I walked, they made a second echoing bang.

The guy from one flight down yelled up to where we stood, "I feared it was a herd of wild Trojan horses, but fortunately we are not at war."

"Ah," the blond boy added, "we can rest at ease. It is only the descent of the fair sex, so to speak." I grabbed the railing as the spiral turned and I teetered against the wall, silencing my aston-ishingly loud foot clatter. I did manage to remember a line from Milton and, leaning against the wall to steady myself, said, "No war or battle's sound, / was heard the world around."

The blond gave me the next line: "Nothing but a battle lost can be half so melancholy as a battle won."

Well, I was out of Ohio now. That was for sure.

I finally made it to the first floor and out crawled the only dou-ble X chromosome I'd yet to see, presumably the New Englander, Margaret-Ann Mitchell. She wore one of those Laura Ashley sack-cloth dresses, drawn in by a a thick black hand-knit sweater and flat boots that looked like they were made by some local New England hippie turned leather worker. Her long, straight strawberry-blond hair was parted in the middle and drooped around her freckled face. Her black gown was also dragging on the ground. She made eye contact with me in the stairwell and blushed to the point that her face matched her hair. "Excuse me," she mumbled and ran off toward the dining room, avoiding any further eye contact.

While I stood leaning against the curved wall of the staircase, trying to get my bearings and to remember where the dining hall was located, the blond guy passed me, accompanied by a dark-haired guy who had also exited his rooms in search of the heifer who was plodding down his stairwell. The blond, whose waves bounced when he moved, carefully pushed open the door for me and said, "Welcome to stairwell number seven. I am Clive Hunter-Parsons and this less-esteemed colleague is Peter Andover."

"I am Helen of Troy," I said, teetering on my shiny red toes.

"Then you won't mind our Spartan conditions," said Peter, the plainer guy who lived below the handsome guy named Clive. Peter could have been considered handsome as well if he had not been standing next to the imposingly tall, willowy Clive. While Clive looked relaxed and perpetually amused, Peter looked earnest, like the men who have their pictures in *The Economist*.

"Reggie led me to believe we might eat together — as a stairwell," I said lamely, hoping they would invite me.

"Not tonight, Helen. We understand you are placed at the high table," Peter said.

"Launching a thousand forks," I added.

Clive, Peter and I walked into the magnificent dining hall with coffered ceilings and walls covered with dour portraits of famous alumni. I always sat under Sir John Willes, Chief Justice of Common Pleas, 1737. All the long, dark tables were lined up in solemn rows with benches. The room actually resembled the one on TV that Robin Hood used to swing through when he'd surprised the Sheriff of Nottingham at mealtime. One huge table at the far end of the room was perpendicular to the rest and was placed on a separate dais a few steps up from the others. You didn't have to be Queen Elizabeth to figure it was the high table. It was filled with white-haired men, some of whom looked older than any professor I'd ever seen, including all those who had crawled up to emeritus status.

Clive tapped my shoulder, saying, "You don't wear gowns at high table."

Uh-oh. I'd counted on this robe to cover my halter-top mini. Remembering the Mary Kay Cosmetic School saying, "Fake it till you make it," I threw the black gown on the chair by the door, strode up to the high table and asked, "Is one of you Professor Beech?"

"I beg your pardon?" one old codger said.

Another smiled and said, "May I offer you a seat." This guy was at least ninety and could have been a portrait on the wall. He could barely stand up to shake my hand. His shirt looked like it had been thrown in the wash with black socks, taken out while wet and then had wrinkles ironed into it. He had cut himself shaving and had a little piece of ragged cloth covering the bloody nick on his scrawny gullet.

We were interrupted by the approach of a fat man with strange lower teeth that actually poked out of his mouth and rested on his upper lip when his mouth was closed. "Good evening. Miss McClure, I presume."

"Professor Beech?"

"Ah, welcome to the adamantine island chained to the shifting bank of the Channel. I see you met our esteemed poet and guest of honour this evening? You've been placed next to him for mutual dining pleasure."

While I nodded assent, the esteemed poet said, "Ye—es." I had never heard the word *yes* spoken in two syllables. Professor Beech scuttled (as fast as a man whose silhouette matched that of Alfred Hitchcock could scuttle) back to his end of the table, saying we would meet in "his rooms" tomorrow afternoon. That sounded kind of creepy to me.

As I sat down next to the esteemed poet, I blathered, "Sorry I'm late. That stairwell is a challenge in these shoes."

"Winding ancient stair; Set your entire mind upon the steep ascent," the esteemed poet said. By this point I was too embarrassed to ask his name. Everyone else seemed to know him.

"*Hey* Yeats." Thank God I'd recognized him. "I love that guy."

"As do I."

"You know him too?" I asked.

"I knew him quite well."

"Me too."

"He gave me much help in dark times," said the esteemed poet.

"Oh. You knew him as in knew the *man* not just the *poetry*."

"If one ever knows another."

"Wow!" Wanting to keep the conversation going, I added my own brush with celebrity. "I knew Marilyn Monroe."

He turned and looked at me with true interest for the first time. "Do tell."

I can spin a yarn for hours, so I told him the full version of when Roy and I delivered Nembutal to Marilyn Monroe while she was filming *Niagara* in the 1950s. I told how she answered the door in a slip and bra and had chipped nail polish.

26

"I *say*," he said. "Do please press on."

Neither of us noticed that the room was quiet and when we finally looked up we met hundreds of eyes looking expectantly at us. The esteemed poet had been introduced to say grace but neither of us had heard.

He stood up really slowly, favouring one leg, and said by way of apology, "The peril of discussing Yeats is that all else recedes."

He was great on his feet, never used a note and spoke in a definitive, yet warm voice for five or ten minutes. He said grace in Latin and in English and then said that tonight might be a perfect night to quote Yeats. He said you can be assured of a poet's genius when he always has a line or two that expresses exactly your sentiments at the present moment. He turned to me and said,

> God be praised for woman
> That gives up all her mind,
> A man may find in no man
> A friendship of her kind
> That covers all he has brought
> As with her flesh and bone . . .

He recited the whole poem and smiled at me as he sat down.

When dinner was over, I helped the doddering poet down the stairs, and while patting my hand, he again quoted Yeats: "And what rough beast, its hour come round at last / Slouches toward Bethlehem to be born."

To this day I don't know his name.

I shake my head now thinking of what the Barson called "my plethora of errors" upon arrival. The seat next to the guest of honour was saved for Professor Beech, who'd been one of the esteemed poet's students, and I had blundered into it. My outfit combined with my Marilyn Monroe vignette was all so wildly inappropriate. Yet no one complained or embarrassed me. In truth, my behaviour in England barely improved over time.

The next morning, after donning half of the clothes I'd brought with me just to eat breakfast, I went to "let" my bicycle in some godforsaken back alley that had no name. Reggie referred to it as "off the map," under the first bridge I would meet after taking two right turns not including the right I took out of the college. Reggie said to go past the bridge, then double back and go under the bridge and there between the river and the bridge, I'd find the shop. As strange as it seemed, there was indeed a bike lean-to under the bridge. The proprietor had a crooked back, presumably from crouching under the bridge for most of his life. As he handed me over an old, rickety bike, I noticed the lifelines in his hands were grey as though his skin had been tattooed with grease. I rented the bike for the year; I asked if it came with a lock. He replied in a thick Scottish accent that nothing in Oxford had been stolen as far as he was aware. He added in his thick Highland Burr, "You'll have to go to the United States of America to get your bike stolen." I asked if there was a light. He groused that it was a generator light, which worked when I pedaled. "If you learn how to work, light will be shed, now won't it?"

He began to explain how the bike worked. I rolled my eyes and told him that I'd been riding a bike all my life and knew how to do it. He said that Americans, "who think they've invented the wheel," often have a problem with English brakes. I rode away while he was still going on because he wouldn't stop, and besides

I couldn't understand what he was saying. I cycled over the top of the bridge and waved gaily to the old Glaswegian troll under it. He just shook his head as he wiped some oil off on his pants, shiny with layers of accumulated toil.

I loved physical activity and bike riding was the best since it combined exercise with transportation. In Oxford, almost everyone rode a bike no matter if you were twenty or eighty. The university was made up of different colleges that were spread around the town and some were quite far apart. Although you were housed at a certain college, you could have courses at other colleges so everyone had to cycle. Little old women in thick Marks and Spencer flesh-coloured tights rode a bike to the shops. Men with cigarettes perched on their lower lips drove along in dress trousers and tweed jackets and Dubliner wool hats.

There is nothing more gorgeous than an English morning. The sunlight sparkled off the icy gauze of early morning dew on the crunchy greens. Everything was fresh and clear and the colours seemed supersaturated. A bracing English morning could wash away all sins, no matter how mortal, from the night before. The colleges all had manicured lawns and the shops looked Victorian, with many small rooms lined in wood — just as I had imagined. I sped along the road, going faster and faster. I decided to go to the post office, which I had seen right across from the Trinity College gate, and send my parents a postcard to let them know I'd arrived safely. Actually my mother had never asked me to do this, but I continued the form as though we were a normal family instead of one where my addled father thought J. Edgar Hoover was a vacuum and that President Johnson said no Irish Catholics could drive until the war in Vietnam was over.

At the age of twenty, I still loved the rush of speed. I was now going at full tilt, not slowing down for the one-room post office. I was speeding up, planning my stunning dismount, when at the last second I pressed back on my pedals with all my might. But the bike didn't stop. It didn't even slow down. There were no brakes, so the pedals just spun backwards. Oh my God, the bike mechanic had said something about English brakes. Where the hell were they?

I hit the post-office window at full velocity and flew right through it, shattering the glass. I went airborne past the stamp line-up and, with a loud thud, came to an abrupt landing against the old mahogany counter. I was bleeding, but I did manage to stand. The postal employee looked at me dripping in blood and said, "Special delivery?" The postmaster came out from the mail-room and quipped, "Americans always want air mail, I'm afraid."

One old woman whispered to another in the line-up. "American, I'll wager, cutting in line."

The other replied, "They're taught that at home."

No one suggested calling an ambulance or a doctor. They acted as though I'd decided to go through the window as opposed to using the door just to save time. The postmaster cleaned my arm off with an old cloth used for dampening stamps. Fortunately it was mostly my coat that was ripped to shreds. There was surprisingly little tissue damage other than a long brush burn on the side of my face. I had a gash on the top of my head, but my hair caught the blood from that. They gave me a "plaster" from a rusty first aid box and that was it. Later, when I went to the doctor in London, he looked at the scar on my head and said, "That could have used a stitch or two — but never mind."

A local bobby arrived with a legal-size sheaf of paper in his hand and said to me, "In a bit of rush, were we?"

"I didn't realize the brakes were on the handlebars."

"Who do you think is going to remunerate the offended party for the window, what with the emergency glass service required and all?"

"Send me the bill at Trinity College."

"You at the college, then?" he inquired, trying to hide his incredulity.

"Yes." My head was spinning and I was feeling nauseous from the bang on my skull.

The two women shook their heads. What was the world coming to if Oxford could let in not only girls, but *American* girls who drove through windows?

"Scholarship student?" asked the clerk who was now sweeping up the glass.

"Yes — well, sort of — partly. Is that pertinent information?" I asked, now seeing double and leaning on the counter.

"Going to be a pretty penny, I can tell you that."

—

By noon everyone had heard about my airmail delivery. Not one person said anything like, "Oh my God, you went through the post-office window on your first day at Oxford?" or "What an idiot," or "How amazing," or "How hilarious," or "Are you all right?" Everyone commented on it but only obliquely. At lunch Clive said, "You are aware that airmail requires a surcharge."

"I didn't go airmail but airborne, which is far more expensive," I retorted.

"Ah, but if you are airborne in a postal outlet, are you airmail?"

Marcus asked.

"A question for Wittgenstein," Peter added.

That afternoon, my tutorial included only one bruised American girl with Professor Beech in his luxurious study. When he saw me, he said absolutely nothing about my injuries. He ignored my shut eye, my bruising and my swollen face. He never alluded to my cranium, swollen to a point on the top, which made me resemble a recent forceps delivery. He proceeded to discuss Coleridge.

Several years later, when I went through my mother's belongings after she died, I found my letter to her describing the post-office caper. My mother loved that letter. She said she opened it in the brain tumour radiation waiting room and burst out laughing. To prevent herself from looking crazy, she read it to the waiting room and they howled too. It really made me feel good that so many people enjoyed the outing. My mother said that my father loved the story as well, and when she thought he might be feeling a bit down she would read him the letter. One of the great things about having no memory is something funny can amuse you again and again. My mother said no matter what the window cost it was worth it.

I did finally receive a bill that amounted to two hundred American dollars, which was a fair chunk of change in the 1960s. When I rode up to the post office to pay the bill, everyone stood back. I approached the postmaster, who said, "It's all taken care of, Miss."

"Who paid for it?" I asked.

"Compliments of the Queen in the year of the Prince's investiture."

"That was nice of her given how busy she must be," I said.

When I got back to dinner, the two-hundred-dollar cheque in my hand, Clive recited:

> This is the Night Mail crossing the Border,
> Bringing the cheque and the postal order,
> Letters for the rich, letters for the poor,
> The shop at the corner, the girl next door.

Margaret-Ann uttered her first word at dinner. "Auden," she said, then spooned in her toad-in-the-hole.

"Oh, was it Auden? Sir Clive, you disappoint me. I thought it was original," Peter responded.

"Ah, Margaret-Ann, you have sniffed us out again. It must be that superior American education," Clive said.

She just looked at them in irritated bewilderment. Margaret-Ann, like me, had no idea how to stick-handle through the labyrinth of English high society. It took me a long time, but not as long as Margaret-Ann, to be able to interpret the subtext. Their tone never gave away their meaning. Once I broke the Etonian code, I realized they were saying that everyone knew Auden's work by heart and it was pedantic of Margaret-Ann to source it for the group. Peter, Marcus and Clive were saying that only an American would believe recognizing Auden should be considered an achievement. To top off such academic delusion, only an American would boast such paltry knowledge.

I had landed with a thud in a truly foreign land. The terrifying thing was they did speak English so you could have the false sense that you shared more than you actually did. George Bernard Shaw expressed my sentiments perfectly: "England and America are two countries separated by the same language."

# <u>foxy lady</u>

*Is it like this*
*In death's other kingdom*
*Waking alone*
*At the hour when we are*
*Trembling with tenderness*
*Lips that would kiss*
*Form prayers to broken stone.*
— T.S. Eliot, "The Hollow Men"

The semester steamed ahead. I almost failed my Old English course, but Clive came to my rescue, as I was honestly a prioress in distress. We had to put on *The Canterbury Tales*, and I had to redeem my bad test performance with a stellar play performance.

I had to play several of the female characters, and Clive devoted untold hours to tutoring me in the accents. He never criticized my tin ear but only said after dozens of mistakes, "Let's try the Nun's Priest once more." He also was invaluable in translating English humour for me. He encouraged me to go over the top with the piece, assuring me that the audience would love it. He also contacted his mother, who had gone to school with the costume designer at Stratford, and she sent up dozens of costumes as a favour. Clive was right about the whole business, and I would never have made it a success without him. His steady hand and constant reassurance when I was on such shaky ground did not go unnoticed. Yet when I told him he'd saved my wild boar, he took very little credit.

The entire stairwell was taking Restoration Drama together. (These are English comedies that weren't funny, written from 1660–1710.) Since we generally had a great time together, we made a group field trip to London to see *The Way of the World*, *The Country Wife* and *She Stoops to Conquer*. We were hoping to catch these in matinees so we could rock on in the evenings.

I had to bunk with Margaret-Ann at a cheap bed-sit that smelled like Shepherd's pie left over from the Dark Ages. She announced that she didn't like my cigarette smoke. I had never met anyone who had said anything against cigarettes before. Peter said just to ignore her, as it was pure hysteria.

At night, Margaret-Ann, in her long white undershirt, flannel pyjamas and long braid, knelt by her bed and said her prayers. When she got into bed, she said to me, "It wouldn't hurt you to pray instead of jumping around like a ninny." When I informed her that it was because of my largesse that she was even included on this trip, instead of shutting up and saying thank you she said, "Well, it shocks me that you went to a Catholic school for years and you don't even pray."

"It shocks me that you study day and night and you still pray. So we are both shocked and appalled by one another." I had had it with her ingratitude and her moral superiority. "Some of the great poets that you love to the point of distraction thought the concept of God was ridiculous. When do you think Coleridge was last on his knees?"

"Wordsworth was a believer."

"And in love with his sister."

"You know as much about Wordsworth as you do about Old English."

I was sick of her sermonizing; I'd had enough of that in Catholic school and I was full to the gills with it. "Listen, your father is a little preacher in Maine who wants his daughter to be a chip off the old block. He reads Donne and is miserable and you read Wordsworth and are miserable. I have news for you. I have no idea if Wordsworth was having sex with his sister, but I can tell you one thing, he was having more fun than you."

"I will someday get a job at a prestigious university."

"And stew in your own juice, praying to some God that depressed your father and will depress you." She was silent and I was still enraged so I threw in, "God is some hellfire-and-brimstone figure made up by a bunch of puritans to keep their peckers in their pants."

"People who live your lifestyle die unhappily."

"I haven't had sex yet or even stayed out all night. I squeaked by in Old English. Gee, does it get any more depraved than that?"

I felt like steam was coming out of my ears. "Listen, at least I could tell my parents I was no longer a believer. They'd still love me. You don't have to be everything your parents are, you know."

"I have heard you talking on the phone in the corridor. Your father doesn't even know who you are." She had no idea my father had a brain tumour but still she was scraping the bottom of a very deep barrel.

"Does yours? Or is he just looking at what he wants to believe is a reflection of himself?" Though tempted to go on, I turned out the light and rolled over to face the wall.

London was then dubbed "Swinging London," and it put New York to shame. I bought miniskirts and bell-bottom pants and a very hairy sheepskin vest that stank and curled when it was wet outside or even just damp in my room. As I came down the stairs in the morning, Clive would yell up, "I smell rancid mutton."

When we were all cavorting down Carnaby Street, we ran into a friend of Clive's from Eton who had, as he said, "defected to Cambridge" and finished last year. He and his girlfriend were going to go to Oxford that evening so they offered us all a ride back even though it would be a tight squeeze. We, particularly Margaret-Ann and I, wanted to save money on the train so we took the ride.

Clive's friends were "mods." The man had on a maroon velvet waistcoat. Under the coat he wore a ruffled shirt and black tight pants with slit pockets. The ensemble was topped off with a flowing purple scarf. No man I knew wore a scarf for decoration. The girlfriend wore a white plastic micro-miniskirt accompanied by matching boots with enormous platforms and buttons and laces.

She also wore a top covered in small mirrors that tinkled like a wind chime when she walked. This couple was amazingly cool and if I thought I could tie my hair on top of my head as she had and look that "happening," I'd have been thrilled.

We met up in Soho and the six of us piled into a miniature station wagon. We were all singing along to the radio as it blasted José Feliciano's version of "Light My Fire." I looked up at a traffic light as José tried to set the night on fire and saw a policeman's face pressed against the car window only inches from my face. I screamed in fright as though I'd just seen Beelzebub, jolting everyone in the car. The dandily dressed driver immediately reached into the glove compartment, pulled out a canister and whipped off the lid to reveal a row of home-baked brownies. He said we had to gulp them down right away while he stalled the bobby. He then got out of the car, slamming the door behind him.

Clive and Peter gulped down two in record time and gave me two, which I wolfed down. As Margaret-Ann chewed on her third brownie, she said in her usual lugubrious tone, "I can't lose my scholarship."

"Then eat and shut your gob," the wind-chime girlfriend said from the front seat without turning around.

We had just finished the last crumbs when the police had us all get out of the car; they took everything out, including the seats. They found the empty canister and asked what it was and the wind chimer said in her upper-crust accent, "Obviously an empty biscuit tin."

Apropos of nothing, Margaret-Ann said in an uncharacteristically cheerful tone to the bobby, "I *love* your hat."

The policeman looked at her, not knowing how to take her.

There she stood in her drop-pleated skirt, red cardigan, navy boiled-wool double-breasted coat and sensible shoes, smiling like she was seeing London for the first time and loving it.

"Thank you, marm," he muttered.

"You know I have always wondered why you fellows don't wear your strap under your chin instead of on it," she said.

"Margaret-Ann, this constable is busy," Peter said.

"Well, it is strange," she said, stretching the word *strange* out like it was elastic. She spoke so loudly and with such eccentric intonation that passersby were slowing down and eyeing the spectacle of all of us standing in a row before the police and the car seats lounging on the curb at Oxford Circus on a bitter February night.

"I am not giving you a ticket this time, but I'm telling you right now, don't go travelling around again with that number of folks in a mini."

We got in the car, and Peter said between clenched teeth, "Quiet until we are away."

Finally, when we turned a corner in Soho, I said, "I like your hat?" and we all laughed hysterically.

"There is no way I can drive to Oxford until I'm straighter," the waist-coated man said. "We all need to come down for a while."

"I have to get back to review my notes for tomorrow's tutorial," Margaret-Ann said.

"Relax. No one ever reviews their notes," I said.

"I'm giving a presentation."

"To one man — your professor. You'll be fine."

"I have to get back!"

"Margaret-Ann! No one is driving us to the train so put a sock in it," I said. The others nodded.

After about five minutes of silence, Margaret-Ann said, "Wait a cotton-pickin' minute here. Could those signal lights be winking at us? I think they *are*."

It turned out this velvet guy was somehow involved with managing some musical performers. He said we could go to a jazz club on the edge of Soho. So we went back to within a block of where we'd started. It was now after midnight.

The club was downstairs in a cramped hot half cellar. It was like being in a basement rec room in Buffalo. There were only a few tables, and the bar only held two stools that were directly under black lights. The only source of heat was the thick cigarette smoke. No one was more than a few feet from the stage. The bouncer, named Crocodile, greeted the velvet-clad dandy as though he were Lloyd George. He even knew the beautiful tinkling girlfriend.

We sat down and Margaret-Ann said with gusto to the waiter, "I'm starving." He informed her that the kitchen was closed.

"Oh no!" Margaret-Ann yelled and dramatically banged her head on the table. The manager just glared at Margaret-Ann, since Eric Burdon was onstage singing "Don't Let Me Be Misunderstood."

As he sang, I wove my way through the thick blue smoke to get bags of crisps for everyone. When I dumped them on the table, everyone dove for a bag.

I popped a crisp in my mouth and started coughing, then choking. I said to Clive, "Are there salt grains the size of dice sprinkled on this chip? I just swallowed one."

Mousy Margaret-Ann, who never spoke loud enough for me to hear everything she said, was yelling to the waitress, "More potato chips over here, *please*."

"She is going to bring you a fried potato. You want 'crisps.'"

I returned my attention to the stage and for the first time in my life I could hear each instrument in the band playing separately, yet I could simultanelousy hear the band as a whole. I was convinced they were playing just for me. My whole body seemed to be rocking with the music, and I suddenly understood what it meant to have rhythm. My entire body felt loose limbed and each joint was moving. I looked around and everyone appeared friendly and warm. Strange for the English. Even Margaret-Ann looked benign. That's when I suspected the brownies.

"What was in those brownies?" I asked the mirror-shirted beauty.

"Hash laced with a bit of my triple-mix fertilizer."

Eric Burdon started to sing "It's My Life." From there we went into "The House of the Rising Sun." I felt the urge to dance — with no need for a partner. So I got up and did a sort of free interpretative number, convinced I looked just like Isadora Duncan.

A thin black man in a large felt black hat with a feather in it jumped onstage holding a guitar as Eric Burdon was singing "We Gotta Get Out of This Place" and played background. Then the feather-hatted man stood up and played "Foxy Lady."

"I remember hearing about this guy," I said. "He was a real hit at Monterey Pop. I wasn't there, but my friend Sara saw him and said he was a total showstopper. Then his popularity just went off the charts. Wait until I tell her I saw him in this London basement."

It was a great night. Everyone was up moving and dancing and the lights pulsed with the music. Lots of people, even Jimi Hendrix, seemed to know the velvet-coated Eton man and greeted him. As Jimi Hendrix walked by Margaret-Ann, she shouted,

"We're American too — I mean as well."

Jimi smiled, waved and said, "Far out, man." He sat down with a woman who had blond hair and bangs that completely covered her eyes.

When Jimi got back onstage for the next set, he said, "I want to do 'The Star-Spangled Banner' for the American girls over there." He pointed shyly to us.

Margaret-Ann dug her fingernails into my arm and screamed, "*That's us*, Cathy!"

Being on hash or whatever was in that brownie and hearing Hendrix's version of "The Star-Spangled Banner" was one of the highlights of the '60s for me. I felt I knew exactly what he meant by every tortured cry of that guitar. The lighting man did "rocket's red glare" perfectly by having red spotlights explode on the ancient rubble stonewalls and the stage. Jimi's rendition was spot on. It incorporated everything that had happened in the '60s: Jack and Bobby Kennedy, Martin Luther King, the riots, Vietnam, Chicago, all of it. It was as though Hendrix was saying, "I know all the shit that has happened, I know what it is to be black in America . . . but hey — it's still a great place to be."

—

Hours later, we stopped in Reading for an English breakfast. You can tell you're still stoned if those rashers floating like pontoons in a sea of grease next to the fried, shrivelled tomato are lip-smacking good. Then you have passed the Electric Kool-Aid Acid Test for stoned.

We finally made it back to Oxford by 8:30 the next morning. We were still a bit high but had mostly come down — all except Margaret-Ann. The Barson, meeting us at the gatehouse, said we were due home last night. Clive gave a big story about how we were fogged-in in London, where we had gone to see some plays for our Restoration Drama course. He blathered on about how we had decided to err on the safe side and stay overnight at his parents' London *pied-à-terre*.

I could tell that the Barson was contemplating informing on us. He hesitated, then turned around and entered our names in the logbook with yesterday's date and said to Clive, "Master Hunter-Parsons, your youth may have the day. Isn't it a shame that youth is wasted on the young?"

As we walked up our stairwell, Peter said under his breath, "Clive, old man, you've donated another bottle of Lagavulin 25 to the cause. That has got to smart. Remember that American Rhodes scholar who offered Barson a quart of Johnnie Walker Red? He just gave him a blurry-eyed scowl. Can't sneak under the wire with the old Barson, can one?"

CHAPTER 4

# when the calves sang to my horn

*Now as I was young and easy under the apple boughs*
*About the lilting house and happy as the grass was green*
— Dylan Thomas, "Fern Hill"

Spring comes early to Oxford and, compared to where I was from, it was glorious. It is like nowhere else in the world, for it's a real season, not like the few weeks in New York when the spring comes late and the buds hurry to open and then are slain in infancy by the rushing hot weather. In England the fruit trees stayed in bloom and fields of daffodils and bluebells grew wild in infinite varieties and lasted for all of the long spring. The slightest breeze tapped their friendliness. Not only did they nod but whole fields would genuflect when I rode by on my bike in the dew-drenched morning.

Spring also heralded the beginning of rowing season. Clive rowed for Oxford in the Trinity College boat and was in the top boat of eight. Eight long, lithe men rowed in a long, lithe boat wearing skintight, short navy unisuits and strange little beanies. The ninth man, who was short, slight and built like a jockey, was called the coxswain. He was crammed into the stern facing the rowers. It was his job to shout out orders at the rowers, who functioned as galley slaves. The rowers rowed backwards so it was up to the coxie, who faced ahead, to tell the rowers what was in their path. He also steered and motivated and yelled out directions and pace to the rowers.

I used to enjoy riding along the Thames riverbank on my bike and watching Clive's boat glide along. The athletic endeavour and the grace while in unison appealed to me. I wished that there could be a girls' rowing team, but I knew that was only dreaming. (Twenty years later, I was part of a women's rowing crew for twelve years, and we raced all over North America.)

One day Clive thundered into my room and said, "It's time for the Torpids. It's a rowing bumps race and our cox has food poisoning from eating at Wimpy's in London. I can't find a substitute. Everyone who knows how to row is already in the race. We need a coxie today or we will have to scratch. Do you think you can do it?"

I looked up from my book blankly.

"I will be right there in front — just inches away from you — giving you instructions."

"Sure," I said.

He explained that the bumps is only done in Oxford and Cambridge and maybe London. It was started because the rivers are so narrow. Everyone lines up in his eight-man boat, bow-to-stern along the bank of the Thames, and then the coxie pushes off with a pole. When someone wants to pass a boat, they bump the boat and the coxie raises their hand and the rowers know they have been bumped and they have to pull over to the shore, letting the boat that bumped them move ahead. Once you're bumped, you are out of the race.

Typical of convoluted English rules, there were over-bumps, side-bumps, bump-up and bump-down. I couldn't grasp the rules. They were way too complicated with a myriad of exceptions. Like the rules in any sport, they make a lot of sense if you know the game, and they are incomprehensible and arcane if you don't. Clive finally said in exasperation, "It is really complicated but you *have* to know the rules."

Picking up on his agitation and knowing I had only two hours left to read a Pinter play, I simply said, "I'll figure it out." How bad could it go? The Thames is only thirty feet wide.

When I arrived, I was a bit taken aback by the hullabaloo. There were cameras and TV crews and what looked like the entire faculty. There were hundreds if not thousands of people in front of the University College boathouse. As we lined up, there were throngs of people with bikes to ride alongside the boats, coaches telling me what to do via megaphone from the shore and rowers asking me all kinds of technical questions about the rigging and the rudder and the bow ball and so on . . . to which I answered, "Just relax, I've taken care of it."

As the horn blew and I poled out, dozens of boats started forward. The best were in front. We were placed in the middle of the pack. (Establishing your position in the line-up is based on a ridiculous number of variables that seemed to date back to all other races you had ever been in and each step you had taken since birth.)

Clive had shown me the two cables on each side of the boat that pull the rudder either to the right or left, and as I steered I drove my guys on. I was a good motivator since I was competitive. Clive was the stroke (lead rower) in the boat, sitting facing me. Our heads were only about four inches apart. My knees were in the way since the coxie is supposed to be tiny like a jockey, but I had long legs. I could feel the sweat spray my way as he flew up his slide and pulled with all of his might on the oars. I was fairly amazed by how muscular he was. He was tall and lean but in that clingy suit I could see that he was solid muscle. Just as I was wondering how I'd missed that he had a gorgeous athletic body, he reminded me, "Remember we can only bump, not smash into the boat in front of us."

"I totally understand." I did everything perfectly and we bumped the guy in front of us and they moved over and we roared ahead.

About two minutes later, I saw a boat coming closer. Then I could hear their coxie scream on the microphone, "Five hard strokes and we've got 'em." They were on our tail and gaining. Clive had told me never to turn my head since it knocks off the exact balance of the boat and slows the speed of the glide. Clive was panting too much to talk. Finally I felt a slight, almost infinitesimal bump. I chose to ignore it. It could have been a ricocheting wake, and I'd never done this before. Clive's face was so red it looked like he had it on inside out. He managed to whisper between staggered breaths, "Were we bumped?"

"No."

"If we were, you must raise your hand and move to the side."

A student with binoculars wearing a Balliol T-shirt yelled from shore, "You've been bumped. Bump-over, coxie!"

A tall man with curly hair and a scraggly beard who was just a few feet away on the bank cupped his hands and yelled in a southern American drawl, "There are no officials here — keep going."

I shouted through the megaphone at the rowers: "We are going to be bumped unless you can give me ten hard pulls right now." I began counting each of the ten strokes and we shot ahead. Clive was giving his all; I could see the veins in his neck popping. The other boat fell back and never regained its lead on us. I bumped several more times as we threaded ourselves along the course. We finished in a really good position. I estimated we were now in the top quarter.

At the end of the race, my rowers (interesting how quickly they became mine) all, with the exception of Clive, crowded around me and congratulated me, saying that tomorrow when the race continued they would start in a great position.

Peter came up to the finish line breathless and said as we disembarked, "Cathy, Cathy, Cathy. You gave those Balliol wankers a run for their money. I thought they were bumping for sure. You really pulled it out of the water."

Everyone toasted me and yelled, "Speech!" I stood up and waved like the queen, saying, "It brings me great pride to be the queen of the bumps."

Clive said, almost inaudibly, "You are truly bumptious." Knowing this to be a term slightly worse than arrogant and egotistical, I was a bit taken aback.

Fortunately at that moment, the American with the Allen Ginsberg beard who had yelled from the sidelines entered the beer tent and strolled by our table. As he shot a smile my way, I said, "Thanks for the tip-off on the officials."

He replied, "Well I had no idea what the hell the rules were, but I figured just keep going until someone tells you otherwise." It was strange to hear a southern American accent at Oxford, yet comforting to hear a countryman for a change.

As he left, Peter said, "He is a big politico around University College. He and some of his American buddies are organizing a big anti-Vietnam demonstration. He worked as an aide for Fulbright in Washington."

"I liked him. I actually picked him out of the crowd as we rowed by. I felt like he was rooting for our boat. What's his name?"

"Bill Clinton, I believe."

—

After a day in the sun at the races, I was exhausted and hoarse from yelling. Clive and I walked back to Trinity without saying a word. Some silences are comfortable while others are fraught, and very quickly you know what kind of silence you are involved in. Finally I asked, "Would it be *bumptious* of me to ask what is wrong?"

"We were bumped, weren't we?"

"No."

"The Balliol coxie gave me a dirty look when we docked."

"It could have been a wake or someone could have been out of sync in the back of the boat. There're a million things that simulate a weenie bump. In my mind, the bump has to be unmistakable."

"*In your mind.* Ah, there is the rub. As a point of information, the bump has to be light or it would harm the scull and the bumper would be disqualified."

"Well, it isn't like we were at the Olympics or even at the front of the line."

"You might have felt differently if you'd been the Balliol boat doing the bumping."

"But I wasn't."

"No, you weren't."

"Balliol could have screamed 'bump-over' or hit us slightly harder."

"They could have, but they wanted to follow the rules. Winning is when everyone follows the social contract."

"Sorry, Rousseau. It was the first time I ever did this and, lest you forget, I did it as a favour to you. I can't know every single nuance and every bump in the road, so to speak. I didn't know exactly what a bump is supposed to feel like. This was all new to me."

"Yes, you did know. Besides you were advised from the sidelines."

"By a Balliol undergraduate. Not an official. As *a point of information*, to borrow one of your favourite phrases, Peter and every other person in the tent thought that I'd done a great job. They don't measure a bump as a wind current or a wake behind a boat. Sorry for disappointing you."

"Don't say you are sorry when you are not and please stop the sophistry." His voice remained quiet, as though we were having a discussion and not an argument.

We walked on in silence until I couldn't stand it any longer. "*Fine*. I felt the bump. I figured they needed one more stroke to make it an official bump. Then I would really have had to acknowledge it. I decided to keep going. I wanted to win the race. Happy *now*?"

He didn't answer. As we approached the gate, the Barson tore out and said, "I heard you gave what's-it to those Balliol wastrels."

Tears welled in my eyes as we crossed the green. I thought of my father and how disappointed in me he would be if he'd heard what Clive had said. I thought I'd done a great job and now I realized I'd cheated, and the pathetic thing was I knew it at the time. I wanted to look as though I could stick-handle through the race. I didn't want to be a wimpy girl. Clive had said exactly what my father would have said if he'd been there and in his right mind. I could hear my father's Buffalo accent echoing in my head: "Hope it was worth it to you."

Climbing up our stairwell, I could hear my leaden feet. When we were at Clive's door, I said, "I cheated and knew it. It was pathetic. Should I tell the officials I was bumped?"

"No. That would create melodrama. Just know that you've been bumped." Then he smiled a sweet, forgiving smile my way, and I trudged up to my room.

The next morning, I lay in my bed, replaying the race. Mostly I thought of Clive and I stuffed together into the tiny confines of the stern. I pictured Clive's firm thighs and the collision of our knees every time he shot up the slide. As I thought about how my hands had rested on his muscled thighs before we began the race, I had my first sexual thoughts about Clive. I wondered if he'd had any about me.

—

I had just begun what was to be my favourite course — Modern British Poetry. The Brits have their foibles, but you could never say they can't use the language. Our poetry fellow never looked in a book. He recited everything from memory (as did bartenders, truck drivers and store clerks). Most of the students did the same thing. When they were called upon, they answered in long convoluted sentences and never searched for words or appeared inarticulate. The Brits could switch disciplines on a dime. If they wanted to make an argument about a critic or a theory of English criticism, they could interweave it with philosophy and history with no difficulty.

Some times of your life are so memorable that you can almost reach into your mind and touch them. The perfect memories are locked in with the horrific ones. It is the everyday tedium that gets wiped out, while the extremes go on file.

I had the traumas burned into my mind as though they'd occurred yesterday. I can remember the weather, the time, what I was wearing, where I was standing and exactly what was said or not said. I can flip through them like shuffling a deck of cards: the day Roy disappeared or was taken away by the two men, having to go to a psychiatrist for stabbing a bully, getting kicked out of Catholic school, Father Rodwick's sexual betrayal, Kennedy's death, the fire I caused at the doughnut shop, the moment I realized my father had lost his mind, finding out that Laurie was married, Splits's murder and the FBI rapping at my door. These traumas were all stored and could pop up in Technicolor leaping across my synapses like a ballerina at any associative moment.

Fortunately memory also has a file for perfect joy. I can still remember hearing Dylan Thomas's poem "Fern Hill" for the first time. I was in my Modern British Poetry class at Magdalen College, sitting right off the cloister on the first floor. The leaded casement windows were cranked fully open, letting in the early morning breeze, and I was looking out on the cowslips that lined the Cherwell River. River daffodils danced to Thomas's lyric as the fellow recited:

> Time let me play and be
> Golden in the mercy of his means,
> And green and golden I was huntsman and
>     herdsman, the calves
> Sang to my horn, the foxes on the hills barked
>     clear and cold,
> And the Sabbath rang slowly
> In the pebbles of the holy streams.

Dylan Thomas's exuberant innocence drove me right back to Lewiston and Niagara Falls, where I had "the pebbles of *my* holy stream": the Niagara Escarpment with its rough cliffs of fossils layered one upon another; the joy of the Niagara River in the spring, bubbling its fury while I stood safely on the warm rocks along the bank; the lemonade on the summer nights when fireflies danced, the ones my dad said only came to the home of perfect girls that looked like peaches in August.

I could still see Roy and me parting the multicoloured

maple leaves that glowed at dusk. I could still hear us singing Ella Fitzgerald's version of "A-Tisket A-Tasket" as we collected chestnuts. I could still feel the stingers on the pea-green chestnut shells that ripped into our hands. We wound our bleeding digits with crimson Virginia creeper leaves. All the way back to work, we admired our mahogany chestnuts that glowed as though shellacked.

The coldness of winter still had a hold of me too: the blinding storms in winter that crusted us all with sleet and knocked those schooldays right off the map; I could still feel the ice that froze the rushing falls in mid air, sending star-studded glitter on our windshield. I marvelled at a force of nature that sent snow from heaven that could bury our footprints in seconds; in minutes our angels-in-the-snow and our ducks-and-geese games would be only memories.

I had no idea then how glorious it was, how I basked in my parents' love like a lizard warming himself on a sunny rock. The dew cleansed each new day, filtering yesterday's folly through the soil. The tragedy is that you had no idea how perfect it was until you realized time was the herdsman. What you once thought was life was really youth, and it was fading. Hearing "Fern Hill" made tears run down my face at Oxford in the early morning of mourning.

You don't feel the steel cable of time. It tightens gradually, link by link, until one day you feel that shackle digs into your breast when you try to take a carefree breath.

And yet life still offered golden moments, like that crisp English morning. I can still feel the bracing air as I rode my bike (now having mastered the brakes) in my heather Marks and Spencer sweater on my way to Magdalen College. Whole fields of sweet peas and bluebells would genuflect when I rode by on my bike in the dew-drenched morning. I could smell the lush green as I sat on a gargoyle stone bench alone in the deer park behind Magdalen cloister. I would read aloud to the deer in the foggy dawn before they'd become skittish and flee. If I talked directly to them, they shied away, but if I read Dylan Thomas to the field, they turned their doe eyes toward me and breathed steam my way, lulled by the rhythm of "Do Not Go Gentle into That Good Night." I thought of my father dying at home, and reading Thomas gave me great comfort:

> And you, my father, there on the sad height,
> Curse, bless, me now with your fierce tears, I pray.
> Do not go gentle into that good night.
> Rage, rage against the dying of the light.

There were three things I didn't know at the time: one was how wonderful the age of twenty-one was with all the possibilities before me. Nor did I know that poetry would never bring tears to my eyes again. The last was that I would soon be reading that poem at my father's funeral.

# "he's willin'"

*"Ah!" he said, slowly turning his eyes towards me.*
*"Well! If you was writin' to her, p'raps you'd recollect to say*
*that Barkis was willin'; would you?"*
— Charles Dickens, *David Copperfield*

I had taken to Oxford. When you sat across from a professor and

you had to fill an hour, it was excruciating to be unprepared, so I

never worked so hard in my entire life — still, I loved every minute

I'd been there. I didn't get a lot of praise for my work, but I did

write a paper on Dylan Thomas that my fellow called "inspired," and he said, in true English style, "That it is an insightful piece is not in dispute, but I have no idea if it would pass the criteria for publication, particularly since the journal in question is American." He suggested that to perfect the article and to verify some of my theories of origin, I should take, as he called it, "a field trip" to Wales to check on the local environs. The idea of seeing some of the places Dylan Thomas wrote about absolutely thrilled me.

My best friends at Oxford turned out to be from my stairwell mostly due to their proximity. Clive I liked a lot. Peter I liked because he was Clive's friend. Marcus was always dour, but I appreciated how he never stepped out of character. Margaret-Ann was the only woman there, and all girls need girlfriends so she was on the list by default. Since the staircase quartet were my best friends, I ran to tell them that I was going on a pilgrimage to Wales, determined to see Thomas's boathouse home and the locales that influenced him.

It was now the last weekend in June, and summer was upon us as the purple clematis wreathed every doorway like a royal Elizabethian collar. I was preparing to depart on a long holiday weekend, but the foursome informed me that it was sheer folly to travel, as it was the week of Prince Charles's investiture at Caernarfon.

"Who's investing?" I asked.

"Charles is being invested as Prince of Wales," Clive said, as though it was *the* biggest deal.

"So?"

"Wales is the key word here," Peter added.

"You know those old biddies who only discuss the bus routes in that Pinter short?" Clive asked.

I nodded.

"Well every one of those women will drag her truculent spouse to the investiture, which is exactly en route to where you are going."

"I want to see Swansea and the boathouse and Augharne, where Thomas lived. I also want to go to Snowdonia. Professor Beech said it's the most rustic part of Wales, packed with people who speak Welsh. It's the best way to take a trip through Thomas's past."

"Cathy, what you don't understand is that Caernarfon is in the northern tip of Wales, which is remote and mountainous. There is one main road to get there. The rest is through winding mountain paths. We are not in America, you know."

"Ah ha," I said, hitting myself Eureka-style on the side of my head. "That must be why I'm eating toad-in-the-hole."

My *parents* worried about things like traffic and the weather. If you want to get somewhere, my theory was you just hit the road. It was the only long weekend we had. Besides, I'd not met one person in England who ever mentioned the Prince of Wales.

On the eve of my June departure, Margaret-Ann, Peter, Clive and I were sitting in the hall at our long Edwardian tables with the straight back chairs eating strawberries and clotted cream from Guernsey. It was the freshest and most delicious cream I've ever had. The English may not know how to heat a room, but those dairy maids that Thomas Hardy talked about knew what they were doing.

Margaret-Ann, as usual, interrupted my tranquility by saying with a great deal of self-satisfaction, "When I checked, on your behalf, train and bus tickets to Wales were sold out for the long holiday weekend."

"So I'll hitchhike," I heard myself saying. *"Jiminy Cricket!* What are you guys going to worry about when you're forty if you're worrying about the traffic in your twenties?"

Marcus sauntered up to our table and said in a casually calculated tone, which for him passed for spontaneity, "Mind if I join you?" Marcus almost always ate from a tray in his room and only joined us when necessary. He said, "I heard your remonstrations from across the room." (In England, that remark is to be interpreted as an insult.) "Not that you were making a spectacle of yourself, since nothing could compare to your airmail parcel, but since it was impossible not to overhear you, you might want to know that the papers have announced that Welsh nationalists have threatened to bomb the railway in Wales and Caernarfon Castle on the day of the almighty dubbing."

"How profoundly moronic," Peter said. "Given Welsh technical acumen, I'm sure they'll blow themselves up first."

"Speaking of moronic," Marcus said as he stole a fleeting glimpse my way, "I have something to show you."

"Marcus, I quake when you join us," Peter said.

"What are you grimly reaping today?" Clive asked. "Come on, man, out with it. I have known you too long. You have not crept out of your lair to peddle some glad tidings."

"Ah, I shall credit you with good intuition. You have gone such a long way on it. I bring an interesting missive from our disloyal colonies." Marcus Aaronson was the only man I had ever met who subscribed to nine newspapers in various languages. The only reason he didn't have one in Old English was because there was no news.

Marcus laid the June 9, 1969, *New York Times* in front of me.

He must have saved it for weeks so he could watch me writhe. The headline, sprawled in huge, depressing black letters, said that the most recent Gallup poll had indicated that President Nixon's popularity was at an all-time high.

The article said that Nixon had disagreed with the tactics of student demonstrations. I said, "Listen to this!" and I read aloud, "Sixteen students from Harvard who had been involved in a take-over of university buildings were expelled."

Marcus said, "I have actually read about those students. The irony was that they were 'old boys.' Their fathers and grandfathers had actually donated some of the buildings they'd occupied. Given the ingenuity of most 'old boys,' they probably had no idea what they were doing."

Clive, knowing that Marcus was really discussing him, said, "Marcus, even as a man of the Tribe, you too will be an old boy some day."

"Aha, you have missed the point of the Chosen People, my good man," replied Marcus. "Only Oxford and Cambridge have fully understood that biblical phrase since I believe they have a quota on those of the Hebrew persuasion."

Peter said, "Speaking of good men, wasn't it Henry Miller who said, 'Who hates the Jews more than the Jew?'"

Clive said, "I notice you have brought us tidings of the colonies but none from the Promised Land. I read this morning that Moshe Dayan has hinted that Israel plans to keep much of the West Bank. Is it possible that he oversteps the original boundaries of Moses?"

I slammed my white plate with its blue Trinity crest on the table. There was a terrible echo in the hall, giant marble-floored cavern that it was. I happened to do this in a moment of silence right before announcements were made by the windbag who ran the junior commons room, the man who was only slightly more of a prig than the one who ran the senior commons room. I looked up and announced, "You guys are so impossible."

"My apologies for having accused you of thought," Marcus said.

"You're such pedants. You," I accused Clive, "and Peter define everything in terms of who someone is based on their exact social status and some complicated system that has more complicated chutes and ladders than an Escher drawing. The U.S. may have its problems, but one thing I can say for sure: Marcus would just be a guy, albeit a grouchy *guy*, from Birmingham."

"No need to be effusive," Marcus replied.

"Shut up. He wouldn't be the *Jew* whose father has new money from the *schmatta* business. You could just be Clive, a guy from Norfolk, Suffolk or some-folking-where."

"Not to be even more pedantic, but it's Cornwall," Clive said.

"The point is you would just be Clive. But now you have to be third-generation Clive hyphenated-name who has *old* money, *landed* gentry, a flat in London — in Kensington no less — which has been in the family *forever*." (I was now doing a really bad English accent.) "How do I know all this? Oh, it just *slipped* out.

"You know when I first got here I was fooled by the fact that we spoke the same language. When you and Peter said you hadn't studied, I, like a lamb to the slaughter, believed you until I failed the first test and you two shone like new shillings." By now I was standing up, pacing and gesticulating. Reggie and the other waiters made only the slightest pretense of wiping down their tables as they listened. "Oh, *sorry*, I forgot I wasn't supposed to mention money. That's left to" — I lifted my fingers and made quotations marks — "'the Chosen People.'"

Margaret-Ann was looking confused, to say nothing of horrified, that I was yelling. So I began addressing her. "You see, Margaret-Ann, if you admit you study then it would mean that you were not born with a perfect memory of modern British poetry. That would not befit your station. Marcus is here on scholarship so he has to study, poor Shylock that he is. He has parents who don't quote sonnets all day long. That means they were tawdry enough to have to work for a living. *How prosaic!* It's vulgar to study. While Marcus is off in his room making up insults to exchange at meal times and finding incendiary newspaper articles, you guys are scurrying back to your rooms to study your asses off. You just make it look inherited. In America, if people study they *say* they study. If they move up in income and educational level in the good old U. S. of A., that would be called *initiative*. In America he'd be called a *self-made man,* not an *upstart.*"

Peter pushed back his chair while saying, "You are throwing a wobbly and it is becoming boring."

"Becoming?" Marcus said.

Peter said in a very quiet, calm tone, "You are bellowing like a fish-wife, Cathy. Something that may be acceptable in the bowels of Buffalo, but . . ."

I was surprised to hear Margaret-Ann pipe up: "Not in front of the servants."

"Cathy, thank you for that précis on English social stratification. No doubt you have revolutionized the American political and social system with all of your . . . concern," Peter said as he stood up.

Marcus said, "Well . . ."

I cut him off. "Oh, Marcus, give it up." I turned to Peter and Clive and said, "Of course Marcus plans to say only snide things. He knows he'll never get into the inner sanctum even if he gets a first with honours, which he will, so he refuses to dance around the edges pleading for inclusion. I'd rather eat in my room than be 'the Jew from Birmingham,' of whom it has been begrudgingly acknowledged, 'No one can doubt he's clever.' Of course he's always marching his brilliance around on a diamond-studded leash. He has to be supercilious and annoying. But brains are all you've allowed him. He's never allowed inclusion. The really sad thing is you've both gone to the same rotten posh school so you've known each other since you were in shorts and knee socks. Every day you both draw your sabres. Every day it's the same bout. Clive and Peter pull the silver spoon number, while Marcus parries with the 'but I'm clever' blow of the shofar. At least in America, we dislike one another for our personal traits rather than our social rank. It's a subtle but important difference, at least to me."

My throat hurt and I suddenly realized I had indeed been screaming. I pushed my chair back and didn't mean for it to fall backward but it did and made thunderous clamour as I stomped out of the dining hall. The cooks were lined up in their white jackets like human swans with their necks craned around the corner of the scullery.

As I passed the door, I heard one hair-netted woman with pendulous breasts say, "My, my" to the carver.

"Some-folking-where? Never 'eard it." The tall, thin carver in the bloody apron answered as they both went through the swinging door back into the kitchen.

I spiralled up the staircase, opened my door and locked it behind me. I needn't have bothered since no one followed. As I lay on my bed, my chest heaved up and down like a bellows. My hands felt tingly, my mouth was dry and my larynx burned. I began to calm down, and I realized I'd had one mighty outburst or, as my mother would have said, "made quite a fuss." *So goddamn what?* I said to myself as I curled into the fetal position and pulled my quilt up under my chin.

Roy had referred to my flare-ups as "tongue flapping"; my father called them "flying off the handle." Neither paid them much heed, for I got over them quickly and forgot I'd been angry. I was never one to, as they say in England, "stew in my own juices." As I lay in bed, I thought how hard it was to explain a bad temper. Your heart suddenly starts to pound and you feel horribly wronged. William James, the first psychologist, asked how we know what we feel. If our heart pounds and our hands feel sweaty and a bear is in front of us, then we interpret those symptoms as fear. Bodily signs of a similar sort also signify rage. Sometimes your body can turn up the volume on all of its vital signs and you act based on your bodily cues or miscues. Only when the internal cacophony quiets down can you look around, assess the wreckage and say, "Wow, that was somewhat of an overreaction."

God knows what this episode had been. An outburst? A flare-up? It wasn't a fight since no one was yelling back. Anyway it gave the kitchen staff something to talk about besides the weather and the investiture. It had to be the most exciting thing in Margaret-Ann's and Marcus's summer. I suspected Peter and Clive were mostly miffed not by what I'd said, but because I'd caused "a scene."

Once I had calmed down, I realized that Clive, the person I cared for most in the group — actually in all of England or, now that I thought about it, anywhere in the world — had said very little during my egalitarian diatribe. He had simply gawked at me as though I'd been speaking Swahili and performing a bizarre medicine dance in a death mask.

Clive had done the most for me since I'd been at Oxford. He'd devoted hours to showing me artifacts at the Ashmolean Museum and patiently explained all of their history. Only graduate students were allowed lengthy appointments to examine original manuscripts at the Balliol library, so he took me as his "assistant" to see Coleridge's manuscripts with his original crossings-out. In my outburst, I'd clearly gone over whatever line was acceptable for him, but hey . . . I sat up and looked in the mirror . . . tomorrow was another day. I'd get up early in the morning, go to Wales and when I got back in four days' time, this dust-up would have settled.

—

I started off at 5:00 in the morning wearing my cut-off jeans, a faded tie-dye tank top, espadrille sandals and a red bandanna on my head. I had a small backpack with only a toothbrush, jeans, a sweater and an old rain poncho I'd found in my closet stuffed behind my gowns.

As I passed the porter's lodge, I popped my head in to tell the Barson I'd be gone a few days. There, parked patiently on the long bench across from the mailboxes, sat Clive with a backpack propped up next to him. He wore cut-off jeans and a T-shirt with the sleeves cut off. When he stood up with exposed arms and legs, I realized I'd never seen him in shorts before or even a short-sleeve shirt other than at the rowing match. I was again hit with what a muscular, tight body he had. I tried not to look at it, but it wasn't easy since his long, tanned legs were splayed across the tiny porter's lodge.

I looked at him blankly. I was sick of being the one who said everything, so I simply said goodbye to the Barson. The red-nosed gatekeeper, who had his back to both of us as he sorted the mail into the ancient nicked wooden slots, said, "Miss McClure, Master Hunter-Parsons is willin'."

I couldn't help but laugh, and then said in my best Peggotty imitation, "Well, he best be moving off then, hey?" At this Clive got up, slung on his "rucksack," as they say in England, and we walked silently down High Street together as the orange dawn set the Bodleian Library spires aflame. We maintained our hush to the first roundabout. I put out my thumb and within seconds a lorry took us all the way to the M40. The driver was a big man with a long, narrow face — so long that it looked as though someone had professionally stretched it. His face was framed by a long black beard and curly black hair on his head. He turned his sunken black eyes toward me and asked where we were headed. (He had such a thick accent that I couldn't understand most of what he said.) Clive responded, "We're on our way to Wales, Snowdonia, then down to Swansea."

"You daft?"

"Why?" I asked, this being the first thing I'd understood.

"Only one road up in there, and all of England and a good chunk of Europe goin' to Caernarfon for the investiture at the weekend. They'll be pulling the cars off the road from what I heard. The trains are already in a muddle."

"Ever try to tell an American woman what to do?" Clive asked in a matter-of-fact tone, as though it was a sociological inquiry rather than a complaint.

"Any woman," the lorry driver clarified, pulling up a hill in his thirteen-gear rig.

After hours of silent travel, he announced, "Tea time comin' up." He actually went to all the trouble of pulling off the M40 to find this little shop that had hot, homemade scones and loose-leaf tea served in a previously warmed pot. When we went in, he took his book, *Thus Spake Zarathustra* by Nietzsche. Clive opened Yeats and I followed suit with Thomas. I had worked at truck stops and I never once saw an American truck driver bring a book. Nor had I ever known a trucker to pull off the highway and lose twenty minutes for the sake of a good cup of tea.

"Well, mates," he said when we got up to leave, "I have some good news for you. I'm going as far as Stoke-on-Trent, so I can just drop you off along the way and you can get a ride west to Snowdonia."

"Brilliant," said Clive.

"How come you didn't say that hours ago?" I asked.

"Wanted to make sure I could read me books as I didn't fancy a chin wag."

"I'm Cathy," I said, hoping that wasn't too much information.

"Rufus."

"Clive." He leaned over and shook hands.

The sun came out and we barrelled on through the Black Country, the industrial wasteland of England, which made Fitzgerald's Valley of Ashes look like the Garden of Eden. It got its name from the nineteenth-century iron foundries that sent black smoke into the air. The buildings were still covered in black soot. Rufus told us everything about the history of making leather, mining lime-stone and coal in the most detailed yet fascinating way imaginable.

He'd inherited his lorry from his father. As the rig shuddered up the hills of Wolverhampton, he reached into the glove com-partment and retrieved a small tape recorder and said that only a sacred few got to listen to his tapes of Roger Miller, a Nashville country and western singer. Clive was a bit lost on this one, but I'd kept an eye on the country and western charts since I'd worked with truck drivers at an all-night doughnut shop in Buffalo. Rufus and I sang along with Miller as he crooned, "Dang Me," "King of the Road" and "England Swings." Then Miller sang one of my all-time favourites, later made famous by Janis Joplin, called "Me and Bobby McGee."

I began singing "Bobby McGee" with Rufus in the lead. I was, of course, thrilled because I was in a truck, in a dirty red ban-danna, as the lyrics suggested. The driver reached in the back seat and pulled out an old guitar, which he said he strummed at night when he was on the road. Clive took the guitar and played beautifully as the driver put on a harpoon, or as he called it a "Texas harmonica," which looked like braces for an elephant, so he could play and drive. We all sang "Me and Bobby McGee" and screamed out my favourite line from that song, "Freedom's just another word for nothin' left to lose."

Later we turned on the radio to BBC and they were having a Janis Joplin concert. This time Rufus was at a loss, and Clive and I could lead the singing. I have the worst voice in North America. Clive suggested there was no need to stop at North America. Everyone did, however, agree that I did a mean imitation of Janis Joplin; the only detectable difference was she sometimes sang on key. We sang everything from "Ball and Chain" to "Summertime" to "Down on Me" to "Piece of My Heart." We sang until we were hoarse and the Black Country was at our backs.

I often wonder why a person remembers one moment and not another. This scene of so long ago is perfectly etched in my mind. I can feel the knot of the bandanna, hear the whistle of the air brakes and the whine of the diesel engine as it climbed the black foothills. It wasn't the scenery, as the Black Country was not in any way beautiful. It was the feeling of freedom — that glorious freedom of youth. I was twenty-one and free as a black crow in a cornfield. I felt it from my heart to my shoes. We were young, on the road; the trip was before us as we wailed with Janis Joplin. We were going to get it while we could.

Sixteen months later, shortly after I'd left England, my father was dead. I was living in Toronto when I turned on the radio and heard the same BBC concert, but now it was called a *tribute* to Janis Joplin, for she too had died. This time when I heard the songs, she seemed to be crying as she sang and her lyrics didn't ring of raucous freedom, but of lonely pain. I remember Roy used to say, "You'd best have fun, 'cause life can turn on a dime."

CHAPTER 6

# adam and eve

*That was the birth of sin. Not doing it, but KNOWING about it.*
*Before the apple, [Adam and Eve] had shut their eyes and their*
*minds had gone dark. Now, they peeped and pried and imagined.*
*They watched themselves.*

— D.H. Lawrence, *Studies in Classic American Literature*

It was dark in the country — like being in the middle of a black
cylinder. Suddenly life is a deprivation chamber and since you
have nothing to look out at, you have to look inward. There are
no clues from the outside world anywhere.

Clive and I inched along, hoping to find something to hold

onto. We desperately needed somewhere to crash. I actually hadn't thought of sleeping arrangements until that moment. I figured since he sprang his attendance upon me, he could figure out the hotel arrangements. I was, however, getting nervous. It was the era of free love, and people who were free enough to hitchhike around Europe and travel with male companions usually slept with them. I was sure that Clive had no idea I was a virgin. As my best friend Leora had said, I was a package of extremes. Margaret-Ann, on the other hand, was a dead giveaway.

Being a virgin was getting beyond boring — it was almost an albatross. I guess I still bought the notion that the first time was supposed to be special and with someone you loved. I knew that was a hangover from the '50s, but I couldn't feign the casually cool attitude practically every other woman my age who knew how to walk, talk and spin a birth control wheel seemed to have mastered with aplomb. Now people just "got it on." As Janis Joplin said, "Get it while you can." It was a right of passage, and I'd become stuck in the doorway.

I have to confess that, in retrospect, I wished I'd slept with Laurie, my first, and thus far only, love. At least I'd been with him for years and had loved him or thought I had. He wasn't the man I thought he was, but my sexual organs would never have guessed that. Besides I could tell by the way he touched and kissed it would have been great. What had I been thinking? What had I been afraid of? Maybe somewhere under all my bravado I was afraid the gates of Paradise would slam on me. I was afraid that St. Peter would meet me at the entrance of the kingdom of heaven and say, "You did *that*?" Somewhere in my ex-Catholic heart a nun's voice tremulously warbled, "Eternity is a long time, Catherine."

I don't think it helped that the first time I saw a sexual act was witnessing a gang bang at age thirteen. My girlfriend and I hid in a closet to spy on her older brother's fraternity meeting. The first order on their agenda was to bring in a pathetically deluded neighbourhood girl, and then all of them proceeded to have sex with her. When they were finished with her, they left her in the rec room and went upstairs for pizza. They told her to go out through the garage.

Probably the circumstance most responsible for my sexual squeamishness was that I was an only child who was close to my dad. I didn't have childhood friends or siblings who could initiate me into what post-pubertal behaviour was supposed to be. I had no idea what was normal. My father yelled at me only once in my life and that was when he caught me, at age thirteen, slightly flirting with a boy at church. He said he was ashamed and humiliated by my behaviour and that I was not a girl he wanted for a daughter. I never forgot it and flirting inevitably elicited dread and anxiety thereafter.

Shame and humiliation are scars for the mind. They lighten and fade with time, but they are always a part of you. Whenever you look at one of your scars, you remember exactly where you got it. You may forgive yourself, but shame will not be erased.

Little did I know I had nothing to worry about, since we couldn't find anywhere to stay. We were caught in the worst traffic jam in English history. They were now turning Europeans away at the Channel, every pump was out of petrol and no reserves could be delivered on the stymied roads. The M40 looked like an auto-wrecker's field where people had willy-nilly abandoned their overheated and gas-depleted investiture-seeking vehicles. I had no idea at the time, but it would take us weeks to get back to Oxford. Helicopters were dropping off food and the police were turning everyone back where they could. Potable water was a crisis, and the police were on the radios, asking homeowners to take in stranded wayfarers.

I couldn't imagine what it took for Clive not to say, "I told you so." I know I could never have managed to keep my mouth shut. We, unlike most people, had made it as far as Snowdonia in the depths of the night. The police turned us back there. No one could go on to Caernarfon.

We walked on and on in the dark in search of shelter. Now I knew how Mary felt on Christmas Eve. We approached nine farms to ask for lodging but all were full. We'd walked for miles into the depth of the forest. We felt our way along in the gloom and heard a dog bark. Clive said it didn't sound like a coyote or wolf and guessed there was a farm in that direction. We followed the barking until we came upon a tiny farmhouse. The woman said she had no room. As we walked away, she yelled something at our backs, in some foreign language that sounded as though it had no vowels. I recognized the words "Charlie's investiture." As we felt our way down the dark path, she began squawking and pointing to the barn. Clive made the sign for sleep by resting his head on his two folded hands. She nodded, pointing more insistently to the barn. She yelled some further directions, which we didn't understand. I was so hungry, cold and grateful; all I could do was smile at her. After entering the barn on my legs that shook from fatigue, I grabbed a blanket off the closest horse, figuring he couldn't grab it back, covered myself with straw and was "spark out," as they say in England, in seconds.

This was the closest I've ever come to communing with nature. I was a city girl who did sports in arenas. I had never been camping. My mother said people who camped were loopy. Her view was why save a whole lifetime for a house so you can sleep outside on the weekend? And the camp food, that dried stuff that grows like a man-eating plant when you add water, was, according to her, out-and-out scary. She said it was bad enough to cook on a stove, let alone an open fire. My father had been in complete agreement. After all, you could get poison ivy and as he said, "Thank the good Lord for campers. How else would druggists sell calamine lotion, bug spray or antibiotic ointment?"

I was having my first real outdoor adventure. Needless to say, I was shocked when bleating awakened me. I opened my eyes and there, in the next stall to mine, was a sheep looking down on me. All I could see was his head sticking through the wooden slats. I swear he smiled at me. I yelled over to Clive to catch the grin and he said he'd seen it. It was a real smile. I said no one will believe it back at the Bear, our local pub, but Clive said he'd back me up.

"How did you sleep?" he asked.

"Great. I hope I didn't give birth to the Christ child in this manger."

"Magi are forever late," he said.

"Bloody foreigners," I said as I brushed straw out from my hair. By now I could do a fair Oxford accent.

The farmer, who hadn't even seen us the previous evening, rang a bell as he swung the barn door open and grumbled in some foreign language, which the sheep seemed to understand. Clive said it was Welsh for breakfast. All the sheep stirred and bleated. After propping the door open with a pitchfork, the farmer walked away, carrying a big pail of feed. The sunlight streamed in the door, forming beams that shot through the hay like lightning. The scene reminded me of the cover of my robin's-egg-blue childhood Baltimore Catechism with an illustration of the Holy Ghost, in the form of a dove, perched in the white clouds bursting with beatific sunbeams from the heavens. The sun shone on the sheep's wool, making the lambs warm to the touch. Petting their wool was just like cuddling a stuffed animal, and when you snuggled close to them, you could feel their hearts beating and be warmed by their breath.

Since we'd arrived on a moonless night after wandering in a forest, I was not sure exactly where we were geographically when I woke up. We were somewhere in Snowdonia, Northern Wales's huge provincial park with the Cambrian mountain range as its backbone. Tiny, ancient towns dotted the landscape and cultivated farms were tucked in between the mountains. The whole area was criss-crossed with trees and fields that made me realize that the colour green had infinite variations. Streams meandered through the forests and were so clear you could see the forest perfectly reflected in them.

I walked out the door, and there before me lay a Welsh paradise. The sheep were filing out of the barn and the sheep dogs were barking, running around them in circles, nipping at rams that dared to stray in another direction. Wow, a dog with a job. That sure beat my lazy dachshund, Willie, who slept in all day and only woke up to growl at the mailman; at dusk he would bark at my mother until she put down the top on the convertible and took him for a ride.

Opening the door of that barn was a magnificent moment

for me. Suddenly I knew what the poet Gerard Manley Hopkins meant when he said, "The world is charged with the grandeur of God." It was the first time I had seen God as separate from organized religion.

The wildflowers were drooping with perspiration, exhausted after a wild night. As I continued to walk away from the barn, I saw the wheat was as high as the little stone farmhouse with its milk-paint-blue Dutch door. I cut through a field of purple lavender. The smell was so strong and intoxicating my eyes watered.

Clive, forever the Renaissance man, acted as though he was born there in the folds of Snowdonia. He had the sense to go right into the hen house and search for eggs. Some of the eggs were actually warm. He went up to the farmhouse and handed them over the top of the Dutch door. Inside, the peat fire had the warmest and most inviting smell, like incense from the earth.

We wound up staying in their manger for over two weeks, maybe more, since we were trapped in the mountains while the investiture traffic was clearing. The owners, Hiral and Aarowen, wouldn't take any money for our stay and refused the offer of work, although we did as much as we could. They danced in a small circle to indicate we'd entertained them for our keep.

We decided that since the traffic was still not cleared we might as well do some sightseeing in the area. As I packed, which meant putting an anorak and a toothbrush in my bag, I told Clive that I wanted to go mountain climbing. Although he agreed that mountaineering sounded perfect, he was worried that we didn't have the right equipment. Clive gestured his concern to Hiral by pointing to his shoes and then mimicked falling down a mountain. Hiral scoffed at Clive's trepidation by waving his hand and shaking his head. He drew out a map and indicated that Tryfan was the spot to go.

Thus began our trek through the forests. I remembered reading Heidi when I was a child and longing to experience the mountains. I had always loved climbing. I think it was genetic. My mother had made the mistake of reading Jack and the Beanstalk to me when I was three, and the following day I climbed to the top of our cherry tree and wouldn't or couldn't come down. My parents had to call the fire department. (My mother said if they could come for a cat, they could come for me.) The next day I did the same thing again, and my parents had to put stilts around the trees to keep me off them. They got me a climbing gym at age four. When I did a 360-degree flip over the top of the swing and got a concussion, I had to stay in the hospital until I knew my name. When I said, "Eisenhower," they said, "Close enough" and sent me home.

What do you do when you like climbing, but you live in a city with no mountains? You become a pole vaulter like my grandfather, a high hurdler like my father or a high jumper like me. I had expressed a desire to climb mountains for as long as I could remember. I even dressed up as a Billy Goat Gruff for Halloween. However, my mother, a lover of the level surface, nixed the idea, saying if God had wanted us to climb mountains, he would have given us cloven hooves.

As Clive and I began climbing Mount Tryfan, we came across varying patches of blooming phlox growing over the stones; the green mountain side was flecked with white and gold, purple and blue in a careless smattering of wildflower glory. We stopped and ate our cheese and bread that the farmers had packed for us and sat down in a valley in a crevice of the mountain to eat it in the sunlight. The ground was warm and there was no wind there. A creek rolled through the valley, which Clive said was drinkable since it was mountain run-off for the spring. We lay on the ground and stuck our heads in and lapped up the freezing water. As I threw the water on my face and then lay fully sated, sinking in the toasty moss, I said, "You know, Clive old boy, I won't forget this moment. If this stream was like memory and over the years it dried up, I could still dig through the silt and find this one moment."

After seven hours of hiking, we were still ascending. The wind had gradually picked up and was now circling near the peak, making a sound like a Jew's harp. Either the wind was drying my throat, or maybe it was the thinning altitude, but I was parched.

We had reached the cairn, the pile of stones that indicated you were almost to the top of the mountain. The temperature had dropped enough that there was some snow and the steepness had increased. Instead of grass, there was only shale and stones to grasp. It was now so steep we had to go on all fours and find protruding stones or stumps to use as handholds. One mountain climber scaled the shale beside us. He was the National-Trust-English-tramper type, equipped with thick mountain climbing gloves with traction grip, hat, boots, anorak and a detailed summit map hanging in a plastic sleeve around his neck. No one had told me you needed a map or that it was colder at the top and you had to expect incredible wind pressure. Clive said we needed to go back as we weren't dressed for the summit or for the scramble needed to get there. He also pointed out it was colder in Snowdonia compared to Oxford. I said we were almost to the top. He pointed out that summits were deceiving. The narrowness makes the top seem closer.

He assured me it was much farther than I thought. "Summits narrow for a long while. Everyone thinks it's over the next crag but it isn't." He said we had hours left. But, Christ, I'd come this far and I knew we could make it. He said we had to think of coming down, not getting lost in the maze of valleys and turnoffs, and it all had to be done before dark.

What a worrywart. I mean, really, coming down was no big deal. It wouldn't take any energy at all.

He screamed — to be fair to him you had to scream over the cacophony of the wind currents — "You know the problem with you? You make rashness sound like adventure. There is a fine line between the two. These winds are unusually high and the direction keeps changing. We need to return *now*."

"So? Don't come," I said.

"Please don't go from ballsy to batty, Cathy. You don't have to be the reincarnation of the American spirit. It can be tiresome."

"Go back," I said.

"Well, then I'd be a cad, wouldn't I?"

"No, we would just be two people who made different decisions."

"This is just one of those reckless moments of youth that is in truth very treacherous."

"You're getting into some British snit about this and I'm not interested."

His face now looked really angry for the first time. I continued in a less provocative manner. "This needn't be a point of national character. I am taking the risk to go to the summit; you have assessed the risk and don't feel comfortable with it. End of story."

"I have climbed the Matterhorn. I know the danger signals. I will not blindly follow an inexperienced climber wearing sandals into high winds with no ropes. This is my final warning or you will go ahead at your own peril."

The wind was howling around us now and I was really cold since I had stopped climbing.

"Everyone has gone back due to wind," he pointed out.

"Join them," I said and turned around and continued climbing.

"Just one minute, Cathy," Clive screamed. He had to scream since the wind was now circling like a hungry wolf and screeching in protest as though I'd stolen her pup. He was holding onto a rock to stay upright and said, "You are making this all very difficult."

"What is so difficult? I never asked you to come."

"Why do you think I came on this star-crossed venture?"

How the hell did I know why he came? "Look, Lord Whimsy, I am not playing 20 Questions with you on the top of a windy cliff."

He screamed across a large fissure from about eight feet below me but the wind was suddenly wailing so loud that I couldn't hear what he said. His arms were gesticulating wildly and he was going on and on. I indicated by holding my ears and shrugging that I couldn't hear him. I turned around and began climbing up.

I didn't look back until I got to the top hours later. The distance to the peak of the mountain was exactly as deceivingly far away as Clive had suggested. When I reached the summit, I looked down at my hands and was surprised to see them bleeding onto the crumbled shale. I guess I'd lost feeling in them. I looked around. No one else was there. I was puzzled since the pinnacle wasn't that large. I should have seen the mountain climber in the wool hat since he hadn't passed me coming down. I was also inexplicably shocked that Clive had left me. I was mistakenly lulled into believing the British gentleman training would supersede all else. In a way I admired that he left — after all, he said he would. For the first time, I began to worry about my safety because I knew that it would have had to be truly hazardous for him to bail.

The peak of the mountain was covered with large boulders that were hard to crawl over, including twin monoliths named Adam and Eve. Clearly, the monolith had at one point split and now there were two slabs separated by a gap. Hiral's map had a sidebar that indicated that it was a tradition to jump from one to the other. (I now understood what Hiral had tried to indicate by jumping from his couch to his chair.) You had to hurtle only about four or five feet, not an outrageous leap, from Adam to Eve, but the consequences of overshooting it would be disastrous, as there was a huge drop off on the other side. Intending to jump it, I stood up but was suddenly knocked flat by a gust of wind — I felt my lungs had momentarily become concave. I immediately understood the adjective winded. I had to lay flat, face-down on the stone, since the wind was so strong I didn't dare risk a gust catapulting me off the edge. Listening to the tempest above and below as it blew between the boulders, I hung my head over the side and looked down the mountain, hoping, to no avail, to see Clive. He'd been right, of course. It was hellishly cold. And I was sorry that after getting all the way to the top, it was too dangerous to make the leap from Adam to Eve.

# a shrew in shrewsbury

*We use the word love for the most amazing variety of relationships,*
*ranging from what we feel for our mothers to what we feel for*
*someone we beat up in a bordello, or its many equivalents.*
— Aldous Huxley as quoted by Harold Bloom

I descended as fast as I could, having no idea that it was harder
getting down than going up. Whoever tells you that? I thought it
would be like skiing, where it takes hours to walk up but minutes
to ski down. I was unsure about the footing. Finally, I realized I
had to back down from the summit with my stomach scraping

against the rock. As I undulated down, I heard a rhythmic clack-ing on the rocks below, the sound of large feet clomping. I knew there were no humans, so I was terrified to look below me. When I slithered farther, I saw it was a mountain goat followed by dozens more. The billy in the lead, with his long white hair and curved horns, looked at me with that kind of look that only males can have, which translated to, "So you thought you could climb the mountain and now you have to slither down. You think you're the first woman we've seen do this?"

It actually took longer to descend than to ascend. On the way up, you can see what to grab to pull you up, but it's not so easy in the reverse. I felt around for firm rocks to hold me but sometimes, before I put all my weight on one, I'd hear the scree come loose, then it would plunge down the mountain, pinging on some crev-ice as my head would if I'd lost my footing. The big mistake, well I guess there were a few, was looking down. I hadn't done that on the climb up. I had been too focused on finding the right rock to grab to pull myself up. Here I was wearing silly sandals with no tread, jeans and a flannel shirt over a T-shirt. I put my bandanna on, hoping to preserve some of the heat in my head.

It was suddenly overcast. God, all I needed was rain. Then I looked carefully at the sky and realized it wasn't really overcast: it was dusk. This whole thing was taking ages. Clive had warned me about this before he bailed. I really didn't blame him. I could only see getting to the top of that peak. Why was it always the reward and never the journey I was after? I swore to God, whom I totally believed in at that moment, that if He let me make it back alive, I'd never mention making it to the top of the mountain. I'd just say, "I went mountain climbing." I also swore I'd never think bad things about anyone ever again, except for Him if He didn't save me.

God didn't seem to be helping, since it was getting darker and I was barely making headway. I started to panic. My heart began racing and I suddenly lost my bearings and had no idea where to turn. Nothing looked familiar. I decided to sit and calm myself. I tried to find an inner calming voice and then I heard Roy from so many years ago. He said when some task seemed too daunting it was best to cut it into bite-sized pieces.

When I was a little girl and I'd said to Roy that we had too many deliveries to make before Christmas and got in what he called "a tizzy," he'd say, "One at a time, girl; one at a time." He would have me grid our deliveries in sections so we would have eight grids of eight instead of sixty-four deliveries. We would go grid by grid. When we finished one grid, we'd give ourselves a treat. His was usually a Johnnie Walker for the cold and mine was a hot chocolate with mini-marshmallows from whatever roadside inn was in our grid. When we were half finished, we had a meal. The deliveries always got done. When I asked what we would do if he got too tired to drive, he said the Rambler was like a milk horse and knew the route. Roy and I would plan our stories the next day for Coke break at the store. They were always based on our adventures, especially at Christmas time, when we would sometimes get to customers' houses at midnight and we'd had many Johnnie Walkers and many hot chocolates over many grids.

Roy always came back to me in emergencies because there never was an emergency with him — just a good story. When we hit black ice and almost froze to death in farm country in the famous cold snap of winter '57, he said, "Well, we gots to get out of this alive — it's too good a story to let lie fallow." We did emerge alive, but frostbite bit a chunk off his nose and my ear. When the spring thaw came that year, Roy said we should go back and look for our facial features at the edge of that cornfield among the other ears.

I divided the mountain up into grids: the rocky summit, the crumbling shale, the shoulder, the valley, the snow line, the creek, the narrow ledge, the mountain flowers, the foothills and finally the grassy bottom.

I was so cold my hands were shaking and losing their elasticity and grip. I put them under my shirt and on my still-warm stomach and then tried again. It worked. I finally made it off the rocky summit. I looked at my bleeding nails and fingers and the shrill voice of Irene, the cosmetician at my father's drugstore, came back to haunt me: "Look at those nails! Cathy, please remember those are jewels not tools."

As I worked through the grid, it was getting darker. My third grid down, I was sliding along the narrow path, when I looked across the valley and saw a cat's eyes shining at me. The translucent eyes caught whatever light there was left or else they glowed from within, which was really scary. I guessed it was a mountain lion, though I couldn't see his whole body because it was the same mottled grey colour as the mountain. Thankfully the chasm was too wide even for a mountain lion to jump, but it did give me some trepidation about what was ahead once there was no longer a valley between us.

By this time, it was so dark that only a nocturnal animal could have seen more than a few inches in front of him. Plus each step I took was excruciating. Not having proper hiking boots, my toes kept getting jammed in the front of my flimsy sandals and had to take all of my body weight. With each step, it felt like someone had dropped a large cinder block on my toes and was now grinding it into my entire foot. I had laughed at Clive's hiking boots, telling him he looked like a Hummel figurine. I guess that had been a bit premature. I'd thought the cold had been bad, but I was now relieved that the cold was numbing my toes.

Finally, I made it around the north side of the mountain and as I rounded the west side of the path, I was swathed in moonlight. The heather that had just looked like stubble on the dark side of the mountain now took on a pinkish bubble-gum glow. The gentle wind propelled the heather into a slow-motion dance; it was a sensual Carmen-like tango, its dusky purple haze abruptly changing direction as the wind swirled.

I was almost running now because the pain was too much when I stopped. I needed to get down while the moonlight was exactly on this spot of the mountain. Hours later, I was on the grass and knew I'd make it.

When I was back at the road, which was much farther from the foot of the mountain than I remembered it, I saw a tiny stone house in the distance. When I got there and found it boarded up, I sank onto the steps and nearly cried. I found out later I was on a ridge surrounded by mountain peaks and not in fact near the bottom of the mountain. There were little hamlets in the mountain valleys.

I stood on a peak and saw one light flickering in the distance. I thought it was only a mile, but as I kept going I never seemed to get any closer. My feet were wet from the bog and I was losing sensation all the way up my legs. When I lifted my right leg, sometimes it would fly to the side instead of in front of me. Finally, I found two sticks and leaned on them as crutches.

Like Amahl limping to greet the wise men, I hobbled to the tiny door and knocked. A wrinkled man in a floppy black wool hat opened the door and said in English with a thick Welsh accent, "It's a public house you've come to, lass. Anyone may enter, even an American." His confrère at the door said, "Since when have the Americans knocked before entering?" How did they know I was American? I was way too tired to hear what a bad country the U.S. was or anything about Vietnam. All I could say was I'd lost feeling. The one Welsh man said to the other, "Our dear Lord and the Felinfoel Brewery helped us do that years ago."

As they laughed their heads off and jabbered in Welsh, they helped me hobble over to a roaring fire set in a wonderful old cooking fireplace that was at least as tall as a man. There were two warm milking stools set near the grate. As I gingerly lowered myself onto one, I looked at an old man who sat on the other. He had flowing white hair with just a trace of red left in his beard. He wore a hairy vest and smoked a long pipe with a bevelled stem. He pointed to a white furry dog who slept right at the fire's edge and indicated I should put my feet right on his back. Confused I asked, "Where? On that curly haired dog?"

"That, my sweet darlin', is a sheep — unless you get wool from a dog in the United States of America," piped up another man. Everyone was now crowded around me, howling with laughter.

Finally a young man asked, "Where you from in America?"

"Buffalo."

"The plains where the buffalo roam?"

"No. New York."

There was a hush and the word was passed to the back of the crowd, "She's from *New York*, now."

"Ah, New York is it?" the waitress said, as though that explained everything about why I appeared at the door with crutches in the middle of the night somewhere in or near Snowdonia.

I said I've never seen a sheep up close until recently, nor had I ever seen one in a bar. This tavern was an odd place, a sort of big, snug barn that served alcohol. The ceiling had original beams, and the walls were burned with horseshoe prints and hung with cast-iron tools, the remnants of having once been a blacksmith's barn. There were people from eighteen to eighty in the place and everyone was abuzz as though this was a special evening. The lamb sat next to the fire and its coat was so warm that I could bury my feet into its toasty wool blanket. The bartender made me hot mead with raisins floating on top. It felt so soothing to cup my hands around the hot mug and gulp down the fiery liquid that I could have done a jig if I could have used "me pegs." Unfortunately, they were still ungovernable stumps. I related to the few people who spoke English the whole tale of what had happened. A teenager translated and they were amazed that I hadn't gotten lost. I had never even thought of the possibility of getting lost.

"There are so many crannies in there, wee one," said the woman who wiped the tables. "St. Christopher himself would get lost in its folds."

One thing I was taught by Roy was to watch for every visual sign when you make a turn and then commit them all to memory. He couldn't read, so that's how he got himself around. I never made a turn without committing the corner to memory and now that I'd thought of it, I had never once in my life been lost.

As more people came in, they said a climber from East Anglia in a wool hat had not returned to the lodge and was presumed lost. I said I had seen him and told the mountaineering team when I'd seen him and where. "He was about five hundred feet below the jump from the Eve to Adam when he passed me. I noticed him because he was so wisely dressed and had a map in a plastic sheath. How come no one told me it gets colder on top of a mountain? Isn't it closer to the sun?"

"There's lots you don't learn in New York," the old man with the pipe said to those around him.

The teenager who had translated said, "I'll bet there's lots you do learn," clearly longing to get out of his mountain town with its two buildings.

"Ah, we've lost many a man in that Adam and Eve gap," the old man said.

His crony said, "Many a man, many a man. It doesn't look far, but if you overstep it the results are disastrous with sheer cliffs on the other side."

"*Triw*, Adam and Eve should never have gotten together; that's why the good Lord split that mountain at the top," the woman who owned the tavern said as though she was speaking from experience, and no one contradicted her.

"Shut your clanging cakeholes," shouted an old toothless woman at the bar. "It's the time." As she fussed with the tuning of the television's one channel, I looked around and realized that this was one of those bars hidden from the authorities to avoid paying tax on the alcohol. That's why the men were guarding the door. It was in the mountains and no one knew of it other than the locals.

"What's happening on the television?" I asked. It was way too late for soccer, which the English called "football."

"Why, it's the moon shot!" the old man with the pipe told me.

"It's *Apollo 11* landing on the moon. Doubt they made it. Another Kennedy promise from the colonies fallin' flat on its arse."

His friend agreed, saying, "Why that young Kennedy couldn't have driven straight across a bog let alone get to the moon — not when he was alive and certainly not now that he's joined his maker."

"Nothin' new about an Irishman wanting the moon," his buddy replied.

"This TV gets the best reception in the mountains," another man reassured me.

"Here it is now. Shut your gobs!" the owner yelled.

There was silence in the room as Walter Cronkite came on. With Walter making me homesick and my feet throbbing as they swelled, my eyes teared up. I yelled in a mead-enhanced timbre, "Hi, Walter!"

The teenage boy whispered to the old man, "She knows Walter Cronkite."

Suddenly we heard Neil Armstrong say, "The eagle has landed." The picture moved to mission control in Houston, where all the engineers were jumping up and waving little American flags. Their smiling faces looked like my dad's, and they wore the same thin ties and white shirts. Neil Armstrong bounced out of the lunar module and took a tiny step just to make sure the ground could hold him. He then said, "That's one small step for man, one giant leap for mankind."

Everyone in the bar clapped. I was so proud to be American. Just like when I was a little girl. It had been so long since I felt national pride. *We'd done it.* As Armstrong planted the American flag, a group of Welsh men came over and picked up my stool and cheered me as though I alone had sent men to the moon. The weird thing was I did feel as though I'd done it. They paraded me around with my swollen legs and we partied. Everyone bought me a drink of warm mead. I turned up my nose at the two men who had insulted the memory of John Kennedy. One man stood on the bar and made a toast to me saying, "The good Lord sent a bedraggled American to our manger door to share this great event with us. We can always say we saw it with an American lass."

———

I stayed overnight in an apartment upstairs, where the owner lived with her husband. Miraculously, the whole time I was in Wales, no one would take even a farthing for their hospitality. As I lay in bed, although exhausted, I began thinking how much this moon landing would have meant to my father if he hadn't had a brain tumour. I'm sure he'd watched it, but I didn't know if he would have understood it or remembered it for more than a second. Yet the rest of the world would remember it for the remainder of their lives.

The '60s were drawing to a close. All the men that the counterculture had mocked, the engineering twits with their slide rules and pen holders in their pockets, "the establishment" men who worked hard every day, had made it happen. As I lay there under my frayed quilt, staring at the ancient ceiling beams, I began to feel differently about my idols of the '60s: Eldridge Cleaver, the Black Panthers, the SDS Weathermen and the Abbie Hoffman radicals. They were still activists with legitimate beefs, but they were no longer my heroes. I was growing up — I guess we all were.

Living in England helped me to see what was wonderful about the States. Americans had no class structure — at least not compared to England. In America, if you worked hard, you could get ahead. People were more free and could be judged on their own merits — something I didn't really notice until I experienced the stultifying English class system. When an American talked, you could tell where he was from, but not his social standing. When those American aerospace engineers working on the moon shot talked on TV about what they had done, you had no idea what kind of family they had come from. All you felt was pride in their accomplishments.

There had been many tears in the national fabric: Vietnam, the war that tore us apart, pit brother against brother and child against parent; the assassinations; the race rioting. But with the moon shot we could at least end the era on an up note — one that united us all.

Arriving in Shrewsbury in the county of Shropshire, I couldn't believe that only five days had passed since I'd descended the mountain. I had hobbled through the roads that were still full of abandoned cars, eventually hitchhiking east from Snowdonia. Hitchhiking is for carefree youth, not for the prodigal woman who is walking on crutches one week after nearly having her lower appendages amputated. (Believe me, you don't want the details.) The swelling had gone down, but the skin on my legs had split from having expanded too much and too rapidly and it was still peeling.

Limping and in pain, I stopped to rest my tree-stump right leg in the Shrewsbury's Dingle Gardens. In this sunken garden near a quarry, there was a mammoth ancient tree with a green octagonal bench that encircled the trunk. Since my leg was pounding, I propped it on the bench and wrote a postcard to Professor Beech. I had grown fond of him. The English system was so much different from the American. You could really share a lot with your professor because you had a one-to-one relationship. It was so much better than Psychology 101 in Ohio, where there were 200 students in a huge auditorium and you got extra points toward your grade if you would be a subject in an experiment. I was lucky to have found him. Although he was a repressed, major mothball tweed, he lit up over literature. If I mentioned any pathetic little stray thought, he took it seriously and always found an article on it for our next meeting. He seemed genuinely interested in my ideas. It may have been a good act, as he'd many years to hone his reaction to sophomoric idiots, but I bought it. If I said I admired a particular passage of some writer, he would say, "Oh well if you liked *that* . . ." then he would whisk round his office on a sliding ladder until he ground to a sudden halt when he found something that was always remarkably pertinent. Nothing other than poetry and literature mattered to him. If I mentioned anything other than the written word, he just coughed and muttered, "Quite right, quite right" until I returned to the topic of literature.

I had actually forgotten that I'd stayed overnight in Shrewsbury in 1969 until I unearthed a note folded in a book of Wordsworth's poetry opened over thirty-five years later by my son who used my old volume at university. I can't believe I wrote the following note, considering that any reference to the body made Professor Beech rapidly shuffle his papers and sometimes he ripped them up and threw them away faster than a modern paper shredder. As my mother would have said to me, "What were you thinking?"

Dear Professor Beech,

Well I think my enthusiasms have outdone our one and only Dylan Thomas. While his was libations, mine was mountain climbing. On the way to Cardiff to see Thomas's haunts I began to be overly inspired in Snowdonia. I climbed the biggest mountain — everything here has a Welsh word so who knows what it was called. (Have the Welsh ever heard of vowels?) Anyway I climbed to the top, losing all friends on the way up, and by the time I got down after midnight I was on Welsh crutches (two crooked sticks and a jar of mead). The next morning all of my toenails turned black and the day following that, they all fell off. Apparently I killed the nail beds by putting pressure on the nail all the way down the hill. How come Wordsworth never mentioned his need for boots when mountain climbing? I guess he was only looking at the sky. Anyway, I now have the Byronic clubfoot. Then I developed cellulitis, some hideous infection that makes my leg look like I have elephantiasis.

Lest you think I'm finished with my horror, read on.

Then I got to Shrewsbury, trying to hobble home, and the police had blocked all the exits to the town. No one can get on a highway. The M6 and all the M's are closed. The worst traffic jams England has ever had. Apparently everyone in England went to the investiture. (I will never believe anyone who complains about the monarchy again.) For a country of smart people, it is pretty stupid to have one main road. The police told me that people are running out of gas and food on the all the roads leading to and from Caernarfon.

Anyway that's the lead up as to why I missed our last two

*tutorials and will miss the next one.*

*Wales was amazing. I finally "get" Wordsworth now. I really do. I have no idea why Wales made me finally understand Wordsworth. Maybe it was the first time I saw the religious aspect of nature. Let's hit* The Prelude *hard when I shamble back. I hope you recognize me as the truly transformed nature appreciator. I have been struck on the road to Shrewsbury!*

*This missive is the long way of saying I'm sorry I missed my last tutorial and have been errant — but you're used to it by now.*

*I miss your zinging ladder and your pre-war mud-brown teapot.*

*Your favourite pastoral convert,*

*Miss McClure*

*p.s. Did you catch the moon shot? Now you know why Auden wants to live in America. (Just kidding. Calm down.)*

As I was finishing this aerogram, which must have never been mailed, a shadow appeared upon it. I looked up. It was Clive.

He never looked "on the spot" or, as the British say, "at sixes and sevens" in any way. Everyone in England had nonchalance down pat. He said, "I should have guessed. What an alliterative moment: a shrew in Shrewsbury." I simply looked up at him. He continued in an imperturbable tone. "I have you to thank for allowing me to see the county of Shropshire at such a leisurely pace."

"From what I understand, you may uncover, so to speak, every shrew in Shrewsbury before the M6 opens."

"I believe I've accomplished that." He added, "May I sit down?"

"It's a public park bench." After I moved over, I asked, "How did you wind up here?"

"It's hardly fate. Shrewsbury is the closest connecting link from our ill-fated Welsh tour to the only major highway to get back to Oxford. Nothing is moving on the M6. So we, like the other prodigal sons, are stranded in Shrewsbury until the M6 is running again."

"I guess you made it down the mountain intact?"

"I did make it down. *Intact* will forever remain in question. I informed the authorities you were still up there; however, they had their hands full looking for a missing body," Clive said.

"They found him. He didn't make the leap from Adam to Eve."

"I'm familiar with the gap." Clive said while looking straight ahead. We sat in less than companionable silence for about ten minutes (longer than I've ever refrained from speech in my life) until he glanced distastefully at my scaly, peeling, engorged port-coloured stump and said, "I would never ask you to move that putrescent appendage as it might cause an earth tremor."

"That's nothing. Wait until you see the toes."

"I assure you that I can wait."

We sat there for a while and then he said, "Frankly, you look a bit of a fright."

"Oh no. I'd so hoped to be dazzling on our next meeting. I have no money, haven't had a roof over my head for several nights, have a bad infection and I'm taking antibiotics with no food in my stomach. Should I go on?"

I knew that he was really upset about not being back to run his class. He was a don. He made all kinds of fun of hierarchy, but I suspected that deep down he was frightened of "misbehaving."

I also knew I couldn't keep up with his banter. He was better at quotes, language and mimicking accents than I could ever hope to be. However, there was one thing I did know: I could be craftier and understood people better than he did. I mean, what had he ever had to do but go to fancy schools where the rules were set? He never had to read the public. I'd had to do it since I was four.

"Oh, I just wrote a postcard to Beech-the-Leech. Want to hear it?" I asked.

He settled back on his bench as I looked at the card and pretended to read the following:

*Dear Professor Beech,*

*I have been travelling with Clive Hunter-Parsons. We started out for Wales. He insisted we go to see the investiture. Some very untoward events occurred which I'm afraid I'm not at liberty to discuss at the moment. Suffice it to say I've been hospitalized for an infection in Shrewsbury.*

*I hope that we can make it back on time for my tutorial, although I'm not sure much matters anymore.*

*Your faithful student for whom Oxford seemed so long ago,*

*Miss McClure*

He looked stunned. His mouth became a mean little line. He stood up and said in controlled prose, "I'm afraid that is completely inappropriate, and a lie." His voice was beginning to express the rage he felt. "To say nothing of daft as a brush. Really, woman. Come to your senses." He was white lipped with rage. People who had sat down on the other side of the tree were peeking around the branches.

*"Just kidding."* I handed him the card. He grabbed it furiously and read the real note. He looked at me upon finishing, shook his head in bewildered resignation and sank onto the bench and leaned his head on the tree for a full minute. He suddenly leaned forward, resting his elbows on his knees and supporting his head in his hands. "Got you," I couldn't resist adding.

He mumbled, "You most certainly have."

He didn't say anything for a long minute. His face was ashen and he looked beside himself — almost disoriented. "Of course you know that you *have me.* I have been madly in love with you since the day I saw you immediately following the post-office liftoff." Then he raised his voice and smiled. "You weren't even embarrassed. It was marvellous. And clomping down the stairs in that spectacularly inappropriate outfit for high table. I was gone." He stood up, agitated, and began pacing in front of me. Usually he was very concerned about propriety, but he now seemed oblivious to the pair on the other side of the tree bench who were inching their behinds ever so slightly around the bench in order to see and hear. "I *knew* how stupid this trip was. I *knew* we'd be stuck in some market town like Shrewsbury and not fulfill our responsibilities. *But I really couldn't help myself.*"

He paused. I tried to think of something to say, but I was too shocked. Finally to fill in the void, I said, "Well, I guess you knew a lot."

He didn't seem to notice that I was even there. "You see, I knew you were right when you said we thought only in class terms. I hate to tell you, but Karl Marx beat you to the punch on that one.

We think our parents and the teachers and all our authorities are so ridiculous that we parody them all the time for express amusement. It is all done with an ironic twist, and we all know that. You see, Marcus knows that. That was why he was as taken aback as Peter and I were by your egalitarian soliloquy. He knows it is us playing the game but knowing it is a sick game. What struck me during your berating was how it must look to you. I began to realize that when parody is done on a prolonged basis, it becomes real, or if not real, then it infiltrates who you really are or want to think you are — to say nothing of the whole performance becoming hackneyed." There was a long pause when he plunged his hands into the pocket of his khakis and then, pacing in front of the bench, he said, "I can't marry someone with a string of pearls who's never wandered from Sloan Square."

"*Marry?*" I queried.

"I'm four years older than you. I have to think of these things. We are spectacularly unsuited. I can't argue with you over daredevil things forever. I certainly can't be upbraided in public ever again. I have no idea why I'm in love with you. It's quite daft."

"Maybe it's my legs," I said, lifting up one elephantine stub.

"Cathy, I am trying not to be flippant or quote 'be ironic' or to parody anything, as that is what you have expressly *said* you've wanted."

"I never said that I wanted total earnestness. I simply said that cheap parody was your mainstay."

"What about you?"

"What about me?"

"Don't be a pickled gherkin. You hide who you are as well. You use humour and if that doesn't work, you jump into an outrageous

'American Free Spirit' mode, which, by the way, is no less phony, or I should say clichéd, than my jaded toffee-nosed number."

I thought of all kinds of things to say, but each one had humour or a tad of the outrageous in it. If I was to strip myself of these traits, I couldn't think of a thing to say. Finally, after pondering for a long while, I was surprised at how frightening it was to express real feelings stripped of humour and bravado. Everything seemed to be so *heavy*.

Love? What to make of it? As I sat on that bench in Shrewsbury under that oak tree I was, for the first time, speechless. I had no way to discuss my feelings. I didn't know if I didn't have the vocabulary or I didn't have the feelings. What is love anyway? I thought I'd loved Laurie. My heart pounded in his presence. I loved kissing him. He never objected to anything that I felt or tried to change my mind. We were both involved in the civil rights struggle. He was far more loquacious in print than in person. When we were together, we had things to do, places to go, leaflets to stuff. I'd loved every minute we were together from the moment I saw him. Yet it had all been a lie.

I didn't trust love anymore. Can love be learned? Clive was handsome, very handsome, and had a winning personality — everyone liked him. Most importantly he was kind and generous. Plus he would go far in this world. He would either be an academic or join the foreign service. He was incredibly bright in an astonishing number of areas. He was worth millions but brandished very few possessions in his room or anywhere that I'd seen. He listened, heard what I said about his use of parody and how annoying it was on a constant basis. He wasn't defensive and seemed willing to think about changing. He refused to climb to the summit so he wasn't going to be a pushover. He called me to task, which I knew was necessary. (I mean you don't want the guy to wear the pants but you don't want him wearing a dress either.)

My father said the truth could never get you into trouble, so I tried to explain what was going on in my head: "I don't know how I feel." Then as the ultimate non-sequitur I blurted, "I'm taking antibiotics." He sat down on the bench and held my hand and kissed me very softly and said, "Let's leave it for another day. No one can think in Shrewsbury."

# the joker

*The English are polite by telling lies.*
*The Americans are polite by telling the truth.*
— Malcolm Bradbury, *Stepping Westward*

When we finally dragged our sorry, bedraggled bodies back to Oxford, we were welcomed with open arms. Even the Barson made a fuss about my legs, saying he'd had cellulitis during the war, which had developed from trench foot. He said it was "a devil of a thing." He assured Clive I'd been "first rate" to have made it home on foot. Clive assured him my tenacity had never been in question.

Marcus suggested that the food at Trinity College was already unappetizing and could I please refrain from wearing sandals as my black leprous toes could put anyone off their "spotted dick." (A name for a steamed pudding that only the English could come up with and refer to with a straight face.) When I regaled everyone about the climb up Mount Tryfan, Peter said, "That Welshman was having you on when he indicated it was a good romp, Cathy. How come he didn't go with you? I'd wager he laughed the day away in the pub, telling his friends where he'd sent you." When I looked askance at him, he added, "The Welsh love nothing more than a good one over a pint."

Clive knew this kind of behaviour, which was xenophobic at worst and clannish at best, drove me crazy, so he jumped in saying we'd stayed at their home and the lad seemed on the up and up to him. "After all," he added, "most *normal* people could turn around when they so fancied."

Marcus, who seemed to know about nearly everything while having experienced nearly nothing, said, "I understand real mountaineers jump the twin monoliths from Adam to Eve."

"I could have done the jump if it hadn't been so windy and getting dark. The problem was if you overstepped it you went over a major precipice and if you fell short you crashed down into a rocky crevice."

"A good reason to stay out of Eden entirely," Marcus said.

"Yeah. It wasn't worth it, especially when you think that after that leap I had to deal with coming down the mountain in the dark."

"There has been another expulsion from Paradise while you were away," Marcus said, exhibiting that smile he reserved for when he had privileged information, usually of the desultory variety. "God's eternal justice marches on in our disloyal colonies. I have saved these news clippings for you."

"Oh thanks, Marcus. I was hoping someone would save the press on the moon landing. I haven't seen or heard a bit of news since I've been away. Fortunately, a tavern in Snowdonia had the landing on TV." I couldn't resist adding, "By the way, Marcus, the disloyal colonies you so often deride have made history." Turning to the rest of the table, knowing I was a braggart and not caring, I gloated, "I hope you all watched the *American* moon shot and ate a huge piece of humble pie."

"I wasn't referring to orbiting around Paradise; I was referring to getting unceremoniously kicked out of its wrought-iron gate," Marcus said, sliding the *Tribune* under my nose. I read the bold headlines splashed across the front page on July 18, 1969: "Senator Edward Kennedy reports to Edgartown, Mass. Police report that a car which he was driving plunged into a pond at Chappaquiddick, killing a woman passenger. He fled from the scene, not reporting the accident."

I felt as though someone in my own family had brought shame upon me. He was our last hope for another Kennedy in the White House. My face was heating up to its most vermillion, and I had trouble looking at the members of my stairwell. The one time in my mother's life she had grabbed the ring on the merry-go-round was when she headed up the Kennedy Campaign in western New York. The others had an inkling of what the Kennedys meant to my family and me. I had only one picture in my rooms: my mother shaking hands with John Kennedy in Buffalo.

I thought of how my mother must have felt when she heard the news. The Irish Catholics who led the life she'd dreamt of having: the Hyannis Port compound with servants, the money, the glamour, the family football games, the sailing, the handsome sons who wanted to grow up and serve their country and make a difference. The Peace Corps that my mother admired and would have joined had she been younger was forever linked with the Kennedy clan. My mother had bought into Camelot — had even purchased Jackie Kennedy pillbox hats and two Oleg Cassini knock-offs before "knock-offs" had been invented.

Being stuck in the low end of a dreary suburb of Buffalo and being married to a man who now wore suspenders because he forgot how his belt worked did not add up to a glamorous life. Since we left Lewiston, she had taken interest in so little. The church in Buffalo was too large and impersonal. The garden club had been overrun by the wealthy, who knew each other from the golf club. She never joined anything or went anywhere. Her charmed life of dining out had dwindled to chain restaurants. In the next decade, it would wither to having a Happy Meal at McDonald's early enough to catch the seniors' discount. Maybe that is what it always was, and I was just seeing it for the first time now that I'd grown up, or was growing up. Her props were being stripped away, one by one.

The myth of "America on the precipice of change" was being pulled from under my feet, as was the myth of "my happy family." The small town of the '50s where my parents held a secure position in the hierarchy was gone. My mother's behaviour was more eccentric without my father covering for her, sweeping from behind with a normalizing brush. The money that kept the machine oiled with perfect clothes, cars and the air of elegance was gone. The family myth of strength and security had been dead for years — since we left Lewiston or I left childhood. Maybe it was always a myth. Maybe children have to believe in the infallibility of family and leaders when they're young and innocent. It's too scary not to. To whom would we turn? When these role models disappoint you, it isn't their fault. They just didn't live up to the fantasy that you needed to grow up with. We all build our own ships to sail away on, and they have to be strong enough to sail through the rapids of youth. When we look back, sometimes we wonder how we ever stayed afloat and eventually came ashore.

I had been sitting there pretending to read the details in the paper, but really I was stunned into shock. When I looked up, the dining hall had nearly emptied and only our table was still there.

Marcus said, "Could *she* be lost in thought?" Mixing a sugar cube in his coffee, he added, "Ted Kennedy will get away with it. He knows how to glad-handle and he has those hail-fellow-well-met manners that bought him into Harvard as an old boy, just like all the other toffee-noses."

"Unfortunately, Ted got in over his head as he had the family connections but not enough neural ones. So he cheated at Harvard and was kicked out. He has really been sunk twice," Peter said.

I'd had it. I was so fed up with everything and everybody, I felt like Mary-Jo-Kopechne-goes-to-Oxford. I had swallowed more than water. I had gulped down all the swill that had been thrown at me: lying lovers, fathers whose brains left town, beloved leaders who turned out to be lying cowards.

I never felt sad for long. It was the McClure alchemy to spin pain into anger as fast as I could. It felt better. At least you had someone to yell at — even if it was in your head.

I pushed my chair back to leave, but yelled at Marcus, "Well, gee, thank you, Marcus, for saving all this bilge. I can see you were just licking your chops until I returned. If you don't get an academic job at the end of all this, you could always work for the grim reaper."

Peter, who took it upon himself to keep all discourse from ever erupting with any feeling, abruptly changed the subject. He looked over at Clive and said, "You've been away, ol' boy, so you may not know that it is our little coterie in staircase seven who are to sit at high table with the poet laureate."

"Since Margaret-Ann ate in her room, she may not know about high table tonight. She won't want to miss this. I'll run over and leave a note for her," Clive said.

"I thought we did the high-table bard thing already?" I said. At that moment, I felt like there were enough bad bards in the British Isles that if they only threw half of their books on a bonfire, England would not need central heating.

"This is a new poet laureate: Cecil Day-Lewis," Peter said.

"Brilliant." Clive turned to me and said, "He is a live wire ex-commie Irishman turned establishment — writes great mysteries on the side under a pseudonym."

Since this guy was not your average high-end, often dead-end, poet (I'd heard enough of them to last a rhyming lifetime), I decided Cecil Day-Lewis was worthy of a shower and my new blouse with the tiny mirrors that I'd bought in Soho. It was a straight copy of the one worn by the mod girl with the hash brownies. When Clive saw the blouse, he said it could be dangerous for epileptics to escort me anywhere in the sunlight.

This high table event might even be worth setting my hair in rollers and crawling under my hair dryer with the plastic hood while I read Day-Lewis's *A Hope for Poetry* (1934). Of course there was no real hope for poetry, but these poets all read each other and assumed that, although they had almost no book sales, somehow others secretly read their works or had heard of them through osmosis. They seemed to have no idea that they were famous only in their own minds. One truly minor poet who visited our class said that he believed that poetry was just a powder keg waiting for a spark coming in the '70s. (He thought that people couldn't wait to get home from Carnaby Street to read Tennyson.)

—–

Margaret-Ann and I had to go to extraordinary lengths to get to a ladies' washroom with a shower. To attend to basic bodily functions, we had to walk down our winding staircase, cross the large courtyard, turn and follow the path along the back garden, go behind the chancellor's house and then ascend another staircase in the new wing. If it rained, we actually had to wear our wellies and macs over to the shower. The new wing was still under construction and the heat was yet to be hooked up. However, it was the only shower for girls. On a few occasions in the winter, the drain had iced over and we had to hack away the ice so the shower could empty. Fortunately now it was summer — for what that's worth in England. Margaret-Ann and I sometimes went together so one of us could hold the flashlight or, as Margaret-Ann called it, "the torch." (She loved using English terms.) I also toted a red metal toolbox that contained all my bathroom supplies and makeup.

As the hour of high table with the poet laureate approached, I donned my shower trek attire and closed my door and headed

down to pick up Margaret-Ann. Since the new wing was still under construction, pipes were scattered everywhere and there were
no curtains yet on the windows, but the glass was shaded. The
showers were not like showers in dormitories in America where
there were many sets of faucets on the wall in one big room with a
drain in the middle. This was a large room with individual marble
showers with curtains for each cubicle. It was typical of England
to have the shower curtains up before installing the heating. Each
shower had a bench in it so you could be seated while showering,
which seemed strange to me. (Who sits in a shower?)

Margaret-Ann and I got into our separate showers. I remember
distinctly that I was singing "Mellow Yellow" in an English accent
when my curtain suddenly whipped open. A man stormed into
the stall. He slammed me against the marble, seized my breast and
twisted it painfully. I grabbed the glass bottle of green Prell Shampoo and hit him over the head with it as hard as I could. It spilled
and he slipped. As he tried to get up, I kneed him in the groin.
Margaret-Ann was now in the middle of the room screaming, "Get
out!" He looked completely shocked to see her there. He stood up
and grabbed my arm and began pulling it behind me as he tried to
grab the other one. Blood was streaming from his head, obscuring
his vision. I screamed at Margaret-Ann to go for help. She ran out
and screamed down the hall of the empty building.

The intruder, who looked about middle age with salt and pep-
per short curly hair, was English, with a round, florid face. He
was of a huskier build than most English and wore a blue cotton
shirt with a button-down collar. Not the shirt of a workingman.
I remember thinking that. I didn't notice anything more. As he
heard Margaret-Ann's piercingly loud, unearthly shriek retreating

down the hall, he looked around the room like a caged animal. He still had a hold of one arm and was trying to twist it, but I kept moving around so he couldn't keep it behind me. He tried to get closer to me, and I attempted to hold him off. The blood was mixing with the Prell on the floor, making a purplish brown colour.

Suddenly Roy came into my mind and I remembered something he'd said to me in grade four: when you hit a bully, you have to use something sharp — you'll never overpower him. As the blood was running into his eyes, I realized he was momentarily unable to see, so I had a second to act. I wriggled out of his grasp and I ran for my red toolbox that I used to carry my bathroom products to hit him again with the edge of the metal. As I picked it up and got ready to swing it, he rubbed his eyes with both his hands. Breathing heavily, he looked at me with fury in his eyes and ran out of the room. I will never forget that look. It was as though he knew me. His face registered bewilderment, then shock over a betrayal and then just plain rage. I straightened up and tried to put on my red shirt but my one arm wouldn't work and I'd cut my feet on the broken glass.

Finally the Barson and Reggie came running down the dark hallway of the vacant building with Margaret-Ann, whose tiny body was naked other than the suds she had on her head. The suds made her look as though she were wearing a white Marie Antoinette wig. By now my legs were quivering like they had the time I had hypothermia as a child, so I sat down on the wooden bench near the row of sinks. The three of them stood just inside the door, looking at the shattered glass and the blood. The Barson said, "No worry, my dear. We have everything locked. He can't get out."

I guess that was supposed to be comforting.

Reggie saw my hand hanging at my side (I later found out I had a rotator cuff injury) and silently helped me slip on my long T-shirt, which I primly tucked under me with my one working hand. Reggie began cleaning up the glass. I said, "Leave everything for the police," and I threw Margaret-Ann her Laura Ashley shift with the pink and white flowers.

The Barson said, "Oh, there is no need to overreact just yet. Steady on, we'll have the bloke in a matter of minutes."

"Either you call them or I will," I said, still panting.

"Oh we will," Reggie spoke up.

I began to calm down and said I was going back to my room to get dressed. I looked at Margaret-Ann, who was holding the towel rack and shaking so hard the chrome rack was making a rat-a-tat sound as it quivered against the tile. She whispered, "I had to run out without my clothes."

"Of course you did. You saved me from being raped. Thank you. He knew you meant business and that's why he took off." She was still naked. She seemed in shock. She was holding the shift I'd handed her as though it were a crunched-up Kleenex. I pulled it over her head as best I could with one working arm. "There, now you're dressed."

The Barson said, "I didn't let anyone in who wasn't authorized. It's not easy with this addition and the roofing on the old building being worked on and ladders everywhere. Still, there were no strangers."

"It doesn't have to be a stranger," I said.

Margaret-Ann went into a lavatory stall and began throwing up. I held her head and helped her down the hall as best I could. She said, "I feel decidedly unwell."

The Barson said, "I wouldn't make hay of this until we've some facts. No point in stirring up trouble with the poet laureate on his way."

As I held Margaret-Ann and guided her back to her room, Peter and Clive came out to see what had happened. Peter said, "You were walking so slowly across the quadrangle, I could tell something was wrong."

"There was an attempted rape in the girls' shower in the new building," I said as I led Margaret-Ann into her room and helped her cover her wet shift with a blanket. Peter and Clive followed us into the room.

"There was no rape!" Margaret-Ann yelled at me as though I were the rapist.

"I know that," I said quietly. "The guy forced his way into the shower and grabbed me, and Margaret-Ann went for help. I cut him with a shampoo bottle; he got scared and ran away."

"You don't *know* he became frightened," Margaret-Ann screamed hysterically at me. "This is pure supposition."

There was a knock at the door. I jumped and my heart began to race. The door opened and Reggie entered, accompanied by what I presumed were two plain-clothes policemen, although everyone in England wore plain clothes so it was hard to tell. In fact, they both looked surprisingly like the intruder. I decided to call him "the intruder" since "rapist" set off Margaret-Ann.

The police asked me what had happened. I gave a description of the man and the event. Then Margaret-Ann gave her version of the story. She had remembered brown unlaced work boots. I hadn't seen them.

The policeman then asked if we knew him. When we both

said no, he asked if we were sure about that. When I said I was positive, he asked if he could possibly have been a man I'd met in London when I'd stayed out all night there. Perhaps I hadn't remembered him?

He also asked why we were alone on a building site. I explained that was where the girls' shower was located and we were told to use it. Then he asked the strangest thing in a tone I had come to really dislike. "You were nude at the time, then?" He looked at his mate in a knowing way.

"Yes, I said I was taking a shower. Even in England one must disrobe." I really didn't like this guy. I was fragile and I looked him right in the eye to let him know I wasn't putting up with any of his bullshit. One thing I'd learned about England: yelling was frowned upon. What really frightened the English was getting "called out" as they referred to it, by someone who was one step above them in the elaborate hierarchy of British life. I quietly said, "I have no intention of having an assault in the afternoon and then someone acting as though I'd been doing a water dance in the nude on a construction site." I snapped into what had become my new English self, complete with Oxford accent. "May I speak to your superior? I don't care for your line of questioning. I am not feeling protected, which is, I believe, the job of the police."

"I don't think that will be necessary," he said in quiet terror.

"I'll decide what is necessary. I called you — now I'll call the chief inspector." I stormed out of the room, went to the Barson's office and called the chief. He was there in fifteen minutes. He entered Margaret-Ann's room, where we sat with the plain-clothes detectives, Reggie, the Barson, Peter and Clive. The chief inspector was old, with white hair and a moustache that still had some blond hair in it, and wore a suit with a matching vest. He said that he would take over from here and never once looked at his underlings as they departed. He sent everyone out of the room except for Margaret-Ann and me.

I told him what had happened. He never asked me about the flunkies and I never mentioned them. He went over every detail. Margaret-Ann simply couldn't answer. The only thing she could continually say was "I had to run out disrobed or it would have been too late."

He said, "Of course you did. You were brave and did the right thing. Catherine was brave as well. She never ran away and left you there. She took him on, which I would venture to say took him by surprise. Catherine, I suspect he was watching your room and knew when you put on the red long shirt you were going to the shower. I imagine he had no idea you picked up a friend on your way to the shower. So I'm moving you two up to the top floors and putting my men in one of the downstairs rooms for an unspecified time or until this rascal is apprehended. If you are going anywhere in the evening, please don't go unaccompanied or else tell our man. I will introduce you to him presently, and I will be back in the morning. Do you think you need a doctor's care? We can have one brought in here promptly." When I assured him I would be all right, he said, "I think you need to rest now."

Margaret-Ann didn't say anything when he left, not even good-bye.

—

Peter, Reggie, Clive and the Barson helped us switch quarters. At about a half hour before dinner, I was lying listlessly on my new bed. My body ached all over and my arm now moved only in sudden jerks. Far worse than my physical injuries was my state of mind. I was upset but felt I had no right to be. I was almost as upset by the police insinuating it was my fault as I was by the attack. Clive entered and said quietly, "You had best get ready for dinner. We are at the high table in less than half an hour."

Now, nearly fifty years later, when I look back on that moment, I wonder why it never occurred to me to stay in bed. Why didn't I say, "I don't feel up to going and talking and being pleasant to the poet laureate and pretending that I feel just fine one hour after an attempted rape. My breast is swollen, all black and blue, my shoulder hurts, my arm will not move in any requested direction and my feet are scored like a country ham." For several years after that, my heart pounded when I saw the Prell Shampoo commercial on television. When the pearl dropped through the green viscous liquid, it felt like fingernails screeching down a blackboard until the pearl finally hit the glass bottom.

However, I felt I had to do what I'd committed to do no matter how much turmoil I was in. So I must have shovelled all my pain and fear in with one long swallow and said, "Right. I'll be ready in a few minutes."

No one had answered at Margaret-Ann's door, so I moved on without her. As I descended the stairs, my legs were a bit shaky, which I thought was odd. Still I walked in red patent leather stacked heels on lacerations that opened with each step.

I was seated across from the new poet laureate, Cecil Day-Lewis. As he greeted me, I wondered why, if someone makes it to the lauded position of poet laureate, don't they get their teeth fixed and buy a jacket that fits?

He was craggy but handsome and wore his bow tie with

aplomb; he was also charming and engaging and had more animal magnetism than most men have in their sixties. He really knew how to tell a story. They all began with famous people: "When I was fettered to Auden before I found my voice . . ."

I noticed I was having trouble following the conversation. I seemed to be out of sync. I heard someone say Day-Lewis had written *The Magic Mountain*. "Wait a minute, Thomas Mann wrote that," I said.

Clive snapped, "*The Magnetic Mountain* is what the poet laureate wrote, Cathy."

"Oh sorry. I'm not myself tonight," I said in a daze.

"Feeling indisposed?" Day-Lewis asked kindly. He was the first person other than the chief inspector to speak solicitously.

"Yes." He looked at me to go on. Finally I said, "I was assaulted in the shower today and I seem to be a bit dazed."

"Appalling ablutions," he replied.

There was an embarrassing silence. Clive finally said, "Really, Cathy, we have a poet laureate here, not Florence Nightingale." Peter began a discourse on *The Magnetic* or *Magic Mountain* and everyone rushed forward with their literary quips.

It was as though I had defecated on the table and now they all had to whip into gear and sweep it away. I was terribly embarrassed and realized I'd done something awful. I was only trying to explain truthfully why I didn't hear the title correctly. I didn't say a word the rest of the night. After dessert, when I felt I would not make "an issue," I excused myself. Reggie must have been told to walk me back to my room so I wouldn't be out alone at dark. As we got to my door, he said, "I'm ever so glad you gave that guy a bit of welly today. Not many English girls would have done it."

I curled up in my bed, in my unfamiliar room, holding one of my fuzzy slippers with a donkey head perched over the toe or, as my father called them, my donkey-hote slippers. My mother had said that they were far too big to pack — they did take up half the suitcase, but I guess I knew that I might hit a low like this when I had no one to turn to. I wasn't calling my mother or father. They had enough on their plate.

As I held my donkey, I began questioning myself. Although my long red shirt came almost to my knees, maybe I shouldn't have worn it to cross the quad and trot around to the shower. Maybe my short skirts were provocative. Why had I been alone in a big, empty building? The windows were shaded glass so that wasn't the issue. Why had the first policeman wanted to know why I hadn't run away?

Now there had been this whole embarrassing fracas at dinner. No one other than Reggie acted like I'd done the right thing. I mean I wasn't the rapist. Why was it so bad to have mentioned it? Maybe I was making a mountain (magnetic, magic or otherwise) out of a molehill? The British fought in the war and had the black-outs — I guess I was overreacting. It was hard to feel so raw, so emotionally wronged, yet have all of surrounding society tell me to "put a sock in it."

The next morning, I felt a strange combination of anger, embarrassment and shame. Reggie knocked on my door. "I've brought you some tea, Miss." He came in and brought the paper. He said that, much to everyone's shock but mine, Margaret-Ann had pulled up stakes and vanished. A cab picked her up with all of her belongings. She left a short note for her don. He said, "It's ever such a pity as she was in line for a first."

Reggie opened the shade and continued, "The High and the Broad are swarming with jam sandwiches." I imagined Wonder Bread sandwiches piled to the top of the streetlights, but I later found out that jam sandwiches were police cars — white cars with a red band circling them. "I saw them on me way in this morning. I also heard from me mate what works at All Saints that somethin' happened in town last week when you was away. The Barson heard the bobbies banging 'bout it on the phone in his gatehouse. He said something about the rapes around Oxford. He said he had another for the map. That's what he said: rape and then map. He was quite certain about them words, he was. They're trying to keep it down, but they knew better than to try and shut you up." I nodded listlessly. Seeing I wasn't myself, he said he'd take his leave.

By breakfast, Clive tried to be chipper. Marcus said that Reggie had blathered on to him how Margaret-Ann had left Oxford. "One less to compete for a first," I said, reading his mind.

I had learned my lesson. Shame is the most effective teacher. I never mentioned the assault again. I was a bit reclusive for the next while and managed to get a lot of work done. No one ever asked what was wrong. They simply made small talk at meals.

The inspector eventually came to me, saying they had found, as he called him, "the joker." The man was a roofer who had come in from a city up north to get work. He had a wife and one son, to whom he faithfully sent a paycheque. There was roofing tar on the floor of the shower that had washed off him with the shampoo so that had narrowed their search. He also had a gash on his forehead. He had actually brought a dry-cleaned shirt in his bag with him to work that day. Apparently, he'd been looking in my room for months. My assumption was that no one could see in the top of my window. He, however, stood on a turret at Balliol College and watched my every move after the other roofers had left for the day. He knew that when I took the red box off the window seat, I was going to the shower. What he didn't know was that on that particular day I was picking up Margaret-Ann to go with me, which threw off his plan. He had been in and out of the college wall on a ladder used by the roofers.

I didn't have to go in and identify him. When the police confronted him, he confessed to my attempted rape and to several actual rapes, the latest of which he managed successfully two weeks previous to my attack. He admitted that he had been waiting for me at my usual 11:00 p.m. time to buy my two cigarettes from the vending machine on the Broad. However, when I hadn't showed as I'd been stuck in Wales, he was angry at my refusal to follow my usual pattern. According to the inspector, he felt "stood up," and he had brutally raped another woman who had the misfortune to buy a cigarette at 11:30 that evening. She lost an eye as well as her innocence in the attack.

The police moved out of the residence, much to everyone's joy, since many wanted to smoke dope and carry on. I could tell they blamed me for the shutdown. The underlying idea was "before we had American women here, we didn't have any of this trouble."

I worked my tail off for the rest of the summer and kept a low profile. I felt it was my high profile that had led to trouble. No matter what you look like, if you are one of two women and you have crashed into the post office and had armed guards in your stairwell, you stand out.

Fall edged its way back onto the calendar and caught me in my summer clothes, shivering on my bike. I guess I should have expected it, but, like aging, you only realize it has arrived when it inconveniences you and you are unprepared for it.

As we were soon to discover, the blustery winds blew in more than the fall. One day when we were enjoying the first log fire and the fermented apple juice called "scrumpy," in walked Margaret-Ann. She looked more delicate, thinner and less rested than when she went home to "recuperate." No one ever mentioned what she went home to recuperate from. They'd saved her room for her and even left up her pictures of John Donne and his religious cronies.

Fall was the perfect biking weather, and we all rode across fields and through forest on rights-of-way paths to get to the Trout Inn in Wolvercote, about three miles from Oxford. We would have a beer in the amazing setting of this ancient building by the Thames River, where peacocks roamed and men played at archery instead of darts or the jukebox. The turning leaves were glorious, subtler than the magnificent display in America, but stunning in their display of refined colours.

Apparently the Trout Inn provided the inspiration for Lewis Carroll's *Alice's Adventures in Wonderland*, and according to some it was the meeting place for Fair Rosamund and King Henry II. I believed all of the Trout's lore because it was magical for me as well. I used to sit on the river wall and watch the Thames rush by. There was something about the rushing water that reminded me of the Niagara Falls of my youth and made me feel warm and at home.

One thing I'll say about Clive, he knew when to back off. Since "the untoward incident" and his attempt to get me to not appear "unseemly" in front of Cecil Day-Lewis, he simply came to tea and meals and often walked me home from the library and rode his bike to the Trout with all of us. Other than that, he kept to himself. He was preparing for his M.Phil. examinations, so he was really working hard, which even he admitted.

Once at dinner, Peter said, "Jane Cromwell and Fiona Wright are in from Cambridge. Her brother is a cox for the Dark Blue. They rang yesterday and suggested meeting up."

Clive said, "I don't think I have the time."

"They're expecting to get together. Why not? It'll be a corker. You don't have to make a night of it."

"No, I told Cathy I'd help her with her Romantics essay."

"Go ahead," I said. "I only wanted you to proofread it."

"No, you didn't."

He was right about that.

"Suit yourself" was all I could manage to say.

We worked all day on my essay and then took our bikes through the forest to the Trout Inn. I got a flat tire, so we had to walk home. As we strolled through the woods, he said, "You know, I've really tried not to be a cad and I must tell you it has taken quite a bit out of me."

"Gee, I'm not a cad, and it was easy."

"Well, having had a few pints will make this a bit easier. You haven't been a cad exactly, as I believe the definition is gender specific, but you know how I feel about you, yet you have never once alluded to it." I just kept walking my bike, not knowing what to say. He continued, "I know you were upset about that unfortunate business back in the summer with that joker, so I have tried to back off."

"'The unfortunate business' I should have only mentioned to

Florence Nightingale?" I inquired.

"Cathy, England is drastically different from America in that discussing a personal matter at a formal dinner with someone you have never met would have been considered" — he paused — "ill advised. I was only trying to save you from embarrassment."

"How chivalrous." After walking along the winding path in silence for about five minutes, I just couldn't resist trying to figure out exactly where he thought I'd gone off the rails. "I don't want to, as you would say, 'have words,' I just want to understand the situation. You thought I was uncouth?"

"Well, that would be close to what it would have appeared to others."

"I think there is far too much couth in England."

We walked along, looking at a cloud passing over the moon for quite a while, and he said, "You know before I met you, I used to be Jack the lad, or quite the man about town, but I no longer feel the urge to . . ." He didn't finish the sentence but only ran his hand through his thick blond hair.

The moonlight was flickering through the trees, and as the woods opened we came to a narrow meadow with a thatched roof cottage at its edge. As we looked down on the meadow of wheat, it glittered golden or yellow depending on how the wind was blowing it and how the moonlight caught it.

"Let's sit down on the edge of this copse and have a fag."

He lit both of our cigarettes and we smoked silently. He looked into my eyes and slowly leaned over, gingerly kissed me and then kept his arms around me. On the one hand, it was lovely since I hadn't kissed anyone in a long time, but that kiss made me realize it would still be a long time before I'd be over Laurie. I guess your first love or first kiss is always the one that knocks you flat. Probably Clive was proceeding tentatively because of "the untoward incident." Not many people would have had the decency to avoid all contact until I showed signs of being my old self.

I decided to give it time. I had no idea how I felt about him. I was certain of one thing. I didn't want those girls from Cambridge honing in on him.

Sexual attraction is such a strange thing. Clive was handsome, with his lion's head of blond hair, bright, kind and we always had enormous amounts to say to one another. Why is it that some men only need to look your way and you feel rocked, while others fail to register on the Richter scale? Chemistry is a peculiar but accurate term to describe this phenomenon. You can mix hydrogen and oxygen and get water, or you can add temperature and pressure to the same atoms and get the hydrogen bomb. Once that critical mass is reached, it is hard to stop the chain reaction. The way Laurie would walk with that sway back or smoke his cigarette down to the filter was thrilling to me. However, even a moron knows that is not what makes a relationship work. A man like Clive who understands when I have period cramps too awful to move, buys aspirin from the Barson in the middle of the night and delivers it, is a far better bet for a lifetime partner. The heart is an odd muscle. It is a stubborn little fellow. It can be pushed and cajoled, but only so far. You can tell it whatever you want, but you can't make it listen.

CHAPTER 9

# <u>reparations</u>

*After loss of identity, the most potent modern terror, is loss of*
*sexuality, or as Descartes didn't say, "I fuck therefore I am."*
— Jeanette Winterson, *Art and Lies*

Margaret-Ann, who never was particularly robust, seemed more

wan than ever. She was still praying, and every Sunday she would

march off to not one but all of the morning services at Trinity

Chapel.

It was Sunday and none of the shops were open, so I was forced into Margaret-Ann's rooms in hopes of scoring a Tampax. She said she could never use anything as "invasive" as that sanitary protection. She proceeded to give me some pinned-up gear that must have been used in the Middle Ages when menstruating women had to jump over hams during a full moon. "Margaret-Ann, you are carrying this troglodyte thing too far."

"Take it or leave it. I have to start getting ready for chapel services," she said as she put on all of her makeup, which consisted of Chapstick.

"For God's sake, Margaret-Ann! Does God really need you at *every* service?"

"For *God's sake* precisely," she said while tidying her already immaculate room, where her pencils on her desk were even lined up according to size.

"Why don't you stop belabouring this whole church thing? Reading all those religious poets is so depressing and they never say anything new."

"There is nothing new. If you prayed more and did less running around chasing your own tail, you'd understand that."

"I mean it's not like I'm saying get married and procreate. Why not have a date? How about that nice single divinity student?"

"It isn't like men would look anyway."

"That's not true. You give off the don't-look-my-way-I'm-too-hung-up-for-the-dating-world look to anyone who glances your way. Your body language screams, 'I only have chemistry with my bible.' You could be pretty and even sexy if you didn't wear those baggy Laura Ashley dresses. Empire waists went out with Josephine." Margaret-Ann sighed and rolled her eyes. I pushed on.

"You have a great figure buried under those folds. You could do something with your hair. Take it off life support and set it in orange-juice cans. Give it some oomph. Who makes a pass at a woman in thick tights and Wallabies? And you don't wear make-up. Fine. But you wear makedown."

"What are you talking about?" Margaret-Ann asked, genuinely bewildered.

"You have gorgeous skin and eyes. You wear loose powder. My grandmother wore that. Even my mother wears pressed powder."

"For your information, it absorbs perspiration."

"You don't have to be in Vienna to know that your extreme religiosity is a defence against . . . I don't know what: dating, sex, the whole kit and caboodle."

I don't know why I bothered badgering her on a daily basis about this, since I really wasn't *that* different; maybe I was appealing to the sexual prude that lived within me who'd refused to leave graciously and would not give up the tenacious grasp she had on my frontal lobe. Whatever the reason, I was like the Elmer Gantry of Oxford on the topic of getting Margaret-Ann to give up the bible and live. Margaret-Ann was a pain, but she was the only girlfriend I had. When you needed a Tampax or someone to button the straps on the back of your swimsuit, she was the entire gene pool. Besides she was the only American other than that Clinton guy, and I rarely saw him.

One day she went to a departmental wine and cheese with her entire Tudor Songs and Sonnets class to welcome some visiting pastoral poet. Her don plied her with sweet wine and I believe she got a little tipsy.

She appeared at my door red-cheeked and flung herself on my

bed with uncharacteristic abandon. She said that maybe I was right and that her religion just wasn't cutting it anymore. She was beginning to see that by preparing only for the afterlife, she had missed out on this life — or what there was of it in England.

I was barely listening to her as I placed my basket of clean laundry on my bed. While folding my underwear and putting it in my dresser, Margaret-Ann droned on about her life draining away. Although it was boring, it was better than listening to her go on about how I would regret not studying for Old English, which was one of her favourite rants. I reminded her that she was twenty-one and hardly ready to hang up her dancing shoes. I pointed out that at any point in her life she could just lean over and kiss the divinity student and he'd probably be thrilled. I had no idea why I spoke to her as though I was such a woman of the world, when the truth was I would no more do the things I was suggesting than I would tumble over Niagara Falls in a barrel.

As she lay on my bed, tears were languidly falling out of the corners of her eyes. Having no idea why she was so upset, I said, "Okay. So he's not your type."

"No, it's not that. I guess I need to tell someone."

I didn't say anything since I could see she was upset. "I know I should be braver like you were with —" She hesitated, and then whispered, "The joker." This was the first time she'd ever mentioned "the untoward incident" as it had become known.

"Margaret-Ann, no one expects you to be Maid Marian. What is it?"

"I have cancer."

*Cancer.*

I turned around and stared at her.

"It was in one breast and they gave me radiation. They thought it was only in one spot. I just got a letter from the doctor saying now it is in the other one and spreading to my lymph glands and there is probably little point in operating. They said it was 'more virulent than it appeared upon biopsy.'"

"Can't you get your breasts removed? I've heard of people doing that." Actually I'd only heard of one person doing that: my mother's best friend. She was the only other woman in my mother's math class at the University of Buffalo. She never married because, as my mother said, "How could she take off her clothes?"

"It would have to be both breasts and it is probably too late now. It's just a matter of time."

"God, that's awful." I flopped down beside her. "I'm sorry."

"It's the way it is." After a silence she added, "Besides as George Herbert said, 'The lion is not so fierce as they paint him.'"

"Is that why you were home so long?"

"I guess so. I was tired. I seem to have a second wind; I think it is like nesting. Before birds give birth, they run around with amazing energy and build a nest, and when they are going to die, they fly around frantically getting food for their young or getting all their ducks in a row or whatever it is that they do."

"What can I do for you?" I asked.

"Nothing really. As you have suggested, I've been reading Nietzsche's *On the Genealogy of Morals* and Freud's *Moses and Monotheism.*"

Only I could have taken away the solace of faith from a dying woman and rubbed her nose in Nietzsche.

"He is not the most uplifting read," I said with the British flair for understatement.

"You know, he might be right. Maybe good and evil *are* no more than 'God's prejudices.' He makes a brilliant argument for pointing out that this is all there is."

"Come on, Peggy Lee made the same argument and she wasn't brilliant."

"Then I finally read Hume, as you suggested. The empirical argument against God is hard to refute. By the way, thanks for the copy of Bertrand Russell's *Why I Am Not a Christian*. He writes so simply yet cogently. All the literature you gave me and all the discussions we had added up." I sat trying to think of what to say. She added, "I think you're right. There is no God and organized religion is a crutch." There was a long silence. I just sat next to her with my clean socks in my hand. I couldn't leave since it was my room.

"I guess because my father is a minister, I was never exposed to the other side," she said.

"I'm sorry. It was so ridiculous to push all that philosophical bilge your way." Hesitantly, I added, "Especially at a time like this."

"This whole . . . episode would have been easier had I religion to prop me up. However, it can't be helped, can it? Once faith is gone, it's not coming back. I guess that's why it's called the *gift* of faith."

I had no idea what to say, clearly having said enough for a lifetime.

"It's not just the religion, the praying. Hume is right. You have to be dogmatic to be religious. I'm sick of myself." Before I had the chance to say anything, she started hammering her fist on the bed and murmured in an agonized gasp, "Cathy, if this is *it*, then I've spent all my energy reading, *preparing* to live, and not *living*. I always thought I'd live, whatever that means, later. Now I'm going to die with a perfect CV."

"But, Margaret-Ann, you're forgetting that you've loved your reading."

"I thought I did at the time, but now I realize that all that religious writing was preventing me from true understanding. Schopenhauer said it best: 'Religion has always been and always will be in conflict with the noble endeavour after pure truth.'"

"Margaret-Ann, Schopenhauer never had a friend, let alone an attachment. He died alone in his bed — sitting with his poodle."

"So Christ died on the cross. What's your point?" She leaned back on my bed and smiled for the first time since coming in to my room. "Well, we did have one good night. Remember when we had those unusual brownies in London and went to see that guy Jeremiah Hendrix in that club downstairs in Soho?"

"They were drugs, and his name was Jimi, and you're right it was a great night." I was surprised she'd thought so, since she worried the whole time about getting back for class. There was a long silence and we heard the college bell tower ring the half hour. Usually it sounded so cheerful; however, today it seemed to ring balefully, announcing the marching of time. Margaret-Ann and I looked at each other, both beginning to realize we were being trampled under it. I looked out the window at the glorious Cotswold limestone building that usually took on the glow of the evening light, but now it looked prison grey. I thought of taking her hand, but I figured neither of us would feel comfortable with that.

"There is one thing you can do for me," she said almost in a whisper.

"Name it." I was relieved since I had been stupid enough to interfere in her belief in God, right when she needed Him. I owed her some form of salvation. I swore to myself no matter what she wanted, I would just make sure I did it.

"I want to have sex before I die just once . . . with Jimi Hendrix."

Sex with Jimi Hendrix. Holy shit.

"Margaret-Ann, that is no problem. None at all."

After agreeing that I would never tell anyone that she had cancer or that I was the Pandarus in this modern version of *Troilus and Cressida*, I set to work learning everything about Jimi Hendrix I possibly could. It was before Woodstock made him a superstar. I went to the library to look up all the books on him in the card catalogue. None.

Next I looked up the articles on him in the *Readers' Guide to Periodical Literature*. It took me a full three days just to find all of them in the various out-of-the-way holes where they were located and copy them. I was not a reader of *DownBeat*, *Rolling Stone*, *Good Times*, *Cheetah* or *Disc and Music Echo*. It wasn't easy finding the Jimi Hendrix Newsletter or the *Groupie Diaries*. Although he was everywhere in the underground press, he was just beginning to make forays into the mainstream media. Within the last year, there had been articles about him in *Time* and *Newsweek*.

I now understood how groupies found their man. You didn't have to be Sherlock Holmes. You just had to read the press, know where he was and knock on the door.

An article, in a magazine appropriately titled *The Realist*, inspired me. It reported how two teenage groupies, one the daughter of a policeman, carrying black attaché cases, followed Jimi Hendrix from his performance in Chicago to his hotel between shows. They met him in the lobby and told him they wanted to take a plaster cast of his "rig." (The rig I was picturing was a surrey with the fringe on the top as in *Oklahoma!*; however, I soon figured out it was British slang for penis.)

These groupies had a collection of rock artists' rigs immortalized in plaster. Apparently Jimi thought this was a fabulous idea and immediately said, "Well, come on up, girls." The girls explained that he had to be hard before they did it and he assured them that was never a problem. He invited them both up to his room. The major presses picked up the picture of "the plaster casters" and their handiwork. *Newsweek* reported that it was a nine-inch-long, very thick rig, while other rockers' plaster rigs looked shrunken. After Jimi Hendrix, no other rocker would ever submit his rig for casting and the girls had to make a graceful retirement.

Not only was he perfectly equipped for the job, it was clear that groupies had no problem getting into his room. In fact, he welcomed them in groups or singly. His security wasn't anything special once he was away from the performance venue because no one ever knew exactly where he was staying. He had about nine different places where he flopped in London. I mapped them all out.

As far as I could figure, we had two shots at making this happen. He was appearing in London at Royal Albert Hall, and if we missed him there, we could go catch him on the Isle of Wight, where he would be performing at a music festival. I needed all the ammunition I could get because this man was unpredictable and always on the move.

The concert was in a few weeks and I had to get Margaret-Ann in psychedelic shape by then. I dragged her into London for clothes and makeup. I got her outfitted in a pair of wide, hip-hugging bell-bottoms made of carpetbag material and black patent-leather boots. I talked her into buying a tie-dye T-shirt and a buckskin vest edged in long flowing fringe. I got her hair cut all one length with fringed bangs and tied a large Indian scarf dabbed in patchouli oil around her head as a hairband. It tied on the side of her head and flowed down her back to her waist. She looked totally mod, but with enough hippie Indian to appeal to Hendrix. She was a little reluctant to go braless, but I told her that men didn't wear a device holding their testicles in the air, so why should we wear bras? We compromised by going braless but putting Band-Aids on her nipples. When she was all done up, I thought she looked pretty damn happening. Besides, judging by the pictures of the groupies I'd seen in the *Groupie Diaries*, Jimi didn't seem all that fussy.

I realized I had to get her used to her new look before we got to the concert, which only gave me a few short weeks for an identity change. Thus far it had been amazingly easy. I bought liquid eyeliner, mascara and lipstick combinations of Swinging Pink and Blasé Apricot topped off with a white lipstick called Pearl.

I got her all dolled up for our dry run, which was the wine and cheese before a high table dinner. Fortunately our stairwell was not at the high table. She had a little trouble with her high heels and couldn't make it across the Trinity quad without slithering along the brick wall and then collapsing when she hit open air. She couldn't grasp that she had to push out her rear end in order to balance. (That's why high heels were invented: they made women stick their rear ends out. Once the bustle went out, high heels came in.) After three tumbles where she was splattered across the cobblestones, I gave up. I substituted leather strapped sandals made by some man with a waist-length beard in a Carnaby Street basement. The sandals, which laced up her leg, looked like ones

Christ would wear for the Wedding at Cana.

We walked into the party and perused the room full of fifteenth-century religious poetry scholars and I was immediately hit by a tsunami of asexuality. However, Margaret-Ann thought it was dandy. A divinity student rushed over and plied her with sacramental wine and then asked her to go to a reading of minor seventeenth-century religious poetry at St. Regis on the weekend. This was all accomplished within ten minutes of our arrival.

It worked.

After a few glasses of sherry at the wine and cheese party, we bounced home for dinner. We were a bit late and Marcus, Clive and Peter were already on their dessert or, as they called it in truly infantile English fashion, "their pudding." As we sat down, Marcus looked over for the first time at the revamped Margaret-Ann and, in shock, uttered the first genuine remark I'd ever heard him make in what must have been his original Manchester accent. "Have ya gone mad as a box of frogs, woman?" He looked over at Peter and Clive for confirmation, but they were stunned into silence.

—

Finally the day of the big concert arrived and Margaret-Ann was fairly comfortable in her own skin. She was never really comfortable in her old drop-pleated skirts and cardigans either, so it really wasn't that hard to make a switch. I was surprised by how little she complained and sermonized. She seemed to fully concentrate on what I said had to be done. I guess Johnson was right when he said nothing concentrates the mind like facing death. She now had three new outfits and had even managed to mix and match on her own. She could apply her own eye makeup without looking like a raccoon and she could walk in small heels without looking as though she were in *The Mikado*.

I wish we could have gone into London a day ahead and stayed overnight for a dry run of the plan, but neither of us could afford it. I carried a folder with all of the information we needed. I was amazed at how calm she was on the day of the concert. It was clear that Margaret-Ann had complete faith in me, and I didn't even let myself think that the plan could fall through.

As we sat at lunch at a King's Road café in Chelsea, sharing an appetizer and filling up on bread because we couldn't afford a real meal, I went over all the logistics with her one last time. Then she wanted to know what to do when she got into the room with Jimi. I wasn't going to get into that. Jimi could take over from there.

I had gone over the plan a thousand times. We knew that he was staying at the Cumberland Hotel. I had ascertained this by calling each hotel in the area of the Royal Albert, saying I was part of the Jimi Hendrix entourage and Dick Katz, Jimi's agent, told me to drop off his Stratocaster guitar in person in the afternoon. (I'd read it never went by air freight.) The first four desk clerks said he wasn't registered and the fifth, at the Cumberland Hotel, said he was registered to arrive on the day of the concert and be in by 3:00 p.m. So now we knew he was staying at the Cumberland Hotel, only a few short blocks from the Royal Albert Hall. There were two concerts scheduled: one at 8:00 and the other for midnight. He would have to come back between sets and toke up or lie down, shower and change clothes for the last set, or do whatever guys do. I read he always returned to his room between sets to avoid the crowds. That's how the rig cast girls got him — in the lobby, between shows. Why reinvent the wheel? If we missed him between shows, we could catch him after the last show. However, that was more risky because he might go out straight after the show and not return, sleeping in any number of places. These hotels have detectives, so I knew she couldn't camp out all night waiting. There wouldn't be a crowd at the hotel. If someone had truly cold-called, the hotel would have guarded his privacy by saying he wasn't registered. All the uninventive groupies would be waiting for the limo out in front of the stage entrance of the hall or rushing backstage.

I'd carefully studied the map and surmised that he would be taken by limo back to the Cumberland along the edge of the park and then up Park Lane and dropped. We could get there much faster because the vehicles had to go around Hyde Park but we could cut through it on foot. If we left before the encore and ran, we could get to the hotel first. If we walked fast, we could do it in less than a half hour.

As soon as we entered the concert rotunda, Margaret-Ann said she felt like she had been there in a previous life. I said, "You've seen it in Hitchcock's film *The Man Who Knew Too Much*."

"Oh right! That was another life," she said.

The concert was amazing. All the Brits stood up when Jimi played his freaked-out version of "God Save the Queen." A joint had been passed our way and Margaret-Ann toked with the best of them. We were stoned — what else would you do at a Hendrix concert? The smoke was so thick you could get a contact high. When he played "The Star-Spangled Banner" with true Hendrix intonation, we stood up and cheered, "Hey, Jimi, we're Americans, man. Don't worry, buddy! You're not alone." He actually looked our way and smiled, probably because we were screaming and jumping up and down with imaginary Stratocasters like the

Cheech and Chong Oxford roadshow.

Getting stoned really buggered up the plans, which counted on timing. During the encore, I said, "Let's go."

"Why not go backstage?" Margaret-Ann asked in bewilderment. I could tell that the dope was like catnip and we really had to hold onto each tiny thought before it slid away.

"Margaret-Ann, listen! Just follow the original plan. We aren't in any shape to make updates."

We pushed our way out of the rotunda and darted across the street to Hyde Park. As we neared Longwater Pond, Margaret-Ann said, "Oh, let's take a minute and look at the Peter Pan statue. It's just over there."

"Grow up. We're in a hurry. Move it."

As she stepped up her pace to a canter to keep up with me, she said, "Did you know that J.M. Barrie, the author of *Peter Pan*, lived very near Kensington Gardens and paid for the statue to be erected? He used to walk here regularly and was inspired to write Peter Pan from what he saw here. All of the terrain we are now walking through is described in the book."

As the Marble Arch appeared, Margaret-Ann said, "You know that used to be called Tyburn Gallows, the city's main execution spot until 1783."

"Margaret-Ann, shut up and concentrate. When I want a guided tour, I'll get on a double-decker bus. "

Once I saw the hotel in the distance, I calmed down. We'd made it. We started chuckling about the concert and how we had made our elaborate plans. We laughed about our maps and clandestine phone calls to the hotel. Either we were totally stoned or it was nervous giggles, but we started to guffaw so hard our eyeliner was running. I tried to stop howling as we hit the steps of the Cumberland, which was clearly a posh hotel. We were moving at such a clip that as we entered the revolving door we went so fast we found ourselves on the outside again.

"Oops," she said, annoying the doorman who was dressed like Jiminy Cricket.

Out of breath, we finally made it in and sat on a liberty-printed bench located between the elevators. This way we couldn't miss him.

I gave her the final pep talk. "Remember, you're here to have fun. If it's not fun, just leave. You have your ticket and it's open ended."

Margaret-Ann laughed and nearly fell over as she said, "I'll be open ended."

Yikes. She was really stoned. I went to get her some water. When I approached her with the glass, she looked at me with a furrowed brow and asked, "Well, should I tell him I haven't done this kind of thing before?"

"It's up to you. Just play it as it lays." The strange thing about this entire venture was I was really nervous that he wouldn't show up and I was terrified he would show up.

About five minutes later, Jimi Hendrix came ambling through the lobby. He wore a purple shirt, maroon leather tight pants and an electric blue scarf on his head. As he headed toward us, Margaret-Ann said the most ridiculous thing I have ever heard. "Hi, Mr. Hendrix. Long time no see. We're journalists." He waved as he went by, hoping to get on the elevator before we interrogated him.

In a panic, using the groupie voice that I had no idea lived inside of me, I said, "Yeah, Jimi. Like, we used to work for *DownBeat* magazine, but we were, like, too upbeat so we were fired." He started laughing and kind of twirled around.

Margaret-Ann realized her error and made a quick recovery. "Yeah, now we're just party girls."

"Well, come on up and party then," he said smiling and holding the elevator with his foot.

As Margaret-Ann got in the elevator, I said, "I'll order drinks from the bar."

The elevator door closed and I didn't see her again for two days.

—

She came sauntering into the Trinity dining hall after a very long weekend, looking absolutely radiant.

She virtually bounced up to our table and sat down. Marcus, the perpetual black cloud, said, "You are aware, I assume, that the world's authority on John Donne was here giving a guest lecture and you missed it."

"I was having sex with Jimi Hendrix and you missed it," she said in the same tone she used to describe an excellent book she'd just read.

"Margaret-Ann, seriously, where were you?" Peter asked. "We were a bit worried about you."

She spoke completely nonchalantly. "No, seriously, I was having sex with Jimi Hendrix in London."

"What exactly do you mean by *sex*?" Marcus thundered.

"Marcus, you need to get out more," she said, buttering a dinner roll.

"The deflowered prodigal returns? Fine. Have it your way," Marcus said.

No one, except me, actually believed her — so we all simply

changed the subject.

As it turned out, Jimi Hendrix died within the year from an overdose while Margaret-Ann is still plugging along over forty years later. Marcus heard about the cancer and contacted his brother who was head of Sloan-Kettering Cancer Center in New York. Margaret-Ann was one of the first people to have a radical double mastectomy. She had massive dosages of radiation and ongoing chemotherapy. At one point, she looked more dead than alive. However, she made it.

Both Marcus and Margaret-Ann became academics in the same American city. They remained lifelong platonic friends. Neither married nor had children. Every once in a while I see one of her articles in the *New York Review of Books*.

# cherry run

*Thou art thy mother's glass, and she in thee*
*Calls back the lovely April of her prime.*
— William Shakespeare, "Sonnet III"

Within the next few weeks, the winter frost was threatening, yet

the flowers still held their heads high. We needed to wear our

sweaters as we crossed the deer park in the morning. Clive was

getting ready to sit his exams. I have to say, he was a pretty cool

cucumber. He never missed buzzing out to the Trout Inn when we all went; however, he was fairly preoccupied for months on the most important test he'd ever take. Of course, he'd get a first with distinctions and whatever other accolades they could dig up from the sixteenth century. He had mostly put our relationship on the back burner because he had to study, which was fine with me. I needed time to think.

The day after he finished writing his finals, he said, "Well, before the cold sets into Cornwall, we should probably get out to Cherry Run. I've told my parents all about you. Actually that's not technically true; I've told them a bit, which is more than I've ever told them about anyone else. Anyway, they must meet you."

"Uh, okay. Is Cherry Run the name of your town?"

"No. It's the name of our estate in Cornwall."

"Oh my God! It's the old Manderley estate. Your mother was Rebecca and Mrs. Danvers raised you. No wonder you're so cruel."

"Don't be potty. My parents won't know what hit them." As I wound up my stairwell, he shouted, "You do know you're marrying me, right?"

"Not until you've come to see Clapboard, my home in America."

*Meet his parents? Marry?*

When I wrote to my mother about my upcoming visit to Cherry Run, I expected her to be her usual blasé self. However, just when you think you know people, they step out of character, reminding you that humans are essentially unpredictable. She was, in her words, "tickled pink" about my upcoming estate visit; she sent me reams of advice for the first time in her life, which she labelled *estate planning*. She even drew little pictures on graph paper showing me possible silver settings that included oyster forks and which to use first. This from a woman who said, "Oh, for heaven's sake," while continuing to page through her *National Geographic*, when I went over the Niagara Escarpment and nearly fell into the Niagara River on my sled in the dead of winter. Stumpy, who was known as Trent before he went sledding with me, was less fortunate that day — his sled went airborne into the river, which gave him frostbite that claimed his fingers. Her sudden estate enthusiasm reminded me that she had in fact been on a downward mobility trajectory since she'd married my father. Her relatively well-off family died young and to her credit she never once in my entire life mentioned what her family "had been."

A week later, I had a break, so Clive and I sped out into the countryside in what I described as a "green sports car" and he called his "roadster." It was a British racing-green Austin-Healey two-seater convertible. We wound along a road in Cornwall flanked by a white cliff with black veins on one side and the ocean crashing on rocks on the other. The ocean looked like white clouds rushing toward the shore then breaking into rain upon the rocks. I actually felt the spray from the ocean at a few points. The mist on my face reminded me of Niagara Falls, and I felt almost at home.

We were singing along with the Animals, when we turned onto a long drive cutting through huge expanses of green lawn dotted with wild-flower gardens and circular English tea rose gardens. Clematis, trumpet vine and climbing hydrangea intertwined over fences leading up a gently rising slope to a massive yellow-brick house. It had wings for Christ's sake! Richard Adams had designed it in 1762, and it was grand in a way that nothing in America could ever be as grand. We continued up the driveway lined with arching cherry trees with burnished orange leaves just beginning to drop. I thought it must be magical in the spring with the millions of white blossoms in a row. You could have a wedding here and never need confetti. We passed a ruddy-faced gardener in old wellies perilously perched on an ancient ladder. He leaned back while holding huge, cast-iron pruning shears, which must have been about six feet in length, and waved to us, and then snipped off a branch.

A pretty woman, somewhere on the dark side of forty, tall with pale blond hair pulled back severely into a French twist, was waiting as we pulled into the semicircular drive under a portico that must have originally been for carriages. The arch had a magnificent leaded-glass lantern that hung down on ancient wrought-iron chains. The woman wore sensible Ferragamo flats, a linen blouse with flat pearl buttons and a navy linen skirt. Draped loosley around her neck was a Hermès scarf with a horse head and horseshoes pattern. The outfit was casual, yet elegant. As she walked toward the car and smiled, I could see she had once been very beautiful, but something had happened to one of her eyes. It was a bit cloudy and didn't scan as fast as it should. It pierced her otherwise Grace Kelly–perfect looks. I'll bet her dance card had rarely been empty.

The father was something in the British hierarchy but I didn't know what. (Duke? Earl? Viscount? Baronet? Lord? Knight?) God knows what she was supposed to be called. I couldn't call her "Lady"; it was too much like *Lady and the Tramp*. I decided to never call her anything.

Even though Clive was an only child, I assumed he couldn't be that close to his mother since he went to boarding school practically the day he left the nursery. That was the first mistake I made at Cherry Run. Unfortunately, it wasn't the last. In retrospect, I think it should have been named Cherry Run as Fast as You Can.

I could tell from the way she wonderingly eyed me, she was trouble. She hugged her son and tears came to her eyes. Clive said only, "Steady on, Mother." A man who looked distinguished but older than Clive's mother stood in the giant double-door entrance. He had grey hair combed straight back and bushy black eyebrows. He wore khaki pants, a grey plaid Viyella shirt — an homage to country-casual Americana — and a navy sports jacket with some sort of gold braided letters on the pocket.

He said, "Wiggles!" Believe it or not the name "Wiggles" had been Clive's mother's name since childhood. "My dear, really, unhand the boy so he may fulfill his social obligations," he said, eyeing me as I stood ignored and leaning against the car door.

"Oh, of course. How discourteous of me," she said.

"Mother," said Clive, and then he looked up the stairs to the bushy-eyebrowed man who was rapidly descending, "Father, this is Cathy McClure."

"*Mc*Clure, what sort of name is that?" the mother asked.

"American," I said. She looked expectant so I felt I had to further delineate myself. "I guess Irish American." I had never really thought of myself as Irish, but I could see that just *plain American* wasn't enough information.

"Isn't America marvellous, how everyone simply arrives and feels such a great part of it," Wiggles said.

Into the portico came another woman, looking nearly as old as the wrought-iron lantern and wearing a black blouse and skirt and really strange shoes that looked like lunar walking gear. They were rounded in front and laced up the side. She had stringy, greasy salt-and-pepper hair and a leathery face.

Clive's face lit up. He hugged her for a full minute and said, "Titty, how are you?"

Had he said "Titty"? No! He couldn't have. That would be beyond the pale. He *must* have said Tatty.

"Cathy, this is my nanny, Titty."

"And mine, lest you forget," his mother added.

"Ah . . . Cathy the American," Titty said. "We've heard so much about you. You're a lucky girl to have caught our Clivester. He's a real fine chap, he is." Titty was still holding him and flattening his hair with her fingers. "Oh, I'm so glad my Clive boy is home — and brought an American. My, my. I'm ready to take on my third generation," she said, the first person to look directly at me.

"Titty, let's not get ahead of ourselves," the father said, jumping down the stairs to help fetch the bags.

"Where is Henderson?" the father asked the mother.

"Archie, he's trimming the fruit trees before there's a frost," she answered as though he should have already known that.

"Whose rucksack is this?" he asked, holding it up at arm's length with two fingers. It was at this precise moment that I noticed, for the first time, that I had never washed it in all the years I'd owned it. It was slick with baked-on dirt and grease.

"I can carry it," I said, taking it off his pinky.

"Oh, I wouldn't hear of it," he said taking it back. Clive had his head in the trunk of the car and was sorting out bags when his mother said, "Archie, let . . . Cathy here, carry it. You'll throw out your back. People in America are used to doing things on their own. They think it's their personal right, isn't that so, Cathy? May I call you Cathy?"

"Sure."

I grabbed my backpack and Archie, his head in the trunk, said, "Where is your luggage?"

"On my back," I replied over my shoulder as I walked up the stairs and into the house with my filthy rucksack hanging off one shoulder. I couldn't believe I hadn't even stepped over the threshold yet and already my lineage had been questioned.

When I went in, a woman who seemed at least openly hostile said, "Your room will be in the west wing. Would you like me to escort you?" Looking me up and down, she added, "I assume you want to freshen up."

Clive said, "Hello, Mrs. Clifford." She smiled slightly, almost shyly, and said, "Welcome home, Young Clive."

I could just imagine someone in Buffalo saying, "Welcome home, Young Cathy," or how about "The Cathster."

"She is in the bluebird room, sir," Mrs. Clifford said to Clive.

"Why there? It's so far away," Clive said.

"I was given the guest floor plan and prepared the rooms," she said, as though she had only been following orders.

I wondered who else was coming since they needed a floor plan for all the guests. I hoped someone, anyone besides me, was visiting.

Clive led me upstairs and along a wide, dark hallway that turned and then led up another flight of more narrow stairs. We made a ninety-degree turn and began going down another hallway. The room I was staying in had beautiful hand-stenciled blue wallpaper with birds standing on twigs. It had twin beds with the same fabric on the bedspreads and on the drapes and even on the window seat that accented the beautiful bay window, which was divided into hundreds of diamond-shaped leaded-glass pieces. As the afternoon sun sat in the west, the light shone through the window, turning the blue birds on the seat and on the bedspread almost orange. The floorboards were wide and waxed and strewn with hooked rugs in bird themes. There was a huge vanity that had the same blue bird fabric as a skirt. When I sat down, I realized you could move the fabric away and there were all kinds of drawers behind it. One drawer was a built-in jewellery box all lined in pale blue velvet with six separate rows. There was a reticule holder and collar box. I stuffed my bikini underpants into the collar box.

The bathroom, which was connected to the bedroom, was a scream. It had the same blue-bird shower curtain and drapes and a needlepoint rug that looked like a series of Audubon prints all meticulously embroidered to show various species of blue birds. There was rich dark wood and all kinds of built-in cupboards from the ceiling to the floor. The odd thing was that although I could find the sink and huge tub, I couldn't find the toilet. I mean how many places can you hide a toilet? I checked for another room. My mother had warned me about this British nonsense called a water closet. There could be another small room, which housed only the toilet. In these old houses, toilets were added later. It would be just like the cyclopean mother, Wiggles, to force me to the rooftops with the gargoyles in search of a toilet. Then days later when they found me, I would be as insane as Mr. Rochester's wife and have wet pants.

After going over every square inch, I finally decided to follow the plumbing from the ceiling. At long last, I found an unobtrusive flush cord hanging from the ceiling above a flat, highly polished mahogany wooden linen or blanket box, which had three deep drawers. I attempted to pull open the drawers but realized they were fake. I jogged the top slab of the trunk and found it moved. When I picked up the lid of the box I found a hole in the middle, which presumably was a toilet. You had to make sure you sat in just the right spot on the wood. I guess this room was attempting to make the point that really no one in the aristocracy in England excretes waste material. Only a few even know where to find the toilet. The Hunter-Parsons hid their toilets and had a nanny in the nursery named Titty for two generations. Freud could have had a field day.

I have to say the grounds were the most beautiful I had ever seen. They had the perfect combination of manicuring and wildness. As we walked around, Clive showed me what flowered and when. It was organized so that something in each grouping was flowering at some point from early spring to late fall. It was times like this when I liked Clive most. He shared the love his parents had for flora and fauna. No wonder he knew so much about the farm in Wales. No one ever left the house without taking one of their drooling dogs with them. Clive showed me the plants that were chosen for colour and texture and their reaction to sunlight at specific times of the day. We sat down on an eighteenth-century stone seat to admire the aster and lily borders. The lilies, now on the wane, were in colours and combinations I'd never seen before. I said to Clive, "Your mother doesn't seem thrilled by me."

"Oh, she is, or she will be in time. She is the type who likes to get her bearings first."

"Then there'll be no holding her back?"

"She's concerned with *who* you are in that annoying English way that we've talked about. I'm not doing any more imitations of her as I used to. She is my mother and has her foibles just as I'm sure yours has."

"You're right, of course. If you met my father now, you'd find him doing a bad imitation of Nietzsche in his last year." I should not have added but did, "He has an excuse."

"So does she. She has been raised to believe in all her hang-ups just as you and I have. I have had you to bludgeon me about my assumptions and elitist behaviour, even as satire. She never sees anyone who has ever questioned her beliefs."

"What about the BBC?"

"She thinks they're communists."

Clive, of course, was right. It never went anywhere to criticize anyone's parents. I was being far too touchy. In a way, I admired Clive's defence of his mother. He was now twenty-six and had outgrown finding fault with her. I remember my mother saying once that the way a man treats his mother will be how he will eventually treat you — that was such a terrifying statement that it always stayed with me.

— ⁃ —

I was down for breakfast the next morning at 5:30 a.m., partly because I'm an early riser and mostly because it was so cold I could see my breath and thought I should move before frostbite set in. (I had no idea at the time that you could ring down for tea.) While at Oxford, I had already realized that there was a direct correlation between how much cold you could handle and your social class. The upper crust always called it "exhilarating" or "refreshing" when it was freezing. Clive warned me that it got cold at night and remained "bracing" through the early morning, but it could be as hot as blazes in midday in Cornwall.

When I got downstairs, there was already a fire blazing in the main hall or whatever it was called. As I sat by the fire, I had such chills I could hardly feel the heat. My ankles felt itchy. That nineteenth-century bane, chilblains, was taking on real meaning. I needed a game plan before I was relegated to do some needlepoint in a back parlour. This Wiggles woman was trying to kill me.

I decided that the best thing to do was to out-English them. Never act cold, tired or sick of the hairy stupid, yappy mutts they kissed on the mouth. I also realized a lot of social messages were delivered through the dogs. In terms of delineating my social standing, I would be ingenuously honest, even outrageous. That should just about cover my battle plan.

I decided to find the library and get a volume of poetry and read while I waited for everyone to thaw out and get going. Christ, if I were in a real house, I could just make myself a coffee. Who even knew where the kitchen was? I wandered around but never found it. If you lived in a one-room shack, you could have a cup of coffee when you woke up, something that I considered to be an inalienable human right.

I found a door ajar and discovered a library. Not just any library, but one that was as large as one of the college libraries at Oxford. Built-in bookcases with bevelled-glass gothic doors lined the room. Each cupboard had green felt on its shelves so as not to damage the books, and each shelf had recessed lighting so the books shone in a beatific light. It had a cathedral beamed ceiling, and a circular wrought-iron staircase led to a balcony lined with another full set of bookcases. A large table in the centre of the room was piled with books, most of them with bookmarks in them. In the far corner near the windows that looked out on a courtyard sat a high-backed leather chair and ottoman. By then, the dawning sun was casting a thin magenta glow along the treetops and would momentarily shine through the open casement window. To my surprise, there sat Clive's father, Archie, hunched over some small, decrepit book.

"I'm sorry, I didn't see you. I thought you were part of the furniture," I said, realizing that didn't sound quite as I'd meant it.

"Old enough to be. How was your sleep? Stimulating air cleared your head after all that petrol?"

"It was perfect. I've never felt so refreshed," I said as I walked around the room, looking at his collected works. The books almost all had leather covers. A humidifier hummed, a dozen little gauges and indicators fluctuating like those on a life-support machine in an intensive care unit. I was really in awe. If I had this library, I would never leave it. I swore that with these reference books and these perfect surroundings I'd write the great American novel.

"Look at the collected Jane Austen!" I exclaimed.

"Oh, they are not first editions, but they are beautifully illustrated," he said.

I sank into a chair that looked as though it had been upholstered with a Persian rug and eagerly pulled myself up to the big table. Archie opened collection after collection for me. He had the keys for all the glass bookcases on a large oval ring. Some of the keys were over six inches long.

While looking through the bookshelves, I found a first edition of *Middlemarch*, when it was serialized in eight half-volume books. I just couldn't be quiet when I found *Bleak House*. I bubbled over in amazement when I saw the first edition with the original illustrations. "Wow, this is a great illustration of Mr. Guppy when he declares his intentions for Esther! This is exactly how I pictured him."

Archie did a perfect comic imitation of the unctuous upstart Mr. Guppy, preparing the ground for his proposal to Miss Summerson. "My mother has a little property . . . She is eminently calculated for a mother-in-law . . . She has her failings for who has not — but I never knew her to do it when company was present . . ." I mentioned other illustrations, and Archie quoted the relevant scene in perfect accents. As I looked around the room, I could see from the cracked spines the books had been read. Even the books on the shelves had all kinds of papers stuck in them with tiny notes neatly sketched in fountain pen.

"Now I know why Clive can quote from almost anything."

"Wiggles has upbraided me for what she refers to as my 'wanton quoting,' but to me there always seems to be someone else who has said what I was thinking so much better than I could have ever said it."

In a large folio box, I found another illustration of Mr. Guppy from *Bleak House*; this was one of Mr. Guppy rejecting Esther after she is scarred by smallpox. The illustration wisely does not show Esther's face but only Guppy's repulsion. The viewer is left to imagine the disfigurement. Archie picked up an expression on my face that I'd let slip and said, "Cathy, my dear, is something troubling you? I hope it isn't anything I said." He looked into my eyes in a really caring way. I realized how sensitive this man was. Only a slight, I thought, imperceptible glimmer of distress had shadowed my demeanour, yet he'd caught it. I decided to be honest and let my guard down, for there was something I liked about Clive's father.

"No, not at all. I remember this passage so clearly when Mr. Guppy rejects Esther due to her facial scars. I too have facial scars from acne and this passage leapt out at me a few years ago — I knew exactly how Esther felt. Losing Mr. Guppy was no sacrifice, but having to endure the disfigurement hit so close to home."

"Women are so unnecessarily cruel to themselves." He placed his hand on mine and looked genuinely puzzled and upset. I could see where Clive got his sensitivity and kindness. Who knows? Maybe my scarring was almost gone. The beholder is the worst judge of his or her own disfigurement, for perfectionism wreaks havoc with reality. "I have not seen any scars on your face. In fact, when you smile, this entire wormwood library looks to me to be a multicoloured carousel."

At that moment, Mrs. Clifford appeared at the door to mutter that food was on the buffet in the morning room and was getting cold.

"Why, thank you, Mrs. Clifford. That is most kind," he said as though she had said, "Good morning! Breakfast is served."

"Why not show me the Thomas Hardy before we go?" I suggested.

"Oh, I was saving them for tea time. They are really my favourites."

I was in heaven as he opened each book. I had pictures in my mind of all the characters in the books. It was wonderful to see a true artist's rendition of psychological traits. "Take a gander at Arabella. How risqué. Amazing!" I could tell, by the rise in my voice, I was getting way too excited, or as my mother called it, "rambunctious." Clive thankfully called it "alive."

"It is astonishing, isn't it? You know, Hardy actually saw these and approved of them." He was gathering illustrations of Hardy's poems and taking things off shelves in a great rush. He was a bit doddering on foot, but he really knew how to leap around the library. It's wonderful to share an interest with another, especially when neither of you are feigning enthusiasm. We went on at length about how we interpreted each character and how we would have drawn them. We were totally engrossed when Mrs. Clifford came and began pacing before the door like a golden retriever that was barred from the stick she was meant to recover. Finally she said, "I was sent with a message, sir."

He jumped up and said, "Oh quite. I'm dreadfully sorry." As he dashed around, locking the bookcase doors at breakneck speed, he said to me over his shoulder, "Cathy, we have been dawdling." He used the same intonation for "dawdling" as one would use for "murdering."

I wondered who ran the place. Couldn't you have breakfast when you wanted? As he locked the last cabinet, he said, with his back to me, "Cathy, I realize I am egregiously overstepping the bounds of a polite host, but may I ask for your indulgence or, as you say in America, to 'go easy' on Wiggles. Clive is her only son. Whatever she appears, well . . . it's just fright."

While rushing to breakfast, which took five minutes to walk to, Archie explained that in the summer and early fall they ate in the morning room, which gets all the morning sun and opens onto one of the prettiest gardens. It was once the vestry — I guess there was once a chapel as well. We turned the corner to the morning room, and there sat Clive, all showered and shaved, and his slim mother looking pert in her sweater set and flesh-coloured riding pants.

We sat down to the quilted tablecloth and Waterford goblets, and we were told the food was on the sideboard. I started enthusing about the books and the illustrations. Instead of joining in, Clive looked pained. I got up to get my cold, dry, crustless toast that I wouldn't give a teething baby, and he got up as well. As he stood behind his mother, he pointed to the fresh flowers that festooned the room and then pointed at the back of her coiffed head.

When we got back to our seats, I waited a minute so she wouldn't think I'd been prompted and said, "The flowers are gorgeous. They still have dew on them. The colours are exquisite. No wonder you have kept the walls white. They couldn't take any competition."

As she bit into her rusk, she said, "I like to catch the morning dew because the blossoms last so much longer."

The arrangements were stunning and were clearly done with an artistic eye. "I had actually thought they were done by a florist."

"No. I bring in about eight dozen a day and, of course, some greenery as well. The season is so short and now drawing to a close."

"I can't think of anything more wonderful than picking all those flowers in the morning. Do you oversee the gardens or is it all done by gardeners?"

"I have a landscape man, of course, but I would say I devote the better part of the day to the garden in the spring and summer — wouldn't you, Archiekins?"

"Yes, and it would be a shambles without you."

She got her old evil glint back and Archie and Clive relaxed, having shovelled in the fuel that fed her insatiable narcissistic engine.

I was beginning to get the picture. You did it her way, or complimented her on how she'd done it, then she settled down enough to make the day run relatively smoothly, until it needed to be stoked up. If the fuel ran low, then she went on her merry path of destruction.

"Now," she hesitated as though searching for a word, "*Cathy*. I don't know why I have trouble with that name; it is not as though it is foreign. Remember that girl you brought home called Natasha? Now *that* was foreign."

"It was Natashaanlova and it was in third form. We billeted her brother for a cricket match," Clive said evenly but letting her know he was not playing that game. It was a relief to see that he was willing to let her know what was out of bounds.

"Quite right. Now . . . *Cathy*." She looked over at Clive and said, "See I've got it," then she looked at me and continued, "Tell us a bit about yourself."

"Well, I came to Oxford last year."

"On scholarship?" Wiggles said the word scholarship the way an American would say "on welfare."

"Partly." I deliberately remained obscure.

"What about your people?" she asked.

"My *people*?" *Who are they?* I wondered.

"Relations?" She said as though I had trouble comprehending any basic conversation.

"My father is a pharmacist who owned a drugstore in Niagara Falls for many years and now lives in Buffalo, New York, and works in research and development for a drug company."

"Is your mother alive?"

"I was getting to her." *Before you rudely interrupted.* "She graduated from college, what you call university, as a Math major, studied for a Master's in Math and then taught. In fact, she only taught for one day since she said didn't know she'd be teaching children."

Archie laughed. "One day. I say, I like that. It sounds like my career in the foreign service."

"She worked during the war doing the accounts for a munitions factory, but then once the war was over she stayed home."

"Now you're Irish Catholic, as is Darby," she said, glancing at her adoring drooling dog, which I later learned from Clive was an Irish wolfhound, "so I assume you have a large family."

"I assumed Darby was Irish. I had no idea he was Catholic," I said.

"Lapsed," said Archie.

I continued with my illustrious lineage. "Actually, I'm an only child, as is my father. My mother has one sister and her children have mostly entered the religious orders."

"That is singular in this day and age," Archie said.

"So you are from a devoutly religious family?" Wiggles asked. She said the word *devout* as though it was the word *pervert*.

"Yes. All except me."

"Were you adopted?"

"No."

"Often only children are adopted," she said to Clive in response to his long, exasperated sigh. She thundered on, ignoring his blue glacial stare. "Now, let me see. Your father was a pharmacist — a sort of tradesman?"

"I like to say my father was a drug dealer."

"Did your grandparents come from Ireland?"

"No. Both families were in America long before the potato famine. The only one I knew was my paternal grandmother. She was a Math teacher as well. Then eventually in the '20s she was a stockbroker."

"Not a great job for the '20s in America," Archie said. "Though it must have been exciting for a woman."

"I used to go down to the stock exchange with her."

"How novel," Wiggles said with absolutely no expression. "You certainly must know what makes capitalism work — all that wailing for money as the ticker tapes roll."

"Oh I think we all have a fair idea what makes capitalism work," I said, looking around at my sumptuous surroundings.

After a bit of a silence, I added, "Later in her life she was an investor in inventions. She made a fortune investing in Kleenex. She knew just the right moment when America was moving to the disposable. However, she and my father lost everything when they jointly invested in paper underpants. They were both ahead of their time on that one." Wiggles was looking utterly blank, but Archie and Clive were laughing, so I continued. "My mother and I had to wear the paper underpants even though they ripped in half when we genuflected at mass on Sunday." As Archie was howling, Clive leaned over to him and said, "I *knew* you'd like her, Father."

Then I decided to change tacks and said, "Now enough about me. Tell me a bit about you." Clive shot me a please-don't-go-there look. But I figured two can play the same game. I preferred conversation to interrogation.

"Archie, what do you do?"

"Oh, nothing really."

"Oh *really*, Archie. Don't be such a silly sausage," Wiggles said, folding her napkin along its original fold line. "You know that is not true."

Clive said, "You've written thirteen books and you run a large manor and estate."

"Quite right. That's what I do," Archie said with a perfect tone of mock discovery. I had heard that same lovable tone from Clive, and now I knew where it came from.

"What do you do?" I asked Wiggles.

*"Do?"* she asked as though I had posed the most thoroughly taboo question imaginable. This personal violation was compounded by the fact that she had no idea how to answer it. I actually think no one had ever asked her this question before. She stammered a bit and then announced in a frosty tone, "I run the horse farm, ride, breed and jump horses. I don't know if Clive told you or not, but we show and hunt." She concluded with "and I used to race, before the accident." She hastily added, "I also run this home and do volunteer work for the National Trust."

"Where did you go to university?" I asked with false innocence. I knew her ilk went to finishing school and then some horse-jumping academy. *By the way, wily little Wiggles, don't ever interrogate me again or call my father "a tradesman" with that derisive tone or you'll get it again — double-barrelled.*

"I went to what I believe you would call finishing school, worked as a sister in the war, then fortunately married into one of the finest families in England."

Archie said, "That was her first husband."

I looked over at him, smiled and said, "Well, it certainly is one of the nicest." Archie glanced my way with a conspiratorial smile that led me to understand he knew what I was up against.

162

CHAPTER 11

# eye to eye

*And there came to him a sign of man's true home. Beyond the*
*ominous and cloud-engulfed horizon of the here and now, in the*
*green and hopeful and still-virgin meadows of the future.*
— Thomas Wolfe, *You Can't Go Home Again*

One morning at breakfast, Mrs. Clifford said, "When the Taylor-
Deeks come tonight, should I serve the consommé first?"

"I beg your pardon?" Clive said. "The Taylor-Deeks? Here?" I
had learned about a year ago that among the English "I beg your
pardon?" translated to "What the hell are you doing or saying?

And whatever it is — it is totally unacceptable to me." When I'd first arrived in England, I had no idea of the English connotation of the phrase. Assuming they had not heard me, I would repeat whatever it was that had already enraged whomever I was talking to.

Darby picked up the emotional timbre and began barking to warn of the danger that he felt in the room. (Not bad for an *Irish Catholic* watchdog.)

"You see, now you've all got Darby going." Wiggles turned to the scowling housekeeper. "Mrs. Clifford, you've given away our little surprise." Mrs. Clifford just looked at her as though she were speaking a foreign language. "Philomena is home from school, as is Noddy, and they are coming *en famille.*"

I hadn't seen Clive angry since we were near the top of the mountain in Snowdonia, but I could see the same storm cloud rising behind those blue eyes that were getting darker by the second.

She twittered on, "Well, you've grown up with them. I thought it would be nice to see them and for them to meet . . . our Little Yankee Doodle." She'd clearly forgotten my name again but managed to remember "Philomena," which tripped off the tongue.

"Mother," Clive said with an exhausted sigh, "it is all so unnecessary, so totally gormless." After a minute or two in which you could hear people swallow their tea, he added, "I dare say we'll make the best of it." He addressed the doorway. "Thank you, Mrs. Clifford." I had learned that that meant "Get the hell out of here, Mrs. Clifford."

There was a silence at the table. I excused myself, saying I had made a personal vow to read forty pages of Dryden before noon.

As I walked to the library, I wondered what they were saying.

I would have eavesdropped if I could have, but the walls were too thick. Anyway, I was up for company of any sort. No matter how bad the Taylor-Deeks were, they couldn't be worse than consommé, the world's worst soup with nothing in it, alone with Wiggles writhing up my family tree.

I had grown quite fond of Archie. I could see that Clive got his great looks from his mother, but his kindness and erudition from his father. Archie was one of those typical Brits who pretended he didn't know anything; however, I hadn't found any topic on which he didn't have an encyclopedic knowledge.

After riding with his mother, Clive popped his head into the study, saying it was a heat wave today and tomorrow. It was what we call "Indian summer" in America. In a freak accident of nature, it was over 90 degrees Fahrenheit, and England just couldn't cope. Clive said, "The horses took themselves back to the stall and were foaming."

"Sounds appealing."

At lunch the gardener came to the door and said that the men were coming to fix the slate roof and lay some new tiles the following morning. I said, "Tomorrow the temperature will be in the hundreds up there with the slate holding the heat."

The gardener responded, "The telly weather is suggesting not to be out tomorrow unless necessary, but they say they have work up north next week and starting tomorrow suits 'em."

"At their own peril," Archie said. "The job has to get done sometime because there is moss building up on the back wing and the stable needs lead flashing."

"Right then," the gardener said and backed out of the room.

Wiggles said, "Archie, why tomorrow? Chauncey" (one of their

pointer dogs — only slightly less slobbery than Darby and probably an Irish Protestant) "absolutely can't abide those men and the
poor dear will have to be locked up in this heat. You know he'll
bark himself into a lather."

In the afternoon, Archie and I wandered into the dining
room because I wanted to see the elaborate flower arrangements
Wiggles was setting for the evening. At each place setting, a little
silver duck held a card with a name on it in its mouth. My duck
had spelled my name *K-a-t-h-r-y-n*. I was at the opposite end of
the table from Clive. Archie saw his duck flocked next to Noddy
and said, "Dear God, what will I discuss with Noddy? The poor
young lad will be so bored he'll drop into his consommé." Wiggles
looked at him as though he were in a high chair and said it was
never good form to have those who already enjoyed one another's
company next to each another. I guess that was why my duck
was next to Wiggles. She, of course, was at the head and Archie
was at the other end.

Philomena and Clive were placed together at the opposite
end from me. Archie just walked around, viewing the nametags
with puzzlement, and instead of disagreeing said, "I think I'll take
Darby and Chauncey out for walkies."

—

Clive dressed for dinner in a sports jacket with a yellow shirt and
khakis, and his father wore a full suit. It was still about 98 degrees.
I sported my maroon mirrored dress and sandals, while Wiggles
wore an elegant raw silk sleeveless dress in a celery colour. Philomena, the daughter of the Taylor-Deeks, had on a white A-line
dress with black pearls and black pumps — elegant if you're forty
but she was in her early twenties. Noddy was about fifteen and

wore his school jacket. (Did he own no other clothing?) The parents were introduced as Lord and Lady Taylor-Deeks.

Lady Taylor-Deeks said, "Now, Clive, Philomena has led me to believe you have finished your Ph.D. and have already defended."

"So I've heard tell," Clive responded.

"Were you pleased with your results?" Noddy asked.

"Pleased to have more time for cricket and for showing Cathy our fair land," Clive said in his tone of self-deprecating modesty. Of course, no one mentioned he got a first with distinctions. That would have been gauche. After all, it was expected.

"Here, here," Archie raised a glass, trying to get off the subject of his son's accomplishments. "And our little Philly here is in her last year in Chemistry at Cambridge."

I smiled down at her end of the table. She was actually quite lovely in her black velvet hairband and her shiny chestnut pageboy.

Lord Taylor-Deeks sat next to me, swirling his glass of wine and calling it "first rate." He clearly stood by that opinion, as he swilled it all evening. By the time we got to dessert, I had given up attempting to talk to Lord Tanked Taylor-Deeks. When he was dubbed a lord, the sword must have slipped and hit his frontal lobe. Wiggles was engaged in dog and horse talk with Lady Tanked. I had to discuss our incredibly stupid dog Willie for almost a half hour with Lady Taylor-Deeks. I had never discussed him for five minutes in my entire life. She was complaining about her dog's manners when she took him to a pub for lunch while shopping in the village.

Noddy (a family name, I was told) was the only one who showed any interest in me whatsoever. "What state are you from?"

"New York."

"Right on."

Wiggles and Lady Taylor-Deeks exchanged looks. Lady Taylor-Deeks simply said, "Television," with emphasis on the last syllable.

"Oxford suit you?" Noddy asked.

"I've loved it so far."

"Better than American university?"

"Way better."

"Where did you go in the States?"

"Ohio University."

"Now is that on the plains?" Lady Taylor-Deeks asked.

"We're terribly proud of her. She's a scholarship student," Wiggles said.

"Indeed," said the Lady, sending her co-conspirator a knowing glance. Mrs. Taylor-Deeks thought she was deking me out; however, I'd heard that "indeed" said before with exactly that drawn out intonation. I knew it meant "Please don't mistake her for one of us."

I had actually heard Clive and Peter do a riff on this exact conversation, so I knew all the innuendo. I have to say that all of the parody that they'd done on the upper classes and their parents had been truly gifted. The sketches were perfect and their accents for the cook, the gardener, the father and the mother were perfect. One thing I hadn't picked up from Clive was how venal the mother was and how sweet the father was. Maybe she was only venal to me. After all, I could drag him back to the United States to get an academic job at one of the Ivy Leagues. She had no intention of losing her son to the colonies or to a gauche, grasping, loud Irish daughter of a tradesman.

When I stopped to think about it, I hadn't made any female friends in England. There weren't any at school, other than Margaret-Ann (whose life, death and afterlife I'd ruined) and I had no other outlet. I would have been pleased to be placed next to Philomena. We were about the same age and could have chatted.

"Philomena, you must come over and ride with us some morning. You see our little colonial doesn't ride, and Clive is forced to ride with his doddering old mama," Wiggles said.

Clive realized Philomena was on the spot, so he graciously said, "Phil, we would love to have you join us. You could stay for lunch and we could all go into town. So far Father has kept Cathy delighted in the library, but I'm afraid she might be in need of some town flair."

"Be that as it may," Wiggles said. "Philomena, are you still jumping?"

"No. Actually I haven't done that since I was about fifteen. I have spent most of my time in the lab for the last few years."

"You know they asked our little Philly here to go to the Olympics," Wiggles said.

"Not really. It was my horse they asked," Philomena said, smiling for the first time. She was pretty when she smiled. I could see now that she wasn't one of those girls who was so aristocratic that she had been a Sloanie — a snob who wore pearls and ignored the cultural revolution around her since it did not affect the produce at Harrods. She was one of those scientific English girls who always liked smelly chemistry sets and horses. She had never been social and really had not noticed much of what was happening around her. She seemed to be oblivious to Wiggles' chicanery. Wiggles was attempting the double whammy of pushing Clive into Philomena's arms and letting me know she was not going down for the count without a fight. Fortunately, Wiggles was not a multi-tasker.

Since I was so far away, Philomena had to raise her voice to say, "Actually, Cathy, we haven't formally met before, but I did see you at the bump. I used to row as well, so I creased up when you coxed Clive's bumps race. There was a picture in the *Varsity*."

"My God. The *Cherwell* didn't carry a thing about that momentous race, did they, Clive?" I said in mock despair.

"The newspapers! Sir, they are the most villainous, licentious, abominable and infernal. Not that I ever read them! No, I make it a rule never to look into a newspaper," Archie said.

"Richard Sheridan from *The Critic*, scene one, I believe," Clive said.

Clive and Archie often did this quote identification game. It was clearly a way they bonded — like going to see a Yankees game with your dad in America.

I did something that I knew was outrageous but I really didn't care. Between dinner and dessert, while we cleared our palate with lemon sorbet, which I mistakenly called sherbet, I suggested we all change seating. I said I wanted to get to know Philomena better and this would be my only chance. It was true. Everyone looked stupefied and Noddy said, "Spot on, Cathy." I knew Wiggles was angry and that Clive and Archie would have to pay for it, but I'd had it.

As the evening wore on, Philomena and I got on famously. She had been to New York City to give a paper as a grad student, so we had a great talk about that and about being one of the few females in graduate school. Neither of us was going to get snared by Wiggles' folly, nor were we going to let her run the conversation as she had hoped.

Finally Philomena's father, oddly named Rumpie (I wouldn't have deigned to call even Darby "Rumpie," but then what did I know about English nicknames?), suggested the men indulge in a cigar. Wiggles suggested they retire to the conservatory where there was ventilation "if you insist on smoking Cuban leaves," and the women could retire to the west living room.

Wiggles knew that now was her chance to get me alone — without Archie and Clive to cover my back. Philomena seemed to have no killer instinct or any idea what went on when someone was out to squash you like a June bug and only had a few days to do it.

Wiggles, of course, had no idea she had met her match. How could she have known that I'd stabbed Anthony McDougall in grade four with a compass and he'd had to be hospitalized? It wasn't like I'd meant to hit an artery. I didn't think of myself as a mean person, but as Roy used to say when I was eight years old, "Don't get her mad and then run into her in a dark alley."

The four women retired to the west sitting room, which had exquisite floor-to-ceiling windows and simple but elegant furniture.

"My!" Philomena's sherry-sodden mother said apropos of nothing as she crossed her legs and precariously balanced her drink upon them. Philomena, when prompted by her mother to not be "a bump on a log," said she was working in London for the summer for a drug company doing research on another smallpox vaccine in the event one was ever needed.

Philomena's mother leaned forward in her chair and said in a lowered voice, "You know there is a strain of the pox right now in Somalia, or is it Ethiopia, or somewhere like that, so Philly's lab is frantically working on a new vaccine."

"Actually they are not sure about that, Mother, and it is crucial that no one knows about my work as it could cause panic," Philomena said.

"I know that, dear; I'm not telling anyone," her mother said.

Oddly enough I knew a bit about smallpox since I'd taken a course in epidemiology and I had used smallpox as the example on the paper I'd done. So Philomena and I had much to say on the topic.

Wiggles had tried to bring in Philomena, the upper-class horse woman who had so much in common with Clive it was ridiculous, hoping we would have a cat fight, or I would pale next to her sturdy loins and peaches-and-cream complexion. That plan was crumbled when Philomena and I planned to get together in London.

While Philomena was gathering her breath to answer one of my questions on the World Health Organization, Wiggles, avoiding eye contact, played her final card. I have to admit it was good. Let's face it: she had to up the ante.

When there was a lapse in the conversation, Wiggles said, "Cathy, you know so much about smallpox. I wondered if you had something like smallpox when you were a child. Your face is so scarred. You've been so brave to forge ahead."

Looking straight ahead, I said to the original Cyclops sitting across from me, "I'm so surprised you can see my face from where you are sitting."

You can say a lot to a woman, but never point out her physical deformities, especially those on her face. And we both had them.

The party was over.

—

The next morning, Wiggles did not appear for breakfast, and Archie arrived looking quite shaken. Clive came in from riding alone, something he always had done with sweet mama, and we ate breakfast in flowerless silence.

The doorbell rang and Archie jumped up, saying that it would probably be Dr. Stewart.

After I ate, I said I would go and read the newspaper in the conservatory. Clive joined me, looking quite sombre. I refused to inquire and finally Clive said that his mother had a "frightful migraine" (migraine was pronounced "meegrain," which always bugged me). I nodded and continued reading.

Mrs. Clifford arrived, picked the dead leaves off the plants and then said, "Your lass Cathy's things are packed and waiting in the vestibule."

My heart was pounding. I didn't look up from my paper. I wasn't into leaving graciously. Clive looked up from the paper and said, "This is so completely unnecessary."

At that moment, Archie came in and flopped down in a wicker chair. He was, as usual, dressed perfectly (for the 1940s) in a cable-knit sweater vest and tan starched shirt in a heatwave. "Clive, may I see you in the library?"

"Father, I have nothing to hide from Cathy. I don't care what Mother said. *I really don't.* I will not play this game. If Cathy leaves, I leave, and believe me it is all such bollocks. You have been playing this game for years. Mother does and says whatever she wants, and then when someone calls her on her behaviour, she goes to bed for a month. If you had come to London alone every time she ever did that, then she would have given up this charade years ago. I will no longer engage in her ruthless power struggle. She is using the woman I love as a pawn and I won't have it." Clive stood up, tossed his newspaper on the table and said evenly, "It is just not on."

I was beginning to understand why he behaved as he did when I called him on not climbing the mountain in Wales. He'd refused to be railroaded by me. He'd learned emotional manipulation at the foot of the master.

Archie took off his glasses and cleaned them. "I know, Clivester, you're right. Of course you're right. Believe it or not, I have tried to outlast her. But it was all so frightfully unpleasant." After a few minutes of silence, Archie said, "You know she was so beautiful and still is in my eyes. Yet she thinks she is so disfigured from the accident." He looked into my eyes. "It is hard to be a woman of a certain age who was once so beautiful and gay. She has nowhere to turn. She feels so trapped and then unnecessarily lashes out. She doesn't mean any of it. Really she doesn't."

"Since I was a child you would tell me to go to her dressing room door when she was preparing to go out and tell her how lovely she looked. I know it made her happy but it wasn't right."

"I've made a muddle of things. I know. I started it after the accident and I thought it would be temporary."

"Father, the riding accident was eighteen years ago."

Now that they had both been so honest and supportive, I lost my sense of battle and truly felt like leaving. "I don't mind leaving. I really don't."

"No. We'd planned to go on the weekend. It is Thursday. If

mother wants to stay in her chambers until Saturday morning, she can. She has stayed there a lot longer than that."

"Clive, let me just tell you what your mother said, if you will," Archie entreated.

Clive retorted, "It doesn't matter what was said. Something is always *said*. I don't want to hear it. I plan to emerge from this with my scrotum intact."

I had never heard Clive speak of such things. I could see it was also a shock for Archie. After a few minutes of silence, Archie said, "You are right. The event itself is superfluous. The time has indeed come."

Archie looked at me and said, "Cathy, you have youth. Don't judge those who have lost it too harshly. Beauty was all she was allowed in her era."

—

Clive, Archie and I had a wonderful time without Wiggles. It was absolute paradise to have the whole estate to just the three of us. We hiked, ate apples from the trees and picked blackberries.

On the day before we were to depart, we had to cancel our excursion to town due to the revival of the bizarre heat wave. It was the warmest Indian summer on record in a country largely without air conditioning because it so rarely needed any. It was hard to believe we had been chilled the previous week since it was now 99 degrees with no breeze. I couldn't imagine how hot it must have been in London. Italy and France had shut down completely.

I got up early to gather the flowers. It was amazing to have all the flowers one could imagine at one's disposal and all the most beautiful vases in the world. I made huge arrangements of foxglove, nosegays of bluebells and lily of the valley. I stuffed sunflowers together with proteas, nerine and rosehip, then strung ivy on the bottom and ornamental grasses as filler. I have to say my arrangements weren't as elegant as Wiggles's, but they had a certain wildness that I liked.

By about 1:00, my flowers were wilting. The water had become so hot in the window it needed to be changed. I was not in the habit of asking Mrs. Clifford for anything, so I went to the kitchen myself and refilled the vases with cold water.

The roofers were climbing all over the stable roof. I had no idea how they were managing to do the job in this extreme heat with the reflection from the slate increasing the temperature. One of them had been handing up roofing materials to the others on the ladders. He was returning to get another package of slate from his truck and happened to walk by the kitchen sink window when I was filling up my vases. His face was flushed from the heat, he was dripping with sweat and his shirt was drenched. Clive was outside overseeing things to make sure that the roofers replaced the iodized copper on the dormers. I heard the roofer say to Clive, who happened to be passing from the stable to the livery, "Excuse me, guv, I'm knackered. Could I please get a jug o' water?"

As I was about to fill a jug with cold water and ice, I heard Clive retort, "My good man, you may drink from the pipe at will."

It wasn't so much what he said, but how he said it. The supercilious tone was his mother's. The one he and Peter always made fun of. The unconsciousness of the arrogance was what made it so chilling. It had been locked in and set in stone at birth. Carving something new would take tools I did not possess. Clive had only been taking a break while he was at university and carousing with an American — of all things. I could imagine how he would describe our relationship in later years.

I thought of what my father would have said if I brought home a man who wouldn't give a worker a drink of cold water in a glass, who made him drink from the lukewarm dirty hose. He would not have expected that from me.

There was so much that was wonderful about Clive and actually about England. But I could never live here. Isn't all that obsession about class why people left for America? Now I knew why no matter how uncivilized America was pre-1776, and no matter what new tribulations they had to endure, they were willing to form colonies and give equality a whirl.

It was almost two hundred years later, and maybe after another generation or two the class system would loosen up in England. Frankly, I doubted it. Anyway, it just wasn't who I was. You never know what constitutes a deal breaker until the deal is broken.

Clive walked by the window and saw me watching him for the first time. I didn't say anything. I just left the flowers in the sink and went upstairs. While packing, I turned on the radio and the BBC announcer said Joni Mitchell had written a new song and was giving it a dry run on the program. It was called "California." I remember the sun streaming through my leaded-glass windows, lighting the blue bedroom like a cloudless, bird-filled sky, as the words rang out:

> Still a lot of lands to see
> But I wouldn't want to stay here
> It's too old and cold and settled in its ways here
> Oh but California

California, I'm coming home
I'm going to see the folks I dig
I'll even kiss a Sunset pig
California, I'm coming home

From my window, I called out to the gardener and asked to be taken to the train station. I didn't leave a note. Why bother? Clive knew. He never even wrote to ask why. I didn't have to worry about saying good-bye to Wiggles, and Archie had never left the library.

It was time to come home to America.

PART 2

# Cleveland

CHAPTER 12

# the call of thomas paine

*Moderation in temper is always a virtue;*
*but moderation in principle is always a vice.*
— Thomas Paine, *Rights of Man*

Returning home at the end of 1969 to finish my degree at Ohio

University, I discovered the America I had left behind was unrecog-

nizable. The '60s, the hopeful part of the Cultural Revolution, was

over and only the radical fringes and the dregs remained. Madame

Defarge had finished her sweater, and it was starting to pill.

Martin Luther King Jr. had been assassinated as had Robert Kennedy. Ted Kennedy had been implicated in Chappaquiddick, and the Students for a Democratic Society had blown themselves up. There had been major race riots in Detroit, Cleveland and Newark. The Black Panthers were caged, more troops had been sent to Vietnam, and Nixon and Agnew had been elected on a "law and order" platform in a landslide victory. My college graduation was cancelled due to the possibility of riots.

I had to return to Ohio University to organize my student teaching. While I was in high school, my father had extracted a promise from me that I would get a certificate or professional degree. Whenever careers were discussed, he said, "Get a degree that will qualify you for a job that no one could take away." He was fond of saying, "Even in the Depression, teachers had jobs." He maintained that a "solid career" would maintain my independence. I could hear him saying, "Plan your life as though you are going to be on your own. If fate takes you elsewhere, you can opt for plan B. That way you can always have a choice." I wondered what plan B was.

I did a double major, which had entailed taking an extra course each semester, but the educational courses were not onerous. However, now I had to put in a whole semester student teaching to get the teaching certificate. I dreaded going back to Ohio. I probably would have dropped it all since I knew I didn't want to teach, but my father had made me swear I'd do it. There was no way I could renege on the promise. After all I hadn't said one kind word to him since I'd become a teenager and then he got sick and lost touch. This was the least I could do.

Over the years, I'd found the Ohio department of education

had been utterly desultory. It was run by nincompoops, ex-school-teachers who couldn't cut it teaching and had managed to creep back to college at night to get Ph.D.s in things like "curriculum planning" from dimwitted educational institutions. There had been whole courses on things like using language labs and film projectors. The only thing I learned was how to use visual aids that were obsolete before I'd graduated. These same pedagogical wonders came up with the brilliant ideas of having no walls, no real grades, no fixed curriculum, no standardized testing and no memorization of the timetables, and believed children could learn math from their own observation of size and shape. Then, when most kids didn't learn anything, they were passed on to the next grade. Since these mavens inflated grades to cover their tracks, it naturally took a few decades before that scam was up. When children couldn't do math or spell and the SAT scores took a dip, these educational wizards changed the ground rules, claiming that they were trying to improve self-esteem. However, studies showed that not only did students have less self-esteem than they had twenty years ago, but they couldn't even spell the word. I was on the ground floor of the dumbing-down phenomenon.

There was one professor I admired amongst this din of dunces — Professor Narly, who taught the History of Educational Theory. He looked to be on the far side of retirement age and resembled Mark Twain, and with his Virginia accent even sounded similar. He wore a black colonial string bow tie and an antique white linen suit. He had weathered skin and a full white mane. He said he would only discuss educational theories of previous centuries because he felt the present century was in an educational muddle and there was little to be gleaned from it. He chuckled and shook his head as he said, "The inmates are running the asylum."

In his course, I came across Rousseau's educational theory that "benign neglect" was the best learning tool. When I told my mother about the theory, she said she knew she had been on the right track. She used me as exhibit A, saying I'd turned out "just fine" and added, "Thank God I've erred in the right direction." When I asked her if she was willing to overlook me getting kicked out of grade school for stabbing someone, not doing an ounce of schoolwork in high school, burning down a doughnut shop, having the FBI at her door and driving through a post-office window all before age twenty-one, she responded, "You love making mountains out of molehills."

When I got back from Oxford, I heard Professor Narly was in charge of student teaching and called an emergency meeting of all the students who had signed up for high school placement. I drove down the seven hours to Ohio University and attended this meeting with Sara Roth, my one friend at Ohio. We weren't close, since she rarely spent time away from her boyfriend of the moment, but she didn't disapprove of me and we occasionally had a cigarette together before turning in. Sara had lived across the hall from me since we'd been freshmen, and we were going to get an apartment together and student teach at the same school.

I had first met Sara at a meet-and-greet at our dormitory during frosh week. We all had to wear a red construction paper nametag cut into the shape of a chubby bear: hers said *Marilyn Frickin' Monroe*. I asked her if her middle name was *Frickin'* and we had been friends ever since. She was from New York City and grew up on Park Avenue. Her father was a plastic surgeon and she had the nose to prove it. She was beautiful in an exotic way; with long, glistening black hair and a flawless olive complexion, she was mistaken for Joan Baez at Woodstock. I had never met a hippie before and was fascinated by her demeanor. She kept her cigarettes in a Band-Aid case, saying a cigarette case was too bourgeois, only wore attire that originated in India and doused herself in patchouli oil. She was the first woman I ever knew who used the word *fuck* as a positive exclamation, as in, "This burger is *fucking* good!" Unlike any woman I'd ever met, she took the pill and had sex for, as she said, "a *fucking* good time." We both abhorred the provincialism of southern Ohio, and she, like my mother, spoke with an amusing sense of irony. Although their delivery was different — Sara expressed herself with Jewish New York *chutzpah*, and my mother's tone was of the diffident Irish Catholic variety — the sardonic wit was similar.

Sara, who sat next to me at the "emergency meeting," leaned over and whispered, "No matter what they say today, we are getting out of southern Ohio. We go no farther south than Cleveland — as if that isn't bad enough."

Professor Narly said that he had looked at the sign-up sheets and no one had thus far signed up for Thomas Paine, a high school in the heart of the Hough district, Cleveland's toughest ghetto, which had gone up in smoke. He said that this lack of volunteers for the inner city was clearly a sign of changing times. In retrospect, I see that this was one of the death knells of the '60s. He said in his slow drawl, "You all know that there was a time a few years ago when student teachers wanted to make a difference."

Everyone just looked straight ahead, sick of it all; at least I know I was. All the change we, the flower power generation, made was being weeded out by 1970. Haight-Ashbury was now more hapless than happening. Woodstock had turned into Altamont, and the protest leaders were assassinated, dying, crazy or corrupt.

I was getting the niggling notion that maybe I was a spoiled brat, who, along with my Dr. Spock–trained cohorts, had some grandiose idea that we were different from previous generations and could change the world when, in fact, very few managed to do it. It occurred to me that instead of seething in ideological rage, which focused on the inadequacy of the rest of the world, maybe I should just focus on changing myself.

Professor Narly, always the most intuitive of teachers, read my mind. "For those of you who think that the era of political activism is over or that you didn't make a difference, history will judge it and you differently. The civil rights movement resulted in Supreme Court decisions that will change equality forever, as will the civil rights legislation in '64 and '68. More civil rights legislation was accomplished in this decade than in over a hundred years. *You made a difference.* What about the Vietnam War? You changed public opinion. You threw it in people's faces until they couldn't look anymore. It has wound down and will end soon. *You made a difference.*"

Still no one came forward. He took a final shot at trying to get people to teach in the middle of a burning ghetto where even a black mayor couldn't stop the arson and the looting. "The kids at Thomas Paine are the ones who really need good teachers. A great teacher could change the life of one of those kids. Does anyone remember Kennedy's line 'Ask not what your country can do for you, ask what you can do for your country'?" It saddened me that the line that had meant so much to my mother and me a decade earlier was now falling flat.

Sara leaned over to me and said, "At least Hough would be interesting. Besides I'd rather be shot at in a burning ghetto than stay in southern Ohio on the West Virginia border at some Bible belt cinderblock box where they shoot Jews when they get sick of shooting each other and screwing their sisters."

So we signed up for Thomas Paine High School and decided to get an apartment together in an adjoining area called Cleveland Heights. We received a welcoming letter from the school board with a p.s. telling us that public transportation had not yet been satisfactorily restored after the Hough riots. Sara, true to her delusional New York–centric form, suggested we "grab a cab." I decided I'd be best off keeping one of my parents' cars.

Figuring Sara was an art major with great taste, I told her to find us an apartment. I gave her a lecture on getting a cheap place that was no more than a ten-minute drive to school. All she said was "I get it: no ghetto basement apartment and no doorman — something in between."

A few weeks later, I blew into Cleveland in my mother's 1963 robin's-egg-blue Chevy Impala 409 convertible that boasted a four-on-the-floor. Like the rest of my family, it was tired. With a rim of brown rust laced across the bottom, it was carrying the scars of battles with snow, ice and road salt. I'd left my mother with my father's old Lark. I had the trunk loaded for bear, armed with a suitcase full of schoolmarm dresses I'd whipped up over the weekend from some Simplicity patterns.

Clutching the matchbook with the address that Sara had given me over the phone, I pulled into the U-shaped front drive of a truly wacky building — the Alcazar Hotel, a bizarre Spanish structure built in 1923. The Alcazar was on a hill in the middle of

Cleveland Heights. It was Moorish in its design and was so out of place it looked like a Hollywood set for *The Munsters* if they had been doing an episode in Morocco. The five-storey pentagon-shaped building had wings surrounding what was meant to be a lush botanical garden, but I guess the architect forgot that lush and Cleveland are rarely mentioned in the same breath. All the palms and cactuses looked as though they'd been thrashed into a brown-matted straw. The central fountain in the courtyard had no head and was overrun by pigeons.

When I got to the lobby, Sara sat languishing on a large mustard-coloured circular couch that surrounded a dead palm. She smiled and dragged on a Virginia Slim. Before she had a chance to say anything, I said, "What a dump!"

She said, "I know. Doesn't it scream Tennessee Williams? It's so *Night of the Iguana*. I knew you'd love it."

"It's creepy and smells like old carpets."

"I want you to meet Sandor. He was a Hungarian count, but he lost his title in 1956 and is only working here temporarily." Sandor was the eighty-three-year-old bellhop and desk clerk. He worked an archaic switchboard and filled the beaten-up wooden mail slots labelled with Scotch-taped scrap paper. He gave me my key, which was made of thick wrought iron and about six inches long. I said, "What is with the humongous key? It doesn't even fit in my purse." He replied that some people had "eye problems."

I had to unload the car myself since Count Sandor the Bellhop was so bent over, old and creaky, he couldn't even reach the second shelf of the mail slots. As I handed some boxes to Sara to carry up on the elevator, she smiled as though she was tickled pink with her real-estate skills. I tried to burst that bubble by saying, "What were you thinking when you took this place?" Sara ignored me, while Sandor, clearly offended, said in a thick Hungarian accent, "Well, I don't think Cole Porter thought it was a dump when he stayed here and was inspired to write 'Night and Day.'" Like anyone would know night from day in that cavern.

As we got on the elevator, Sara said, "Wait until you see who lives here. Honestly, they scream *Hush . . . Hush, Sweet Charlotte*." The people I saw in the hall made no eye contact and slithered along the walls. They were like vampires who realized they'd mistakenly come out before dark.

Our apartment was as bizarre as the architecture and the other patrons. It had a dark living room, gigantic heavy wooden furniture and brocade curtains with huge tassels. Murphy beds fell out of the wainscoted walls and the kitchen had one of those running board sinks that Ralph Kramden had in *The Honeymooners*. Although the living room was small, there was a huge walk-in closet that had short little curtains on each shoe cubbyhole and rows and rows of old wooden hangers. It smelled like a combination of mothballs, talcum powder and decomposing Old Spice. The dresser had a fold-away mirror surrounded by Hollywood lights. Whenever I put on my makeup, I used to say to Sara in my best Gloria Swanson, "I'm ready for my close-up, Mr. DeMille."

As we drove to Thomas Paine High School for orientation, we saw all kinds of vacant buildings, which made the Hough neighbourhood look like a set from *Gone with the Wind* after Sherman's march. The businesses had iron grates across their fronts and were burned out on the inside. The brick buildings had charcoal on the outside and the wooden stores were just piles of ash. People hung out on the street as though it were still a main thoroughfare, but really there was nowhere to shop — it was just a pile of rubble. A young boy of about twelve sat on an upside down plastic milk delivery crate and sold cigarettes. Another man sat in a lawn chair, selling leather shorts. (Tough sell in January.) Sara said, "Hot cigarettes and hot hot pants. Wow, who would shop here? Hans Christian Andersen if he smoked?"

We pulled into the Thomas Paine parking lot on a freezing winter day, ready to start the January semester. I distinctly remember that "I'm Henry VIII, I Am" blared on the radio. The school looked like an armed camp or a jail. We were stopped in the icy driveway by a policeman posted at the entrance gate. He asked us for identification and then asked why we were there.

He was young and attractive in a Huck Finn kind of way and looked new on the job. While I was searching for my licence among the debris in my purse, Sara and I exchanged a look. It was only a glance, but girls of a certain age share a "glance vernacular." It was like Morse Code that in this case spelled out "This guy is really cute and I'm going for it." I might have been slightly off. It might have meant "Let's have a few laughs before we become teachers and never laugh again."

"We're student teachers," Sara said, tossing her long black hair over her shoulder. A cigarette hung from her lips, and the smoke drifted into her partly closed eyes. Switching to her best Ohio hick accent, she droned, "We're here to carry the revolution into art and literature." She could do a perfect rendition of what she referred to as "defanged bobcats." The policeman laughed at this and said that he was from Chillicothe, the closest small town to Ohio University, and she had the accent down perfectly.

The policeman nodded as I showed him my licence. He went

back to the squad car for a long time and talked on his walkie-talkie.

Sara asked, "What is he doing for so long? Hope he's writing down our home number."

"I swear you really like these Ohio strawberry blonds from hick towns."

"They're exotic if you're from Manhattan." I shook my head, indicating that she was too weird, which prompted her to exclaim in romantic thrall, "Come on! Look at that swayback in those high boots. And that way he wears his hat low on his forehead. And that little Tom Joad westward-ho cowlick. Yuppers," she said, blowing smoke out her nose, "he could eat Cocoa Puffs in my bed anytime."

"You're insane," I said, looking in my rear-view mirror. He was still nodding as he listened to his walkie-talkie.

Finally he came back to the car and said, "Well, Miss McClure, I see from your speeding record you have quite a heavy foot."

Suddenly Sara began singing in a heavy Brooklyn accent,

Dear kindly Sergeant Krupke,
You gotta understand,
It's just our bringing up-ke
That get us out of hand.

He threw his head back and laughed, "Hey, you sound like the guys in the movie."

In the rear view mirror, I saw a long line of cars waiting to get into the gate of the parking lot. He must have too, because he waved us on.

After I drove through the gate, Sara leaned her head out of the passenger side and screamed to the officer, "We live at the Alcazar Hotel. Come and protect us in those big boots of yours."

As we parked, Sara sang, "Officer Krupke, I'm down on my knees," then she looked at me and added, "hopefully committing an indecent act." I just shook my head as we got out of the car. I knew Sara well enough to know that this was not going to be the end of that policeman.

All teachers had police escorts to and from their cars. There were also weapons checks, and many of the students were frisked at the doors. We walked into a room marked *Faculty Lounge* and were faced with a number of unwelcoming black faces. We were told that the faculty lounge we were looking for was down the hall. When we walked into that one, we were faced with white teachers only. Here I was supposed to meet the teachers who were to be my mentors. The head of the English department had a facial tic and about every fifteen seconds his face jerked to the left and he grimaced. He said he'd been there thirty years and counting. He said it hadn't killed him — yet. The other teacher who was to be my direct supervisor was late "that day." The teachers talked about their jobs as though they were doing time in the pen and they hoped that one day they'd be released. They spent a great deal of time discussing how to protect themselves and how to manage the students. In all the time I spent in the faculty lounge, which diminished as time went on, no one ever discussed curriculum. In every hallway, there were two guards who were not police but hired thugs who carried some sort of strange electric cattle prods (the Taser of yesteryear) and bats to keep order. If a kid had to use the lavatory, he or she was escorted by what the students, and eventually everyone, called "the mice," since they wore solid grey uniforms and grey caps. When I thought of the money spent on this manpower, the police in the parking lot and yard and all the attendance officials and social workers, it frustrated me to no end and ultimately made me sad. If they had devoted that manpower to teaching, we would have had a one-to-five ratio instead of one-to-thirty-five.

On my first day of class, Marilee, the young teacher whom I was assigned to work with and who would be evaluating me, dashed into class late. She was pretty in that rubber-stamped Ohio University sorority kind of way and possessed a perkiness that passed for cooperation in undiscerning circles. She told me it was best to "let me handle things on my own" so I could "get my feet wet." I guess I'd run into another believer in benign neglect. That was her way of saying she was hightailing it to the mall now that she had a babysitter. She said she had lots to do to prepare for her wedding. She was marrying some guy from the swanky suburb of Shaker Heights who was doing a stint in the National Guard to stay out of Vietnam so he could take over his father's business. She had actually put his picture up on the faculty lounge bulletin board. She said over her shoulder as she breezed out of the classroom, "Oh, don't send anyone to the office if they misbehave. They're scared of them down there." Without introducing me to the class, she left, swinging her car keys.

I looked up at the newly arrived class of seniors; these were supposedly the motivated kids since they had not quit school at sixteen when they had been legally allowed to. I was twenty-one teaching eighteen-year-olds and some who had failed several times, making them almost my own age. I wrote my name on the blackboard and one lug in the front row stood up and said in a slightly high-pitched voice for such a large man, "Ya want to teach me somethin' tonight, baby?" I let it go. He kept it up, "Honey, I got a real blackboard you can write on," and everyone laughed.

I was not expecting this and snapped into automatic pilot, retorting, "Call me when your voice changes, Junior." I then swung into action and walked to the back of the class and broke up a poker game by ripping only one card. The guy was furious. He stormed out but was booted right back in by the mice. He literally flew by me and landed crumpled against the radiator. No one seemed to take much notice.

After quickly standing up and carefully dusting himself off, he snapped at me, "I was just interactin' peacefully like I'm supposed to be doin'."

"This is a school. We are here to learn how to use the English language and interpret English literature. *Interacting* can be done on a street corner." Now I raised my voice. "When you go for a job interview someday, are you going to tell them you know how to *interact*?"

I walked back up the aisle and caught sight of two pregnant girls, one of whom looked as though she was about to give birth momentarily. The one who was the most pregnant said under her breath to her less pregnant friend and the three ladies in waiting who surrounded them, "Hair dye is for whores, honey."

There was very little point in saying I didn't dye my hair or have sex for money, so I chose to ignore her. But I admit to being shocked. I decided I had hastily judged the walking wounded in the staff room.

A large boy in the front row named Tyrone seemed to be a

class leader. He smiled brightly and said, "Don't mind them girls, Miss. They called the five pillars of salt. They ain't never leaving Gomorrah."

My tone betraying my incredulity, I announced, "Listen, you are graduating from Thomas Paine High School. *Give me liberty or give me death* is carved on the front of your school. If you want to vote for death, then keep on doing what you're doing. Liberty is when you learn something and can make some choices. I'm glad Thomas Paine can't see the walking dead in this place. You had better fasten your seat belts because I have no idea what you've been doing, but we are moving these cattle out of Laramie starting tomorrow."

When I met Merilee to debrief for five minutes at the end of the day and told her about the "interacting misunderstanding," she said, "He was mad because I let them play cards. I find they need time to interact." (She said the word *interact* as though it was a religious term.) "I really think as long as they are not arguing they are learning social skills."

I couldn't understand how her standards had sunk so low. What I really couldn't believe was that she didn't even bother to put on a better act for me. I would have at least faked it and had the student teacher watch a few of my classes until I could creep out the back door. Most agreements are unwritten and this one was "You don't squeal on me and I give you an A." What Merilee didn't get was that, even though I'd never once wanted to be a teacher, I planned on getting an A anyway.

CHAPTER 13

# five pillars of salt

*While we try to teach our children all about life,*
*our children teach us what life is all about.*

— Angela Schwindt

After the first week of teaching, Sara got in the car after a long

day, slammed the door and declared that it was hopeless trying

to teach with no supplies. While rummaging around in the teach-

er's supply cupboard for some art materials, all she found were

piles of confiscated weapons ranging from nunchuks to Saturday

Night Specials. In a back corner under the eaves, she found a big pile of mouldy, tattered copies of the novel *Of Mice and Men*. She brought one home to show me and said as she held it up, "This is a fossil left over from the early days when they had a curriculum." She handed me the faded blue 1948 edition with two old-fashioned-looking, bow-legged cowboys on the cover. Sara added, "Now, tell me what ghetto youth are going to relate to cowboys in spurs? I'm not even black and I don't give a shit."

I knew how powerful that book had been for me when we'd been assigned it in grade school. I'd read it aloud to Roy, who couldn't read. He and I both loved every page of it. In the book, the two main characters, George and Lennie, are itinerant ranch hands who yearn for the American Dream of having a ranch of their own someday. Steinbeck knew how to portray the glory and dignity of America's disenfranchised. Crooks, the black stablehand who nobly suffered loneliness rather than plead to belong to the group of white cowboys, had the same veneer of pride that covered despair, deprivation and loneliness that I saw in the classroom. I thought teaching the book could be perfect if handled well.

The following Monday, I handed out the novel to each student. I thought they would all laugh, but instead they opened the books, ignoring their deplorable condition, and acted as though I'd given them something interesting. I found that most of them stumbled over the descriptions but did far better on the dialogue. When they took turns performing the character of Crooks, they were spot on. I realized from the class discussion that they knew personality types and they really understood motivation. They saw the innocent beauty of the mildly mentally handicapped Lennie, who experienced no racial prejudice. The students saw Lennie as outside of the black and white dichotomy and immediately related to him. They were touched when Lennie unknowingly suffocates the pet mouse he keeps in his pocket, then accidentally kills a woman because he doesn't know his own strength. Nearly everyone had a Lennie, a special needs child whom everyone tolerated in their neighbourhood. We had our first real discussion about character development, foreshadowing and what makes a human responsible for a crime.

The students who were not on drugs or who hadn't permanently frozen from the inside out with freezer-burn rage, which amounted to about half of the class, enjoyed reading aloud if it was dialogue — they liked dramatic performance. I set up different chapters of *Of Mice and Men* to be read with different interpretations, but they all had to be defensible in the book. It worked.

About two days later, I was at a movie theatre with Sara to see *Midnight Cowboy*. I reached into my camel-coloured Ralph Lauren Polo coat to get some gum and felt something warm and furry. It still had a heartbeat. My hand moved down to its wet pink tail. I jumped in the air, saying, "Sara, I have some live thing in my pocket. It's pulsating like the tell-tale heart."

Sara imitated Mae West's voice, saying, "'Hey there, big boy, is that a gun in your pocket, or are you just happy to see me?'" and then went back to watching the movie.

After the movie, I made the mistake of pulling the small grey mouse out of my pocket in the lobby. It had by now totally expired. The audience scattered, leaving us with no line-up at the refreshment counter so we could purchase our popcorn in time for *The Prime of Miss Jean Brodie*, our second feature. Sara said the mouse caper was a great trick to get to the head of the popcorn line.

Much to Sara's disgust, I kept the mouse in a baggie in the fridge until the next morning. I wore my same Polo coat to work and left it on the back of my chair. I had Tyrone act the role of Crooks, the black stablehand. Carlson, a large, lanky baritone who was quiet but intense, played Lennie while wearing my coat. I was told by some of the other kids that Carlson had a brother who had been a star basketball player until the year before, when he'd had a high fever then a seizure that left him forever after mentally handicapped. The brother, although older than Carlson, shadowed him on the weekends. Carlson knew exactly how to play the role, how to fidget correctly and mimic his brother's gait and intonation. His performance was mesmerizing, and for the first time even the five pillars of salt sat at attention.

We performed the scene where the hulking Lennie, who loved petting animals, inadvertently kills his pet mouse in his pocket by touching him with too much force. We turned the lights off, pulled down the shades and turned on a huge battery-operated light that one of the boys had brought from somewhere. The light shone on Carlson as he walked over to George, Lennie's partner. Carlson, as Lennie, reached into his pocket and pulled out the dead mouse and put it in front of George, who was played by Tex. The whole class gasped, and I nodded to the players to continue with the scene. Carlson played Lennie with such angelic innocence that when he said, "Oh now, George, look what I gone an' done," he had us all in his pocket; there was spontaneous clapping from everyone when the scene finished. I thanked everyone, saying that the rodent donors had chosen to remain anonymous, but I wanted to thank them for the mouse or we would never have had such a marvellous scene.

When we did the section of the book where the tartish wife of the boss's son comes on to Lennie, I was shocked that Yvonne, the most pregnant pillar of salt who usually kept her eyes on the clock and sighed heavily whenever I spoke, offered to read and act the part. Tyrone said she wouldn't even have to act. Yvonne pulled a knife out of her sock and tore across the room toward the offender as everyone laughed. I caught Yvonne by the arm and sent her back to her chair. (I didn't want to call the mice to throw her around since she was pregnant.) Something let loose in me. I had yet to get angry and I just let Tyrone, a well-known Casanova, have it: "How dare you say one word to Yvonne about her condition? If you were a woman, you would be sitting in the same condition many times over."

Yvonne, picking up on my tone, interrupted me to say, "You sayin' I made some mistake? I want this baby. I'm marryin' this father soon as he gets hisself sorted out." The boys in the back seats snickered as she continued. "I ain't made no mistake. I don't want to be old like you and have some baby when I'm a granny." The rest of the class made an mmm-mmm sound: Yvonne had pushed a boundary with me and they knew it. I chose to let it go — the idea of being pregnant in high school was so awful to me that I thought she had the right to live any desperate fantasy she wanted. I kept Yvonne after class that day to apologize, saying I was sorry that I'd made assumptions about her pregnancy that were clearly unwarranted. I'd embarrassed her instead of helping her. She stood with her arms on her hips and snapped, "Not only you got the wrong idea, you gone and gives it to the whole class. Now I gots to live that down. From now on, keep your nose out of my business." I decided that was a good idea. I think she was shocked that I had apologized, but she didn't want to lose face so she said, "Yeah, you went around putting my business on the street. Now you tellin' me you *sorry*." I offered to say something to the class the next day, but I realized it would have brought more unwanted attention to the situation. She said, "Forget it. You gone and done enough," and stormed out of the room.

The next day, Yvonne told Tyrone that she was going to play the part of the farm owner's wife and she didn't want "no manner o' thing comin' out his big mouth." I was surprised that she wasn't just bowing out. This time everyone was respectful or at least quiet.

Carlson played Lennie and Yvonne played the farmer's wanton wife. This very pregnant girl was perfectly able to play the part of an evil femme fatale. She changed the words only slightly to enhance the performance. She cuddled up to Carlson and said that she knew what it was like to touch soft things. She said her hair was not nappy but soft, just like his baby mouse. Then she picked up his hand and ever so gently put his hand on her hair. She said, "That's okay, sugar, just feel how soft that be." I have seen many versions *Of Mice and Men*, but I have never seen one that approximated the intensity of Carlson and Yvonne.

Although there was a part of me that winced seeing a pregnant teenager attempt such outrageous flirtation, rubbing her body against a boy's and making every word and movement a sexual innuendo, I admired her guts. I would have been terrified to flirt with a man at any time, let alone while pregnant and in front of a crowd.

Two months later, when Yvonne had her baby, she went alone to the hospital, was home for two days, gave it to her tired mom to raise and returned to school on the third day, not wanting to miss the prom. The boy who got her pregnant asked another girl to the prom and left Yvonne on the sidelines.

——

I opened the next unit by announcing that we were going to do poetry. The class groaned and one student threw himself into the aisle with his arms and feet in the air as though he were a dead rodent with rigor mortis. I handed out a mimeographed sheet with a poem.

I read the first of several verses aloud:

> Love the lie and lie the love
> Hangin' on, with a push and shove
> Possession is the motivation
> that is hangin' up the Goddamn nation
> Looks like we always end up in a rut (everybody now!)
> Tryin' to make it real — compared to what?

No one got very excited until they saw me unveil the expensive record player I'd borrowed from Sara and lugged into school. I put on the record by the jazz greats Les McCann and Eddie Harris, who had recorded the lyrics. The class had a completely different reaction to the song, which had a strong staccato rhythm. Those who had tripped over the words while reading them could suddenly read every word as they pounded out the rhythm on their desks. A few of the tough guys from the back row, the Huey Newton clones who wore black berets and bullets over one shoulder, nodded and for the first time participated by reading another verse aloud:

Slaughterhouse is killin' hogs
Twisted children killin' frogs
Poor dumb rednecks rollin' logs
Tired old ladies kissin' dogs
Hate the human, love that stinking mutt (I can't stand it!)
Try to make it real — compared to what?

I was confused. How could they not read a poem, but then be able to read it when put to music? I realized that day that performance was something they liked, and could do, and that they learned far more with this auditory approach. It was the motivation they needed for their reading.

As time went on, I realized they also liked to have a say in things, and I had them vote on the best poem of the day. In order to nominate a poem and place it on the board, you had to have good reason for why it was superior and then we would vote for the best of the day, best of the week and best of the month. The kids called it "Pimp My Poem."

Every day on the Gestetner, I would run off purple copies of poetry by both black and white authors. I had each student start a poetry notebook that they were to decorate in Sara's art class. When Sara's father heard of the lack of resources at Thomas Paine High School, he offered to pay for the poetry notebooks. He used a phrase I'd never heard before when I thanked him on the phone; he said, "Not to worry. I can write them off." I bought beautiful notebooks with unlined pages. Each had a lovely red ribbon bookmark. Then I bought gold stick-on lettering and personalized each one.

The kids were not used to school supplies; they were all silent for once and just spent time looking at them. One kid complained, "Hey, I got a dud. Mine's blank." When I told them that the notebook was for their poems and to record their favourites, they were delighted. I announced in our poetry unit that we would learn how others wrote poems, then write our own and bind the whole project together. We'd also perform the poems in front of the school. I arranged with the principal to do an assembly. He said he usually had to bring in outside speakers for assembly because counting on the students had led to "scheduling issues" and "disappointments." However, if I really felt I could bring this "poetry party" to fruition, he would pencil in the date.

I had Sara on board, and she had her art class work on the set design using old wood she found backstage in the auditorium. With some supervision and encouragement, the natural builders emerged and the sets were constructed and painted. She even found footlights locked under the floorboards. One of her boys had that lock picked before the janitor could get there with a screwdriver. The lights were covered in dust and cobwebs but they worked.

Once in a while, one of the kids would put me down, but I always had a worse put-down for the offender. I tried to make my rejoinders amusing, but my comebacks could sting. It was an unorthodox form of discipline, but it was all I had in my juvenile armoury — and it worked. If you, as the teacher, showed any vulnerability, you were toast. I think I finally made some in-roads with some of them because I really worked hard and listened to them. I actually found them and their learning styles interesting, and I think they sensed that. I got the toughest boy, Tyrone, on my side and the rest fell into line like dominoes. That is, all except the five pillars of salt.

I always thought I was hard to ignore, but they managed it. They burned me off their frozen psyches as though I were an unsightly wart. I tried everything from talking to them one-on-one to calling their mothers or grandmothers, but they never thawed.

Something I never would have figured out on my own, but began to understand through their daily voting process, was that their love of poetry was colour-blind. With all the talk of black power and black literature having a voice, these kids paid no attention to whether a poem was written by a black or white poet. If it rang true and used language imaginatively, they liked it. They had amazing bullshit barometers. They had seen a lot and knew emotional truth when they heard it. Their all-time favorite poem, which they used to introduce their show, was "Richard Cory," written by Edward Arlington Robinson in 1897.

> Whenever Richard Cory went down town,
> We people on the pavement looked at him:
> He was a gentleman from sole to crown,
> Clean favored, and imperially slim.
>
> And he was always quietly arrayed,
> And he was always human when he talked;
> But still he fluttered pulses when he said,
> "Good-morning" and he glittered when he walked.
>
> And he was rich — yes, richer than a king —
> And admirably schooled in every grace:
> In fine, we thought that he was everything
> To make us wish that we were in his place.

So on we worked, and waited for the light,
And went without the meat, and cursed the bread;
And Richard Cory, one calm summer night,
Went home and put a bullet through his head.

When the class heard this poem, they stopped in their tracks. It didn't mean that much to me. I had just included it randomly, but they loved it, exclaiming as though they were at a corner church revival meeting. One student said, "That poet lived a *life*." We had our longest continuous discussion about that poem. I think I won them over that day because I could learn from them and they realized they had something to teach me. I said, "There is a reason why this poem struck a chord with everyone in here, and this class is not over until I learn what it is."

Tex, a quiet tiny boy who the nurse told me suffered from sickle cell anemia, spoke for the first time: "They is the poor people who is watching Richard Cory — the guys on the street. They got nothing. They be cursing for a piece of bread. They watch this guy strut his stuff — he ain't mean or nothing, he just rich — got it all. Then he blows hisself away." With that, Tex imitated blowing a hole in his head. Finally they'd found a poem from their point of view. As Alphonse, a boy who made lots of money at poker in homeroom, said, "Don't be thinking them Richard Cory dudes got the world by the tail. That envy can eat you up — and it ain't even true."

Later at our show in assembly, Alphonse walked across the stage in a bright green pimp suit, which he said was just "hangin' 'round his house." A "heavy lid" was donated by Smalls-all, another short, delicate boy who limped. Someone else brought in his brother's fancy walking stick and diamond-studded cuff links. The class stood behind a semi-transparent screen in silhouette and recited "Richard Cory" as Alphonse strutted across the stage, greeting imaginary people left and right, and then pulled out a gun (a prop not hard to come by; they were locked away in every supply cupboard) and pretended to shoot himself in the head. The kids in the audience went wild. It had struck a nerve. As Smalls-all explained to me, everyone has seen a drug dealer get rich, then get on the stuff themselves and blow their own brains out in one way or another. (The Richard Cory performance wasn't the only memorable part of what would turn out to be a truly shocking assembly for those in front of and behind the proscenium.)

Their second all-time favourite was "The Raven" by Edgar Allan Poe. They admired this poem because, as one of the students said, "You can only read that poem one way, man. Your voice *gots* to sound midnight dreary."

When I asked him why he stumbled over prose and not poetry, he said, "First you got the beat, *then* you got the words. It don't work the other way around." I learned there are ways to teach reading and one should begin with rhythmic poetry — I wasn't accessing half of what these kids could do. These kids were rapping in a pre-rap era.

—

I had become used to my life in the strange Alcazar Hotel. Despite the name, no one ever used the Alcazar as a hotel. It was more of a residence. We were the only two who lived there and approximated normalcy, so you can imagine what the other residents were like. They seemed to cluster somewhere between shifty and bewildered, emerging mostly at night to slink along the wall of the hallway to the ancient elevator. Sara was right when she said it was a whole hotel of Tennessee Williams characters who had been counting on the kindness of strangers for far too long. Some of the women sauntered down the central circular staircase slowly as though they were Loretta Young greeting their guests while the camera panned. They never acted as though they were descending along a threadbare carpet to an empty lobby that smelled of cat urine.

On the first night in January when we'd arrived at the Alcazar, there was a knock at the door. "Oh God, it's Rod Serling from *The Twilight Zone*," Sara said and then made me answer the door. Peering into the dark hallway, I saw a man of uncertain racial origin. He had a white freckled face but a large red Afro that rose up straight on his head as though he were a frightened Raggedy Andy. He was very tall and high waisted, with long, stick-like legs. He wore a faded Hawaiian shirt and high-waisted pants held up by suspenders. He said his name was Merlyn. He came in, glided along the wall and sat in the chair closest to the door. He had a bag of take-out food with him and said he lived next door and that we must be hungry after our journey. He shared two ham sandwiches on Wonder Bread among the three of us. Merlyn said that it was "pitiful to watch the news alone." Every night after that for the entire duration of our stay, Merlyn came over at exactly 7:00 and we all watched Walter Cronkite together. He sat near the door and hopped up the second the news was over. He had a ham radio set in his apartment and often knew the news before Walter, or so he said. There was something odd about him, but we couldn't exactly put our finger on what it was.

Our other almost daily visitor was Bob, the policeman from the school parking lot. Heeding Sara's unsubtle hints, he showed up the first weekend after we'd arrived. He and Sara had, as she said, "gotten it on." When I asked if she was in love with Bob, she said, "What else are you going to do in *Cleveland*?" Since Bob hailed from southern Ohio, he had an Appalachian twang. Sara called him "Hayseed Bob," which was eventually shortened to Hay, a name he seemed to take to. Sara and Hay had sex in the walk-in closet on a more than regular basis. Once I found Hay's badge in my underwear pile. I didn't care if they had sex, but I could never use the closet at night. Whatever I put on in the morning was my outfit until the next morning.

Hay and Sara were completely different types but got on remarkably well. I only saw one altercation. Once after Hay put bacon grease on his white toast and was about to take a bite, Sara said, "Hey, Hay, I can't get it on with a man who uses bacon grease as a condiment." Hay didn't hesitate, just threw the bacon grease in the garbage and asked me where the butter was.

Once I was in the convenience store with Sara and Hay, and Hay spotted Merlyn in the meat aisle. Hay tapped my arm, pointed to Merlyn and put his finger up to his mouth, indicating that neither of us should make a sound. Merlyn was feeling his way along the meat counter with a white cane. He was blind. He had gone through elaborate measures to make us think he was sighted. He said his car was up on blocks when we asked him to drive for take-out. After Merlyn left the convenience store, Hay asked the owner of the store if he knew anything about Merlyn. The man said that he only knew he lived at the Alcazar with the other blind people. He said the hotel had been almost empty so the Society for the Blind rented most of the place. It was for people who were just beginning to go blind through macular degeneration. They lived at the Alcazar, in varying degrees of blindness, and went to a blind school to learn how to cope with their new disability. The clerk asked, "You ever seen them big keys they carry?" He added, "You girls must be the only people paying rent over there."

Every night Sara and I ate dinner at the Brown Derby Restaurant on our way home from school. If Hay wasn't on duty, he met us there. He told us that his mother never once ate in a restaurant in her entire life. Sara asked if she had a mental disability; Hay said she didn't want other people touching her food. She also thought Coca-Cola wasn't good for people. Both Sara and I said we had never in our lives met anyone who hadn't eaten in a restaurant or didn't "believe" in Coke. Sara often remarked with wondrous glee that we could have joined the Peace Corps and gone to "deepest darkest Africa" and not met anyone as exotic as Hay.

We always sat at the booth in the back and on this particular occasion there was a paper covered with tiny, pencilled writing and folded into my napkin ring. It was a nine-stanza poem, which I read aloud to our table. It was so powerful that we were stunned into silence.

I knew right away that Maurice from my class had written it, since he was a bus boy at the restaurant. He had two jobs because, as he said, he had two babies "round the block." (Whatever that meant.) He rarely spoke in class and usually slept in the back row.

As he pushed his dish cart by our table, we all gave him a thumb's up; he nodded his head in his white paper cap, smiled and drove on by.

The next morning, I told the class that I'd chosen the person who would read their poem as the grand finale at our upcoming assembly. I had the boys near the windows pull down the blinds and I asked Tyrone to shine the high-powered light on an empty chair. Then I told the class that I found the poem on my dinner plate and asked the poet to come up and read it. Maurice looked horrified that I'd singled him out, but he reluctantly ambled to the front of the room and mumbled that his poem was in the same style or beat as "The Raven." It was called "Forevermore" and it was from the point of view of the American eagle who cast shadows as he flew over Hough. He said he got the idea for the bird from "The Raven." When the kids heard the first stanza, they began hitting their desks in approval. Then Maurice's voice became more sonorous, and he began rocking as he read. When Maurice was finished, he got a standing ovation from everyone in the class — except for the five pillars of salt. Maurice tipped his pork pie felt hat, like the one Thelonius Monk wore, and let others slap his hand as he bounced in ghetto gait to his seat. The clapping was so loud the mice came in to ask me if it was a rumble. I said, "No. It's just enthusiasm over our poetry unit."

Maurice's poem was similar in sentiment to Allen Ginsberg's lament in his famous long poem "Howl." While Maurice's poem read, "Who ate lead paint to get high, drank thunderbird wine to make filthy laneways into Heaven's alley," Ginsberg had written, "Who ate fire in paint hotel or drank turpentine in Paradise Alley." I told the class that Ginsberg was a man who had won some of the greatest honours in American poetry. We all read sections of "Howl" aloud and the kids nodded and made sounds of assent. Both Maurice's and Ginsberg's poems were chockablock with ghetto images that were neighbourhood mainstays for my students:

I saw the best mind of my generation destroyed by
    madness, starving hysterical naked,
dragging themselves through the negro streets at dawn
    looking for an angry fix,
angelheaded hipsters burning for the ancient heavenly
    connection to the starry dynamo in the machinery of
    night,
who poverty and tatters and hollow-eyed and high sat up
    smoking in the supernatural darkness of cold-water
    flats floating across the tops of cities contemplating
    jazz

I was so sure of our success in the poetry assembly that, in true McClure grandiose fashion, I invited the whole school: from the janitors to all the mice, the police from the parking lot, the principal, our supervisory teachers, Professor Narly, the superintendent of schools and even the mayor of Cleveland! I had also sent home invitations to all of the parents, designed by Sara's art class, and I think the kids actually asked some of them to come.

I reserved ten rows for parents and relatives. While I was cordoning off the seats an hour before the performance, the old janitor told me that I would just look "pitiful" when no parents showed up. He reserved one row in the back, and we had five grandmothers, one mother, and no fathers; not even one row was fully occupied with parents.

As the curtain went up, there was a gasp from the audience as they took in the set — a kind of junk palace in an alleyway, all painted in silver that shone in the moonlight. The lighting man from Sara's class had done an almost professional job. Broken wine bottles were made into a window, which, lit from behind, looked like a church with a stained glass window.

The show was marvellous and you could hear a pin drop in the audience. No one skipped the assembly because word had gotten out that it was not a public speaker but the "homeboys." Even the mice crept in from the halls and parked their bats at the door.

Tex introduced Maurice's poem as "an elegy for the living." (I was pleased to see how Tex had utilized the word *elegy* from our poems.) Sara had the kids do special masks in red so they looked like wolves. The students stood behind a gauze curtain so the audience would see only shadows and a moon with a papier-mâché silhouette of the American bald eagle. Maurice read aloud while those behind the scrim howled at the moon.

For our last number, the five pillars of salt had to do something; they worked so hard at not participating in the work or in the assembly that Tyrone and Maurice just shook their heads. Tyrone said, "Man, we got face out there." Finally they agreed to read "The Raven." Yvonne was to read and the other four were to sing, "Nevermore" in the background and snap their fingers. I agreed.

The five stood together, and Yvonne, their spokesperson, waddled to the mike and said they were going to do a poem by Allen Ginsberg, "one our teacher Miss McClure read in class." I assumed they'd decided to change their routine at the last minute. Two of the girls played backup and the other three read. They had clearly chosen parts that we had not read in class.

I have to say they read them with masterful intonation and expression to fully appreciate Ginsberg's meaning. (Only the highlights follow — believe me, it was worse.)

Pillar of salt #1: "Who let themselves be fucked in the ass by saintly motorcyclists and screamed with joy"

Pillar of salt #2: "Who blew and were blown by those human seraphim, the sailors, caresses of Atlantic and Caribbean love"

Pillar of salt #3: "Who balled in the morning in the evenings in rose gardens and the grass of public parks and cemetery scattering their semen freely to whomever come who may . . ."

On it went. They chose every homoerotic and graphic scene. It was 1970 when gay meant happy and the word homophobia had not entered common parlance. There were grandmothers in the audience who stomped up the aisles and flooded out the doors. The graphic homoeroticism continued to spew from the stage until the audience started booing and yelling.

The curtain came down on more than the show, and Sara and I were called to the office to meet with a bevy of school officials, including the principal and the superintendant of schools.

The first thing I said was that Sara had been in the dark about the content. Then I tried to defend myself, explaining that Ginsberg's poem was a lament about America's disenfranchised. I also explained that "Howl" was a very long poem of almost three thousand words and one could, therefore, take any part of it out of context. The superintendent of schools had one of those red faces that got redder with any exertion: at this moment it turned purple. For a long time, he shook his head and breathed heavily as the buttons on his tight suit pulled across his bulging belly. Finally he said, "Miss McClure, are you aware that we have had here in the city of Cleveland worse riots than anywhere else in the country?" He held up two fingers in my face and enunciated, "*tw—ice.*" He paused to gather more breath, then added, "It is not our desire to make our students howl with rage or to engage in perversion as Mr. Ginsman has done. We are trying to make them into . . ." He hesitated, then finally opted for "empowered, productive citizens."

I was not trying to give any specific message, but only to echo what had touched the students. I tried to explain that if pain and rage were what the students felt, why not express it through poetry rather than burning down their own neighbourhood? Maybe people have to recognize their own rage before they become, as Merilee would say, "empowered"? I looked at the superintendent of schools. "Empowerment comes through education and hard work. I tried to teach poetry and they felt empowered enough to do this assembly. For Christ's sake, we had to clean twenty years of grime off the footlights."

"If you were so eager to build black pride, why didn't you include some black poets?" the black female guidance counsellor asked.

"We did an entire unit of black poetry. Most of the poems that grabbed them and they emulated were not by black people. Actually I admired how they used their gut and did not respond along racial lines. Instead they made non-political artistic judgments. I think that is fairly sophisticated for high school students."

That shut her up.

The superintendent jumped back in. "Clearly those girls hate you or they wouldn't have betrayed you to us," he said with a tinge of pride.

"No kidding. I didn't expect to reach everyone. No one does. I did push them — hard. I'll admit that and they pushed back. At least they got off their backsides. I'll be willing to wager it was more than they've done since they entered this school."

When the superintendent asked Merilee how I had behaved as a teacher, she couldn't answer, since she had never stayed for even one minute of my classes. To avoid taking any responsibility, she cut to the chase. "If Miss McClure apologizes and clearly sees that what she did was wrong, then can we put this unfortunate incident behind us?"

Principal Woldberg said, "Do you see how saying something about giving your semen to people, other men, in public parks, is not high school material — particularly the glorification of that content?"

"Of course I see that. I wanted Maurice, a student, to know that someone who had won the National Book Award and the Robert Frost Medal had written some lines that were similar to his. Yes, an old homosexual Jew and a teenaged heterosexual black man said almost the same thing. I thought that was interesting — and in some way encouraging about the so-called family of man. I also believe it inspired the students."

"Would you do it again for an assembly?" Principal Woldberg asked, fishing for resolution.

"I wouldn't have done it the first time. I would never have picked that passage for an assembly or even to read in class. That's obviously why the girls have done it."

The guidance counsellor spoke again. "Miss McClure, I watched you thinking you were the cock of the walk. You thought we were all lazy and had never tried with these students." I wasn't sure if she wanted an answer, but I thought it best to remain silent. She continued in a slightly higher-pitched and progressively angrier voice, "Do you think we wanted to close the drama department? Do you think we wanted to pay for the mice instead of books? We were once exactly like you. We tried it all. Contrary to your belief, you are not the only educator here — you are just the latest one."

After a brief silence, my curriculum coordinator, Professor Narly, spoke. He pulled out an old-fashioned handkerchief embroidered with the letter N, wiped his face and drawled, "I think there is no doubt that Cathy has been somewhat unrestrained, but what she has brought in poor judgment she has made up for in exuberance. Her excitement has galvanized the students. I have never heard a reading like that rendition of 'Richard Cory' in my life. The scene from *Of Mice and Men* was a masterpiece. Having the crippled boy play the handicapped Crooks was certainly going out on a limb, but there wasn't a peep in the house. Ladies and gentlemen, we have made our point, now may I quote a couplet that is à propos: 'Our youth we can have but to-day, / We may always find time to grow old.'"

The superintendent said, "It's Friday. I believe we will have to meet Monday and make a decision as to whether Miss McClure will be returning."

"Fine," I said and walked toward the door.

"Is there any more you want to say?" the principal asked. Clearly he wanted me to beg for his forgiveness. Or maybe he was really on my side and wanted me to administer an abject apology to placate the superintendent. However, I wasn't nailing myself to the cross. What's the worst they could do? Say I couldn't teach? Hallelujah!

So I turned to the pedagogical posse and said, "No, I have no more to say."

As I walked out the door, everyone else followed since it was Friday at 5:00 and we were still at school. When we went into the hall, at least eight of the students from my class were waiting, led by Tyrone, Carlson and Maurice.

"Gentlemen," Tyrone said with his huge football body squarely planted in the middle of the hall, his hand held up in a stopping motion. "Miss McClure never got into that kind of . . . you know, the nasty stuff them girls went off spouting. Miss McClure just trying to say, 'You think your nerves are tried, read this — then you goin' to find you ain't the only one ailin'.'"

Carlson piped in with, "Hey, you teach Hitler — don't mean you love the dude. You get my meanin' here, men?"

The principal listened to what they all had to say and said, "This is a very serious issue and your feedback has mattered greatly. This is the first time a group of students has ever come to my office on behalf of a teacher."

Then the superintendent, who wasn't giving an inch, said, "I don't believe we have ever had one in trouble."

"Hah," Tex poked his small head around Tyrone's back and started naming off all kinds of incidents that must have happened over the years. Carlson added to the list and then Maurice said, "Jus' 'cause we don't come tear-assin' down to your sorry office, don't mean there ain't been trouble."

With that, the superintendent chose to shut up.

Professor Narly was emotionally overwrought. "Ladies and gentlemen," he said, smiling and shaking the hands of each boy in the group who had come to my defence, "wouldn't it be wonderful if we could help each other out like this on a regular basis?"

CHAPTER 14

# a massacre

Sara and I and the kids made it through the long winter at Thomas Paine High School. If we had not exactly found liberty, we were a long way from death. I had managed to get to spring without another "incident" and we only had one month left to go.

Finally, the May heat melted the ice and even the patches of snow were gone. The top came down on the 409, and the radio blared "Groovin'." The Cuyahoga River was again flowing, although it had caught on fire the previous year. Flames climbed as high as five storeys until fireboats brought them under control. The fire was attributed to waste dumped into the river by the waterfront industries, though no one knows if it started from spontaneous combustion or if it was a welding spark. Tyrone told me that a rival drug gang had thrown his cousin in the Cuyahoga and when the Coast Guard pulled his body out in the morning, he looked as though even he'd been dipped in lye. His hair was even straight.

The tulips and daffodils were announcing the earth was again breathing, and the lilacs were just starting to spread their aroma across Cleveland Heights. All of this heralding of spring was happening everywhere except at the Alcazar Hotel. Nothing was in bloom there. The dead palms paid no attention to spring, refusing any form of resurrection.

One day in early May, Sara and I dragged ourselves home from school on an incredibly hot day. Count Sandor told me that a woman named Baby had called me and wanted me to call her back.

"Baby made a long distance call to *me*? We hardly talked when we were roommates," I said to Sara.

"Why the hell were you roommates for two years?"

"I don't know. She was assigned to my room after my first-year roommate quit school without telling me."

"Remember on the first day of school before you'd met her and she was playing that insane song on her tiny record player and we heard it from down the hall?"

"Oh yeah, 'The Ballad of the Green Berets.' She played that

song *hundreds* of times," I said.

As we waited for the groaning elevator, Sara said, "Remember her ironing board with the special weenie board for capped sleeves? She ironed a blouse every morning. *Who does that?*"

"Remember when she thought a spade was a shovel?" I added and Sara started laughing.

"Oh God, she isn't coming here to visit, is she?"

"She would only come here if it had to do with work and it was paid for."

"Man! Baby was one *strange* chick."

"Actually, *we* are strange and *she* is really normal. Robbie has been her boyfriend since she could talk." Robbie had gone to Kent State on an ROTC scholarship to take Earth Sciences, while Baby studied primary education. She had no money, was in the co-op program and cleaned the slop off cafeteria trays night after night before going home to the good ol' Proctorville farm, and worked again on the weekend. She was the first of her family to go to college. My father would have admired her: she came for an education, worked her ass off and got it.

"Remember when she dragged us to watch Robbie march along in his ROTC suit? He did that little parade thing in the courtyard where he swung his gun around like he was a drum majorette in drag," said Sara.

"They're called drills or manoeuvres," I said.

"It always amazes me what you know."

"It amazes me what you don't know."

"Yeah, like who got you the speed that sped you to Oxford?"

"You're right," I acknowledged as I opened my now-soggy takeout BLT.

We settled down to grade school papers; Sara was in art so she had a lighter load than I did. I had to slog through forty essays on what *Julius Caesar*'s "et tu, Brute?" meant to you. The first essay was titled "A Deal Gone Bad."

When the long-distance rates went down at 6:00, I phoned Baby. I knew she would flip if I called earlier. Clearly this was an important call. Baby never once called her boyfriend at Kent State due to the long-distance costs. She wrote him a letter every night at exactly 10:00 p.m.

She picked up on the first ring.

"Baby, I heard you called. Is everything all right?"

"No, Cathy, it isn't." Her perpetual cheeriness was drained. "One of Robbie and my best childhood friends was killed today. He was in ROTC with Robbie."

"Was it an accident?"

"No. Well, actually, I don't know. The Ohio National Guard at Kent State shot him. He was just cutting through the campus to the ROTC building."

"What happened?"

"*I have no idea.* It was some kind of protest gone wrong." She began to sob. She cried so hard I couldn't understand her.

Sara yelled, "What the hell happened?"

I covered the phone and said, "Shut up," to Sara, then, "Baby, I'm so sorry. What can I do for you?" It all sounded so strange.

"Cathy, would you please go to a memorial for him either at Kent State or in Cleveland? I'm stuck teaching here in Proctorville and I can't afford the money or time to get all the way up there."

"Baby, I'm teaching as well and can't miss school. But I'll go downtown right away. I'll call Case Western Reserve and the other schools and see what they have organized. If nothing is in the works, I'll do my best to get something happening."

"Would you carry a candle?"

"Yes, of course. I'll send you a picture of Sara and me at a memorial if there is one."

"Well, this is long distance so I had better go. I knew I could count on you. Bye."

I looked at my watch. It was two minutes until the CBS news. I walked over to turn on the TV and told Sara what had happened, when Merlyn stormed in, saying, "Did you hear about the slayings? It's all over the ham radio."

"Everyone quiet," I yelled. The news began with Walter Cronkite looking right at the three of us as he announced, "Today the Ohio National Guardsmen killed four students and wounded nine others on the Kent State University Campus. The students were protesting the march into Cambodia, and the National Guard opened fire. We have an unconfirmed report that an ROTC student was a bystander going to class and was gunned down as well."

Sara said, "That must be Robbie's friend."

After the camera panned across students lying dead on the sidewalk, Walter Cronkite shook his head and said, "Well, that's the way it is on May 4, 1970. Good night."

"That's the way it is?" Sara said, staring at the TV in shock.

I said, "It's like not being in America."

Hay called to say he couldn't come over because every policeman in Cleveland was put on alert due to the Kent State "situation."

"*Situation?* Situation my ass!" Sara yelled.

Merlyn said, "That was way more than a situation. At first they thought it was a student sniper but then they found out it was the

National Guard, although they haven't admitted it. Ballistics tests will nail them. I also heard on the ham that ROTC guy was shot in the back."

"The irony is I'd place a high wager that Robbie and his buddy were probably the most patriotic, America-love-it-or-leave-it types on the Kent State campus," I said.

"Well, Robbie's buddy loved it and left it today," Sara said, shaking her head in disgust.

I explained to Merlyn that Sara and I had to get over to the Case Western campus and help organize a memorial protest for Kent State. "Baby can't make it and she needs us to represent her."

Sara and I began bustling around the room packing our cigarettes, when Merlyn asked, "Mind if I come along?"

"Merlyn, there's a lot of shit going down here and we can't play your I'm-not-really-blind game," I said.

"Blind? What makes you say that?" he asked.

"We've had a shock and we can't deal with your *meshugas*. We know you're blind and we aren't pretending anymore. So come along, but get your white cane and take care of yourself," Sara added as we walked to the elevator.

"I'm not blind," he said.

"Save it, Merlyn. We saw you at the grocery store tapping a white cane from side to side. Was that a Fred Astaire number, or are you blind?"

The elevator door closed and we left him in the hall. Sara added, "Christ, I've had enough of ignoring the obvious."

As we were pulling out of the parking lot, Merlyn appeared with his cane at the exit. He hopped in and we sped away.

I remember the night of the memorial well because I described all the people and the action to Merlyn. Thousands of people lined the Cleveland streets and marched silently in the dark, holding their candles. This was unlike other protests I'd attended for two reasons. First, not all the protesters were students. Many were not even countercultural types at all. Some were local citizens. I saw the owner of the deli down the road, and the clerk from the hardware store where Sara bought her roach clip. Second, this was not a protest but a memorial march. There was no talk — only silence, shock and sadness. As we walked along, Sara and many others had tears in their eyes. She turned to me and said, "I mean, this is so crazy. Isn't silent America getting ready to talk?"

Being less than six degrees to one of the slain was all too much. These were deaths on our own soil. I was so relieved my father wouldn't know what happened. It would have hurt him to know that America had sunk this low. I thought I knew what America was and what it wasn't, but suddenly I felt as though I'd been duped. Where were we living? On that walk, I realized how much I loved America. I felt as though I'd had a relative who'd committed treason. How could this have happened to someone I thought I knew so well?

At Thomas Paine the next day, no one mentioned the shootings, and there was no buzz in the school whatsoever. I began to talk about it with the kids in my class. However, they were unmoved. The four wannabe Black Panthers in the back of the room said that now that a few white kids got killed, people were shocked and saying something is wrong in America. One said, "You know how many people got killed in the Hough riots? You ain't hearda none a them and it ain't four — it four hundred." The rest of the class agreed, saying the only difference is that this happened to white people.

I tried to make the point that there was a difference between looting and protesting. One was against the law and one wasn't. They weren't buying it. They were relieved that white America could share their feelings of helpless outrage for once. Tamara, the one girl who was going to college — the one who the others called Oreo, saying she was white on the inside and black on the outside — came up to the front of the room and stood there in her collegiate plaid skirt and perfectly coiffed and straightened Gidget hair. She shook my hand, saying, "Miss McClure, welcome to my world." Everyone in the class clapped.

⁓

Less than a week after the Kent State slayings, I had to go to some distant suburb to Merilee's wedding shower given by her mother. Most of the other guests were young teachers from the school. Merilee and her fiancé both still lived with their parents. However, they had already bought their dream home and furnished it down to the sweet gardenia potpourri. The previous week she'd guided me on a tour of the sterile furnished dream house, which was an ode to Ethan Allen. Merilee described it as "an easy, clean colonial look." They were moving in on the day they returned from their honeymoon in Barbados.

I was surprised that Merilee lived in such an imposing old stone home with manicured grounds. I had the stereotyped notion that wealthy people were bright and worked hard and handed those values down to their children. (My dad used to say when we delivered medicine to wealthy people, "Hard work is how they got where they are today.") Merilee's work ethic was clearly an exception to that rule or else it was skipping a generation. As we sat there watching her open an avocado-coloured electric can opener, one of the shower guests said, "Well, Don is in the Guard and it has been so hard on him being at Kent State, but someone has to defend the country."

"Defend the country? You have got to be kidding. No one in the crowd even had weapons. That was a *massacre*," I said.

Another of Merilee's guests, a sinewy woman who sat in a corner carefully attaching ribbons and bows from the gift wrapping onto a paper plate that would eventually be a bonnet worn by Merilee, said that the country should be relieved that Governor Rhodes had called in the National Guard and that they came willingly.

"*Willingly?* They joined the guard so they wouldn't be deployed to Vietnam or now Cambodia. Who the hell thinks they did this out of kindness?" I asked.

A home economics teacher from Thomas Paine who wore a shocking pink print Marimekko shift with matching hairband said, "Well, my husband is also in the Guard, and he says that they felt they did the right thing. After all, the students were warned to disperse. It was their choice." The other guests nodded in agreement.

"If your husband thinks he did the right thing, why doesn't he and the rest of the Guard come forward and say they did it? In fact, according to the spokesman for the National Guard, no one is even admitting that they were in the front row and no one is admitting to shooting anyone." There was silence, so I took that opportunity to continue. "It is almost a week later and no one in the Guard or the government has even done ballistic tests."

Another woman said, "My brother-in-law was there and he said it was bullets shot in the air that went astray."

"Really? Sixty-seven shots were fired. They shot for thirteen seconds straight. That's a long time," I went on. "Count them: one Mississippi, two Mississippi, three Mississippi, four Mississippi . . ."

"Oh look!" Merilee said, interrupting my counting. "Jessica, how did you know that I was going avocado? Mom, look at this perfect avocado electric knife. It matches the can opener. I love the Formica stand as well."

Another woman tore into me, ignoring Merilee's pathetic avocado intervention. "You know it has been said that those so-called student demonstrators were really not students at Kent State at all."

"What were they — duck-billed platypuses?" I asked.

She leaned forward and once she had everyone's attention she said in a low voice, "They were Jewish professional radicals from New York City parachuted in to Kent State to disrupt." Everyone looked shocked and in the silence she imparted her final zinger. "I have that information on the highest authority."

"I beg to differ," I said. "I met one of the murdered men once. He was a friend of my former roommate. He does not meet any of your criteria. He was not from New York City and was not a radical. In fact, he was a student at Kent State. He was on an ROTC scholarship. He was pro-Vietnam and was not demonstrating, but walking to his botany class and, finally, he was not Jewish." No one said anything.

I was out of control. I kept counting. "Seven Mississippi, eight Mississippi . . ."

Finally Merilee's mother called me into the kitchen and said, "Cathy. It is *Cathy*, isn't it?" She, like Wiggles, seemed to think that "Cathy" was as difficult to remember and pronounce as "Rumpelstiltskin." She wore a petite-sized navy blue wool sheath and pearl choker, and was helmeted by streaked and sprayed Ethel Kennedy hair. She said in a kind, soft voice, "Dear, I'm afraid you are ruining the shower that I worked so hard on." She swept her hand around the kitchen, indicating hundreds of soggy rolled tuna pinwheel sandwiches sitting on blue and white Royal Copenhagen platters. There was a Baskin-Robbins ice cream bride cake as a centrepiece on the table. The face was beginning to melt from a demure smile into an Edvard Munch terrified scream. "I'm afraid that we will have to let history be the judge of the *momentous* Kent State uprising — that is, if they remember it." She took my elbow and ushered me toward the back door. "Now I'm going to let you go." She held out my purse for me to take. "It is clear to me you are not enjoying your-self and frankly," she smiled and whispered as though the empty kitchen were full of people, "I'm not enjoying you."

Shocked, I looked blankly at her. Was she kicking me out? Was I too dull-witted to pick up on it? She then turned to stuff her pinwheels with gherkins. When I didn't move, she said, "I'm invoking my obligation as a hostess to ensure the majority of guests enjoy themselves."

I slowly walked to the 409 and sat stunned in the driver's seat. I had to have a whole cigarette before I could drive back to the apartment. When I gave it some thought, I didn't blame her. If Merilee was going to marry a man who killed people at Kent State, then I was indeed ruining the shower.

When I got back to the Alcazar, I regaled Sara, Hay and Merlyn with the shower details. They hooted when I got to the part about Merilee interrupting my countdown of the shooting spree with the avocado appliance intervention.

Merlyn absolutely loved that story, and when he was in the hospital having yet another eye operation, all he wanted was for

Sara and me to act out the Kent State wedding shower. Sara would pretend to unwrap the avocado can opener and I would do the bullet countdown. Sara pointed out one other upside to my shower blitzkrieg: "Now you won't have to go to the wedding."

Student teaching was actually rewarding, and I have more respect for good teachers than I have for anyone else in any profession. It should be the highest paid job in the country as it is in Japan. It's a hard and often-thankless vocation — way too hard for me, that's for sure.

Sara married Hay the following year. Hay gave up the police force to run a family home-heating business. She has spent the rest of her life in a small southern Ohio town only twenty miles from Ohio Universtiy. She now has a bit of a twang to her New York accent, and she is still teaching art in a middle school. Baby married Robbie and she is now principal of a school near where she grew up. Robbie went back to college in his thirties and is now a veterinarian working with large animals. Merilee is divorced and is a real estate agent.

I have never gone back to southern Ohio, and when I hear a southern Ohio accent, it sounds like fingernails on a blackboard to me. Though my eviction from Merilee's shower was inconsequential compared to the real traumas of my life, being socially ostracized, even from the most dreadful party imaginable, wreaked havoc on my unconscious. I still have nightmares that reenact Merilee's mother demanding I leave, and I have a photographic memory of that kitchen, right down to the Royal Copenhagen china.

PART 3

# Toronto

CHAPTER 15

# a landed immigrant

*The great themes of Canadian history are as follows:*
*Keeping the Americans out, keeping the French in and trying to get*
*the Natives to somehow disappear.*
— Will Ferguson, *Why I Hate Canadians*

When I finished student teaching in Cleveland in June 1970, my future yawned, and even drooled, in front of me. There were only two things in my life that I was sure of: the first was that I didn't want to be a high school teacher, and the second was I wanted no more to do with men. Laurie and Clive, the two big romances of my life, had taken two huge chunks of my psyche. I decided to preserve what I had left.

Since I was going to be on my own, I needed a career that would be all encompassing, as it was going to provide my life's meaning and offer me financial support. The problem was, other than Madame Curie, I had never seen a woman in a career other than teaching or nursing, so I was a bit stumped.

I had written a paper on Coleridge while at Oxford. Clive, who was kind to me, if not to everyone else, had taken me to some of the places that Coleridge had written about. These were places Archie had taken Clive when he was still in short pants. (Clive's father wrote to me for many years after I met him. He never mentioned anyone in his family, but sent all kinds of enormously helpful esoteric Coleridge minutiae.) I wrote a paper declaring that a particular interpretation was incorrect because when I looked at the actual landscape, I could see Coleridge was referring to something entirely different. Professor Beech liked the paper and told me that it reminded him of the work that Professor Coburn, the world's authority on Coleridge, was doing at the University of Toronto.

Professor Coburn had gone to Oxford, and in his meanderings about the countryside, following in Coleridge's footsteps, he wound up at the bard's birthplace. When Professor Coburn arrived in the 1930s, Coleridge's descendants, Lord and Lady Coleridge, were ensconced in the poet's ancestral home. They took a fancy to the professor and let him wander around the home, and in the back of a cupboard he found old notebooks and philosophical lectures that would revolutionize Coleridge scholarship. Professor Coburn was presently editing and annotating these collected notebooks and works. Professor Beech said he would "drop Professor Coburn a line" (the British way of saying he would pull out all the stops for you).

I found out that he did far more than that. He sent the Canadian professor a copy of my paper and wrote me a glowing reference letter. (It's all an old boys' club, especially on the small island of England where they probably played cricket together at Eton in the '20s.) Professor Coburn wrote me a note asking me to apply for a Master's in English at the University of Toronto and asking if I would like to take his course and work with him.

Years later, I learned that Archie Hunter-Parsons had also dropped a line to Professor Coburn. He was well known in the world of the Victorians and the Romantics and told Professor Coburn how much he admired me. I was shocked he'd done that after all the kerfuffle I'd caused. Only once had I casually mentioned to him that I might like to work with Professor Coburn. With two eminent Victorians in my parlour, I wound up with a scholarship to Victoria College at the University of Toronto, where Professor Coburn ruled the roost.

— —

I figured moving to Canada had one advantage: it was hard to screw up there since not much happened. Roy and I had delivered medicine on the Canadian side of the Falls. When I asked Roy why we never delivered tranquilizers in Canada, he'd said, "Canadians don't need them."

My family spent many summers in Canada, at a rented farmhouse on Ontario's Lake Erie (when you could still swim in the lake) with quiet Canadians who collected teacups, admired the British monarchy, celebrated Queen Victoria's birthday and even shopped at a grocery store called Dominion.

It was August 1970 when I rolled into Toronto. I needed a few weeks before school started to get my landed immigrant papers in order and find a place to live. I was relieved I was at a downtown university and I never had to live in a residence ever again. The university was spread over a few city blocks and was surrounded by once stately Victorian homes that had been converted into rooming houses. The streets were narrow and lined by leafy green maple trees that blushed beet red in the fall. Having no idea that there was a university housing service, or that newspapers had sections called classified ads, I decided to find the happening part of town and ask someone where the cool people lived.

Following the smell of incense, I finally hit Yorkville, Toronto's Greenwich Village. While looking at a sign on the Riverboat coffeehouse that said that Gordon Lightfoot and Joni Mitchell had appeared, I heard someone from behind me say with a broad, black Buffalo accent, "*Well*, Cathy McClure, if it ain't the empress from the Queen City." I wheeled around and saw Rick James, an old friend from my high school years. Rick had lived in downtown Buffalo but used to come out to our suburban school parking lot and sell items from his trunk. I assumed his father was a jobber; I had no idea the stuff was hot. He once tried to sell me leather slacks. When I asked him how to wash them, he said, "Baby, they only be a dollar. Just throw 'em out."

Rick was an entrepreneur even while we were in high school. He brought bands to the big summer patios of Buffalo's lake taverns. He had an unerring ability to pick new talent. For example, he brought in Sly and the Family Stone for their first real gig. We saw guys who were on the skids like James Brown and Chuck

Berry before they'd made comebacks. He often contacted me and told me about the concerts so I would get kids from my high school out on a Saturday night.

When I saw him standing there on Yorkville Avenue in Toronto, I screamed, "Ricky James, I don't believe it. I'm not even in America."

He started laughing his infectious, high-pitched screech, which was his signature, and said, "Your dad still the man? He had some real evil horn thing goin' on."

We laughed about the ooga horn and my father's other antics. I didn't bother saying he'd had a brain tumour at the time because Rick seemed to find my father's stunts the most interesting and amusing thing about me.

Rick now had long dreadlocks — way before dreadlocks made an appearance anywhere that I'd ever seen. Rick was sporting a Jimi Hendrix hippie garb of beads, velvet flares and a black hat with a pink feather, an ensemble that appeared to be *de rigueur* in Yorkville.

He'd quit school at fifteen, had joined the Naval Reserve at sixteen at the beginning of his music career, but went AWOL when, as he put it, "weekend service interfered with my ladder to success." He added, "You know me, girl. I got my ear to the ground. I leapfrogged across that border from Buffalo to Canada. I had some happenin' shit goin' down here in Hogtown."

As we walked down the street, he pointed to a bar and said, "I used to play right there in a group called the Mynah Birds. I put together a band back in 'round '65, but get this," and then he shrieked, "we had to advertise pet food! We had to wear yellow boots and black jackets to look like mynah birds." (I later found out that group also included Neil Young and Bruce Palmer, who'd go on to Buffalo Springfield, and Goldy McJohn, who joined Steppenwolf.) Rick started doing an inspired mynah bird imitation and told me he had to fly south to prison for a year for going AWOL. As he said, "Who knew the FBI had wings? I came back and got the Mynah Birds on the road, but we all flew the coop. I been in L.A. for a few years now writing songs and music for Motown. I work with Smokey Robinson and the boys."

We sat on a bench to have a Coke in front of the Riverboat, and Rick said he'd gone to Buffalo to see his mother for the weekend. (I remember that she made a living as an "errand boy" for the Mafia.) He continued, "Not much happenin' in Buffalo since you and me blew out o' town, McClure, so I drove up here to see who still be jivin' in Yorkville."

He looked around at the Yorkville scene, which was nominally still the hip section of town but was just on the cusp of gentrification, and said, "Looks like the Mynah Birds are minor birds now. So, what the hell you doin' in Canada?"

"I'm going to graduate school."

"Hey, I thought you graduated, girl."

The great thing about Rick was you were never sure whether he was out of it or above it. He was either really ironic or a gifted fake.

I asked him for information about living in Toronto and he told me to live in the section of the city called the Annex. (In fact, I still live there forty years later.) He said he used to live in a house on Huron Street called the Crystal Palace because it was packed with speed freaks, but it was cleaned up now and full of "happenin' dudes." It couldn't hurt that Huron Street was the closest to the university's library.

Then he looked me in the eye and said, "Cath, now I'm tellin' you this as an old friend since bobby-sox days, so don't be takin' it the wrong way, ya hear: you gots to know that *no one* in Toronto who knows their ass from Saran Wrap would be caught dead in that American Colonial shit you're wearing. Those threads *scream* yesteryear."

I looked down at my black chinos and sleeveless white blouse with a Peter Pan collar and said, "Lead on, MacDuff."

"MacDuff, I like that. It got a ring. There's only one place to buy clothes. It's Crazy David's." We walked down Yorkville Avenue to the store, and suddenly he turned to me and said, "I got to run." As he ran down the street, he yelled over his shoulder, "Tell Crazy David that I, Rick MacDuff James, sent you. He'll get my meaning." Then he was gone.

Crazy David's reeked of burning incense that made me feel woozy. I spent my entire September rent budget on utterly outlandish hippie clothes — my favourite was a purple vest that had three feet of fringe on it with red beads placed at six-inch intervals. I sounded like a mariachi band when I walked. I bought underwear tops, appliquéd pants and floppy hats in every colour. I bought long Indian shirts with embroidery on the sleeves that Ravi Shankar might wear for a concert.

Crazy David had waist-length blond hair in a ponytail and wore a T-shirt that read, *Turn in, turn on, drop out.* His demeanour was decidedly taciturn. (I later learned that was simply called "Canadian.") I said I was a childhood friend of a good friend of his. He didn't ask who it was and simply nodded. Finally I said, "Rick James sent me here."

"He out of jail?" he asked with such little inflection it was hardly a question.

I never saw Rick James again. However, thirty years later in 2004, I was browsing through *Time*'s person of the year issue, and I saw a full-page spread about him. He had become famous as a rock singer and rock promoter. His famous song, not surprisingly, was titled "Super Freak." He died at age fifty-six. They said the cause was heart problems, but the autopsy showed at least nine drugs in his system.

Following Rick's advice, I rented a room in a boarding house on Huron Street in the midst of the downtown campus. It was a large, three-floor place full of graduate students. My room was a small garret on the third floor. I loved the sloping ceilings and playing the role of the intellectual recluse who had given up all human ties in order to live a life of the mind.

There were four other rooms on the third floor of the rooming house, each occupied by a French Canadian male. I had to share a washroom and kitchen with these four *gentilshommes*. (If you ever think of sharing a washroom and kitchen with four males, think again.) Jean-Claude, who spoke the most English, was working on a Ph.D. He was at the Institute for Policy Analysis at the University of Toronto, retracing the routes of the seventeenth-century French Canadian fur traders, called *voyageurs*. The other three seemed to have a lot of time on their hands and I had no idea what they did. They perpetually jabbered in French about political theory. (At least that is what I assumed from my rudimentary French.) Whenever we exchanged small talk in the kitchen, Jean-Claude prefaced his sentence with "I'm practising my English," as in, "That's the only reason I'm talking to *you*." He would go on about how provincial English Canada was, how uncivil it was not to be able to get wine on Sunday, etc. I usually retorted that if he thought Quebec was so great, why didn't he live there. Once in a while *un ami* of theirs, who said he was doing a thesis on the Basque separatist movement, would come over. He wore a navy blue and white striped sweater with buttons on the shoulder and a beret. He thought he looked like a revolutionary, but in reality he resembled Gordon MacRae in *Carousel*. The only thing I learned from him was where to buy a scrumptious Gâteau Basque. I had enough trouble understanding the Parisian French accent, but this Québécois accent was utterly indecipherable.

Sometimes they would have heavy meetings in the kitchen with a dozen of their other French buddies, all men. If I happened to go into the kitchen to get a slice of cheese, they would abruptly stop talking until I left. Once I came in and one of them asked why I was "lingering," so I said that I paid rent and if I wanted a break from my room to sit in the kitchen to make myself a fried egg sandwich, I would. I could also sit and eat it. I said, "By the way, I didn't know there were so many secrets surrounding the French Canadian trade routes of the *voyageurs* in the 1690s. What are you hiding — a Great Lake?"

What I really didn't like about them was how seriously they took all their little chatter. They wrote FLQ (which stood for *Front de libération du Québec*) in big letters on the fridge. As far as I understood, this was some fanatical fringe group that put bombs in mailboxes way back in 1963.

Less than a week later, the country was in shock when FLQ members had kidnapped the British Trade Commissioner James Cross from his Montreal home. The FLQ tried to set up a trade with the government to get some of their political prisoners released. I had never heard of any FLQ member being arrested.

They hadn't *done* anything. I asked Jean-Claude who the hell had ever been arrested. Had someone been caught selling a *tourtière* with FLQ written in pastry dough?

Refusing to wait for the government to act or even respond, they kidnapped another man, Pierre Laporte, who was found dead in the trunk of his car soon after. Pierre Trudeau, the handsome, randy prime minister, implemented the *War Measures Act*, which gave the police extra power in this state of emergency. Televisions broadcast footage of armed guards rushing up Parliament Hill. Hundreds of people were arrested and detained without charge. Later this became known as the October Crisis, and it made international news. Jean-Claude and his buddies cheered at every new move of the FLQ. The University of Toronto's academic community was outraged at the loss of liberty under the *War Measures Act*. As far as I could see, these FLQ fanatics were like the whiners in a marriage who threaten divorce but never leave. They were all dressed up with nowhere to go. If they wanted to speak French, let them get their own party and secede from Canada — *bon voyage.*

The English Canadians on the second floor of our rooming house made a gesture of solidarity by putting stickers that said *My Canada Includes Quebec* on their doors and cars. The English Canadians got mad at me when I said the separatists were a bunch of delusional terrorists who should break away from Canada or shut up. They said I didn't understand Canada is a bilingual nation. The French on the third floor, where I was marooned, couldn't stand anyone who was English. Needless to say, I was not the most popular person in my rooming house.

I had left the U.S. because I had gotten too involved in politics and was relieved that I was not galvanized by the FLQ. Then on a cold morning in late October 1970, three plain-clothes officers came storming into my room in the middle of the night, trailed by my terrified, pyjama-clad landlord. They shook me awake and said they wanted to speak to me. I was sure they had been searching for me over the Laurie episode, the Black Power connection and the murder trial of Laurie's cousin Splits. I had left the United States for England when I thought I might have to be involved in the trial. I assumed that even though I was still outside of the States they had found me, just like they'd found Rick James, and I would be extradited. For some reason, I was more terrified now than I had been when the whole episode was going on. Maybe it was because they had awakened me from a sound sleep and were invading my bedroom. As I was marched down the hall sandwiched between polyester detectives, I glanced into the other bedrooms and saw no sign that anyone except me lived on the floor. Jean-Claude and the others' beds were stripped and the mattresses were rolled up. The rooms were empty. The FLQ sticker was ripped off the fridge and the walls had been stripped of the *voyageur* and *coureur de bois* posters. When did *that* happen?

The detectives started questioning me about how well I knew Jean-Claude. To my credit, I said I couldn't say anything after waking up from a sound sleep. I said I was getting dressed and having a coffee and toast before I said a word. (I have no idea why I demanded food instead of a lawyer. I guess I knew I had some rights but I wasn't sure what they were.) I had no food in the house so, believe it or not, I was interrogated at Fran's family restaurant. (I figured the worst they could do there was make me eat the Salisbury steak.) I explained that I had rented my room on Huron Street two months ago based on a sign placed in the first-floor window. I said I didn't know anyone who was living there beforehand, nor did I even understand about ninety percent of what they said.

It was one of those good cop–bad cop set-ups, except it was Canada so it was good cop and slightly less good cop. The good cop opened a small spiral notebook and unfolded a note that I had left on a napkin under a fridge magnet. He read aloud:

*Like you guys are so important that you can't shop? I realize that you are too busy gearing up for the revolution, however, when you steal my food from the fridge, please leave all English Canadian products. Don't touch my Canada Dry or my Canadian cheddar, especially the individually wrapped slices, to say nothing of my Canadian back bacon. If you want separation so much why not buy or steal Camembert —*
*P.S. By the way, poseurs, clean your long black hairs out of the bathtub.*

"What exactly does that mean? We know a code when we see one. What did you mean by individual slices?"

I started laughing, and the less good cop said, "Listen, Miss McClure, this isn't *Get Smart*. We are talking about sedition, insurrection and murder."

The other cop said, "If you didn't understand them, how did you know that they were, as you said in the note, 'gearing up for the revolution'?"

"Once in a while they would start screaming, *vive* this and that. They mentioned Quebec separating once or twice. They had silly secret meetings. They clapped over Basque separatism — that sort of adolescent rebellion bullshit."

Then the good cop, who was not as good as he was five minutes earlier, said, "Your past doesn't squeak." A black pool of silence spread over the Arborite table. I was terrified that they had looked into my past and there would be an international incident. "You want a job here, or in any Commonwealth country, you'd better cooperate.

"Your boyfriend, Jean-Claude, is gone. He and his friends will not be returning to Huron Street or the University of Toronto. I would do some serious thinking about telling us everything you know about them. By the way, he is two-timing you with a woman named Renée."

At this point, I lost my fear. Being romantically linked with dreary Jean-Claude was totally off my radar. I was also insulted to be lumped into the all-girls-talk-if-they-are-two-timed subgroup of jealous idiots. I told them I didn't know a thing other than they were happy when they heard the news on the radio about the kidnapping, but they acted as surprised as I was about the killings. They had meetings with other men in the kitchen, but I had no idea what they said.

The almost-bad cop said, "We will get back to you shortly, and I will want to know everything that you have *forgotten* today. If you hear from anyone who was at those meetings, please let me know at this number." He handed me a card and added, "You will have to come to headquarters within forty-eight hours to identify some faces from mug shots we have on file of possible FLQ members. I want to identify this so-called Basque separatist."

I never heard from them again.

—◦—

When I got back to my rooming house, everything I owned was on the porch, neatly placed in liquor store boxes. It was 3:30 in the morning and I didn't know anyone in Toronto. Clearly the Hungarian landlord wanted anyone who brought the police to his doorstep out of his home. North Americans may find police annoying, but Eastern Europeans are terrified of them. I could have called my mother; however, she'd had to put up with my shenanigans since I was four years old, and I decided she'd had enough.

Where can you go in the middle of the night? I sat at the bottom of the steps of my rooming house porch, smoking cigarettes as time ticked by. A German shepherd wandered up and sat at my feet. He looked like some junkyard dog that could take my head off in a second. Fortunately he seemed tired and slightly disoriented, like he'd forgotten how to get home, so ripping me to shreds wasn't his top priority. He just sat there, looking as lost as I felt.

At about 4:30, just as the birds began to stretch, a man walked down Huron Street, then stopped when he saw the dog and yelled, "Mikvah, where the hell you been? Mitzi waited in the lobby, like you're supposed to do when the elevator is out of order. Okay, buddy, next time your sister gets the bone first, you useless, piece-of-shit watchdog." He raised his hand in anger but didn't hit the dog. Then he turned his wrath to me. "Did you lead him over from the park?"

"No. He seemed confused and meandered over here. Then he just sat down."

"Well, this is pretty fucked-up," he said. The man who owned the dog was large with black curly hair. He had eyes with red rims like a white rabbit and arms with tattoos of cherries with the stems still on them. He wore a black tank top with a picture from the

Led Zeppelin album and looked like the kind of guy you would train a watchdog to keep out of your house. Both dog and master looked fierce and dangerous but were slightly off their game.

It struck me as funny that he expected the dog to take an elevator on his own. I said laughing, "Does he take an elevator to work?"

"Yeah, he's in securities," he said. Then he laughed and said his name was Ginger.

"Usually people who are named Ginger have red hair."

"I used to snap at people when I was little, so my parents called me Ginger Snap. The snap got lost over the years." He stretched his pallid arms that were as thick as Popeye's and said, "I haven't been out in a while. Nice to get some fresh air."

He sat down on the step next to me. While patting Mikvah, he asked, "You trippin', blondie?"

"No, I just got kicked out of my rooming house. The police thought I had something to do with the FLQ."

"Those assholes?"

"The FLQ or the police?" I asked.

"Both pigs — different troughs" was his summary.

I offered him a cigarette, which he accepted, lit and then took the longest drag I had ever seen anyone inhale. He was like a human bellows. "Those boxes yours?" he asked, pointing to all my earthly possessions.

"Yeah, mostly books."

He pulled a walkie-talkie out of his pocket and said into it, "Ginger here. Get some guys down to the house across from the park next to the church on Huron. We got some product to move."

What was this guy doing? "Move where? I'm a student. I have

to be near the library."

"It's only four doors up the street — the high-rise at the corner of Huron and Bloor. You can see the university from the window. You can have your own room in my ashram or maybe we will put you in a Zeus."

A Zeus? "What's the rent?"

"Don't worry, blondie, you can afford it."

"What's the name of it?"

"Rochdale."

I had to go somewhere and this Ginger Snap had movers at 4:30 in the morning. I decided to count my blessings. Whatever a Zeus was, I was on my way.

Ginger finished his cigarette and said he had to rush "back to work." The movers, three scrawny space cadets, showed up a few minutes later. They piled my boxes on three red dollies and trudged up the street. When they reached the eighteen-floor high-rise, they brought everything into the lobby, unloading under a sign that read Security. At the security desk sat two guards with long, greasy hair and leather jackets with Vagabonds Motorcycle Club written on the back in fuzzy yellow letters. One didn't have any shirt on under his jacket and the other wore a short T-shirt that read Rehab Is for Quitters. The ripped T-shirt did an inadequate job of covering his protruding hairy white gut. Both of these security guards were bedecked in chains of all sizes and shapes. Behind their desk was a floor-to-ceiling wall mural illustrating smoking motorcycle gangs travelling in packs on huge Harleys with their oily hair flying in the wind. One guard asked why I was there, and I said I wanted to rent an apartment. He carefully went through a box of my books and pulled out Tudor Songs and

*Sonnets*. He showed it to his cohort, who snorted and said, "I don't think even narcs read that shit — go ahead. The rental office is on the second floor." He got on a walkie-talkie and said, "Spence, got one of the Bobbsey Twins down here — wants to rent an apartment." He said this as though it were a strange request, as though we weren't standing in a large apartment building that had rooms for rent. "She seems clean. I think she actually wants to rent an apartment. No need to get out any other wares."

The rental office was a complete mess and had papers piled two feet high over every surface. The floor had booklets piled to the ceiling and narrow alleyways had been left to get to the desk.

By this time, I was confused. Spencer, the man who seemed to run the whole rental office, was handsome and quite debonair. He was tall, thin with fine blond hair flowing past his shoulders. He had one of those Roman noses you find in private school pictures. After we shook hands, I felt on more secure ground. "I am a student looking for housing. What is the exact mandate of this building? I mean, what goes on here? Why are those thugs at the door?" He didn't flinch at all. He said it was a free college where you could set up your own curriculum. He explained that a B.A. required a $25 donation to the college and the candidate had to answer a simple skill-testing question. An M.A. was $50, and the applicant could pick the question. A Ph.D. did not require any skill-testing question and went for $100. (Thirty years later, I was at a philosophy of mind conference in Tucson, Arizona, and I read a résumé of one of the German speakers. In his C.V., he had listed a Ph.D. from Rochdale College, University of Toronto, Canada.) Spencer showed me the degrees and said I could sign up. He also said that they ran an open college with resource people — some from the university and some "scholars of the street." He handed me a sheet with lectures for the following week. They ran the gamut from "How to stay hydrated on speed" to "Hermann Hesse on religion."

He said he had an opening in a Zeus, which gave me my own bedroom, but I had to share a bathroom with six other people and a kitchen and a living room with eight.

"When Ginger sent me here, he said something about an ashram."

"*Ginger* sent you here?" he asked as though the Father, Son and Holy Ghost had sent me.

"Yes, his men carried all my belongings."

"You should have said that downstairs." He picked up the walkie-talkie and said, "That Bobbsey Twin was sent by *Ginger*. Why don't you guys get your heads out of your arse holes?"

"*Wow* — sorry, man" came back as a static blast.

He talked on the phone for a minute and then turned to me and said, "I'm putting you into Ginger's ashram."

"I need my own bedroom," I assured him.

"Don't worry. There is only one ashram per floor. They're gigantic. There are four double-occupancy rooms plus four singles. The bedrooms open onto a huge lounge, kitchen and bath." I looked askance at him. He assured me, "You've got horsehoes up your arse. A mansion is yours for the taking, babycakes."

I thought it sounded a bit too luxurious and so I asked, "What's the rent?"

"We can figure it out later." Then he added as an afterthought, "Not much."

"Do you want the first and last month's rent?"

"No, that messes up my books. I'll get a hold of you when I'm sorted out here." (Apparently he never sorted out his huge piles of papers or accounts, because I didn't pay a cent the entire time I lived there.) "Anyway, I have to get the all-day breakfast and then go to bed so —" he paused, shook my hand and said, "we're square."

When I got to my ashram on the fourteenth floor, I tried to open the door but Mitzi and Mikvah began growling and attacking the door like Nazi attack dogs. Ginger's assistant tied up the dogs and I entered. The inside of the door had lost most of its paint from dogs scratching at it and was completely pitted with bite marks. Ginger, who sat alone at the table working on some papers, welcomed me and said he had several flunkies "consolidating some product and clearing out some rooms." The assistant gave Mikvah and Mitzi my red scarf to smell. I learned that professionally trained dogs need to familiarize themselves with your scent so they don't go crazy when you come and go.

The living room was huge, and one whole wall was floor-to-ceiling windows facing west. They had curtains, but there must have been a small fire because half of them were burned and only their charred remains hung limply. The room had no furniture other than a large table in the middle that could seat at least fifteen people. I said to Ginger, "This place is gigantic. It must be almost a whole floor. Who else lives here besides you?"

"You," he said without looking up.

I went and opened the double fridge to find some orange juice and dozens of rows of bottles with two small pills in each vial. "Is someone here a diabetic?" I asked.

No one even bothered to answer. I went down the hall and opened a door to find a room filled with solid bricks of hash piled to the ceiling. I opened another door and found bales of what looked like marijuana. And on it went. The ashram was large and must have been designed for communal living — nine to a dozen people could have lived there. I actually passed a little phone booth room that had all kinds of numbers written on the wall. Finally, after passing several doors, I found my two rooms. They were clearly meant as two separate living units with a shared bath between them. They were both bright and freshly cleaned. Each room had a built-in desk, ample built-in bookshelves, and picture windows across one whole wall, with a gorgeous view looking south onto the University of Toronto, which was less than a block away. I could see all the way down to Lake Ontario. I used one room as a bedroom and one as my own living room. I was so far away from the communal living room and kitchen that I couldn't hear a thing that went on down there. My rooms and bath were luxurious compared to where I had been living. When retrieving my belongings in the hall, I passed two flunkies carrying scales, bags, tweezers and vials that had been emptied from my room. I unpacked my books and began my life in Rochdale.

CHAPTER 16

# possessing coleridge

*And the Devil did grin, for his darling sin*
*Is pride that apes humility.*
— Samuel Taylor Coleridge,
"The Devil's Thoughts"

I arrived late for the first day of my Coleridge class with Professor Coburn. That's one way to make a stellar first impression. My alarm hadn't rung since the electricity had been shut off in the entire Rochdale high-rise since midnight. It turned out that no one had paid the bill. Spencer, the superintendent of sorts, said he "forgot" and besides he was sick of Toronto Hydro's "Big Brother tactics." Even though I was horribly late, I still took the time to dress in the latest fashion, as dictated by the elusive Rick James.

I tore into class wearing my pink long-underwear top, purple fringed vest and bell-bottom pants made out of an old faded kilim carpet. (Fashion tip: never buy carpet pants unless you want to itch, boil, have trouble bending to sit and have a kilim imprint on your rear end.) On top of my long blond hair, I wore a red felt mushroom hat.

An old woman in a grey boiled-wool suit, like the kind worn by the Von Trapp family, looked up at me and said, "The undergraduate office is down the hall," and continued talking.

"Sorry for interrupting, but where is Professor Coburn? I have to find his class; I'm late."

The old lady said, "I am Professor Coburn and I was, until this moment, conducting a graduate seminar."

"*You're* Professor Coburn?" I can't believe I used that insulting tone. Why hadn't I thought for even a moment before I spoke? It never occurred to me that Professor Coburn was a woman. Recovering far too late, I added, "Oh, then I'm in the right place." I had to walk to the back of the small seminar room to find a chair. I tried to hold my beaded fringes so they wouldn't jingle. As I glanced around the room, I saw less than a dozen people. Every male wore a sports jacket and most wore ties. There were only two women. One looked British and wore a navy blue polyester suit and spectator pumps. Her entire ensemble, mouse-coloured hair and pasty skin made her look remarkably like a female Salvation Army worker. The other was a striking Indian woman who screamed Brahmin. She wore a saffron-coloured sari wrapped around a fitted, short crimson shirt. Her thick black hair was pulled back in a bun, and she displayed a large red dusty dot on her forehead. This was not yet the age of multiculturalism, and I suddenly realized that these top students had come from all over the world and all wanted the one job of working on the famous notebooks.

This had not been an auspicious beginning. I couldn't believe I had adopted Rick James's view of Canadian fashion. He was outlandish even compared to Jimi Hendrix. While I was ruminating on how misled I'd been, I looked up and noticed the class members glancing at me with poorly camouflaged disdain. No one spoke and you could hear the heat going off and then on. Finally, Professor Coburn said, "Now that you have graced us with your presence, perhaps you would like to introduce yourself. Am I to presume that the woman who has burst upon us is Miss McClure?"

I nodded.

"I have already passed around the sign-up sheet for seminar topics. I am afraid that your choices will be limited. Each lecture will be delivered to the class for the duration of the two and a half hours." I had no choice but to sign up for Coleridge's lectures on Shakespeare at Oxford. How boring was that? No wonder no one chose it.

As Professor Coburn continued her lecture, I slumped in my seat realizing I'd made a cockup of my first impression and there was no second chance. I gazed out the window at the red and yellow carousel of leaves and watched the *normal* students casually and quietly amble across Queen's Park to Victoria College. They had not flown through a window in England or worn a clown suit to graduate school and insulted the teacher. Crash landing first impressions seemed to be my specialty.

As the months crawled by, I began to get the lay of the land. I had thought I was going to be pretty sharp, having memorized most of Coleridge's poetry and having a sense of what he was trying to say. Slowly it dawned on me that *knowing* the poetry was undergraduate jejune pap. Everyone in the class had accomplished that. This was a *research* degree and the poetry of Coleridge was never mentioned. It was about researching every arcane fact and exploring every stray whim that Coleridge ever had. You sourced all of his literary antecedents and figured out how Coleridge's poetic alchemy turned the philosophical ideas into poetry. Hours were spent on Coleridge's distinction between imagination and fancy. We also had to know and fully understand his strange autobiography, *Biographia Literaria*, which was more of a group of philosophical essays than it was autobiography. We had to know all the philosophy of Kant, Fichte and particularly Schelling, whose work Coleridge had translated from German. This was not at all what I'd bargained for, but I quickly realized that I had better switch gears from poetry to research while simultaneously sweeping up after the mess I'd made with my dreadful first impression.

The University of Toronto was not at all like Oxford. There I'd felt really liked by all, despite my eccentricities and occasional spats. At Trinity I was just thought of as American and "out there." Plus, I'd had some original things to say and that had gained me some respect. The men at Oxford were not academically competitive with me — they were helpful. They had already competed and won. They'd made it to Oxford, the top of the intellectual heap, and they could afford to be generous to an *American woman*. Despite our personal differences, they were unfailingly helpful and devoted hours to teaching me what I didn't know. Even grouchy Marcus would drop everything to help me with what I needed. I really couldn't have managed without their help.

I could tell that the same was not true here. I could smell the competition the second I walked into the room. There were several problems at the University of Toronto. The first was the program itself. According to Kathleen Coburn, you had only one option as a Coleridge scholar: you must annotate the Coleridge notebooks, which was her life's work and would be the life's work of whoever took over when she joined Coleridge in the sky — which from the looks of her was not far off. (Looking back on it, she was the same age then that I am now.) To me, annotation felt tedious and took the originality out of scholarship. The students were reduced to providing footnotes. We were not to talk of the ideas, but to delineate the minutiae. Professor Coburn had been at this for thirty years. She'd picked the carcass clean of all intellectual meat. Even the carrion was long gone. We were left with Coleridge's shiny skeleton.

We also had to take dry research courses like Bibliography. This was before the personal computer, so we had to have library research skills. I was faced with writing a paper on delineating original watermarks.

The curriculum problems were nothing compared to the students. They fell into several camps. Some had gone to Ivy League American schools or top European universities like Heidelberg or the Sorbonne. Either they hadn't done well and had to be shipped off to Canada for a lesser degree, or they were ambitious and wanted to get in on the Coleridge notebook gravy train. In any case, they were vipers.

Then there were the true lovers of everything Victorian who feigned an inability to function in the twentieth century since their sensibilities rested in the nineteenth. They were the ones who donned antiquated hats, like the Sherlock Holmes deerstalker, or replicated the Keatsian tubercular wan look, complete with wire-rimmed glasses, large scarf, Irish tweed cap and an oversized sweater for the bitterly cold Canadian weather.

The Toronto-born Mr. Thomas Benchman, known as Toady after my first conversation with him, spoke in a phony English accent and, to top his foppery, wore a black cape and carried a walking stick. Whenever we went to plays or talks together as a class, he would always sit next to the professor; then he would turn to the rest of us at intermission and say, "Chaps, may I stand you mead?" Mr. Benchman was the reason no one should take the *psycho* out of sycophant.

There was a third intellectual conundrum, which made the boring annotation, and even the class of vipers, pale; Professor Coburn was in love with, or obsessed by, Coleridge. I now understood why she had gone to his former home for tea and befriended the odd couple. She had been courting Coleridge. She would not tolerate anything negative said about the man or his work. If you did, she would say absolutely nothing, but her jaw would set and her eyes would narrow. She would look away as though you had done something socially verboten. If you said something neutral or positive, she would answer with delight.

It was easy to say nothing bad about Coleridge's *work*; after all he was a poetic genius. It was quite a bit harder to be truthful, yet worshipful, about the *man*, who was an opium addict and an alcoholic. He did most of his best work in his twenties and forever after rested on his laurels and sponged off others. Dorothy Wordsworth, William's sister and a "close" friend to Coleridge, summed up his love life best when she said he was a terrible lover who suffered from gynecomastia (enlarged male breasts) and erectile dysfunction. She referred to Coleridge as "one whose realm is not that of the land twixt the sheets."

As the year wore on, the piddling annotating, the class of vipers and the obsessive, possessed professor were giving me battle fatigue. Yet I couldn't drop out. I had a dying father and a mother who needed taking care of. I needed an academic job, and this one would be a plum. We were the Baby Boom generation. Thousands of us wanted to have academic jobs. I read in *The Grad News* (an oxymoron if there ever was one) that there were enough Ph.D. graduates from Harvard every year to fill all the vacancies in English literature in North America. If I didn't take over the notebooks, what was I going to be — a freelance Coleridge consultant?

With my seminar date approaching, I set to researching Coleridge's lectures on Shakespeare at Oxford in 1818, but I found that most of the lectures had not been preserved. (How would I fill my two and a half hours?) I had to rely on the reactions of the critics and collections of letters, diaries, etc., which gave their mostly negative opinions of the lectures. He was so drunk or high or both on the nights of the lectures, he didn't stay on topic. In his sixth lecture he was, by advertisement, to speak of *Romeo and Juliet* and "Shakespeare's females." Although the audience came to see him on four separate occasions to hear Coleridge on *Romeo and Juliet*, he never got around to it. According to diarist Henry Crabb Robinson, "unhappily some demon whispered the name of Lancaster in his ear: and we had in one evening an attack on the poor Quaker, a defence of boarding school flogging, a parallel between the ages of Elizabeth and Charles, a defence of what is untruly called unpoetic language, an account of the different languages of Europe, and a vindication of Shakspere against the imputation of grossness!!!" Why the audience came again after three of these misfires, I have no idea. The question remained for me — how was I to write a paper on Shakespeare's lectures when they weren't ever on Shakespeare? After struggling with the topic for weeks, I finally decided that I wasn't even in the running for the academic position. There were people in the class who were far more intellectually and temperamentally suited for the job. After this revelation, I felt freed to simply write a three-hour paper including the entire original diary reports, but needed more, so I filled in the missing lectures and their content from my own imagination. I wrote as though I were Coleridge, drunk and stoned, writing about Shakespeare. I had the whole vernacular down pat because I lived at Rochdale with stoned people who always had excuses for not doing anything. I could mimic that and then add a Coleridgean nineteenth-century spin.

I gave my lecture in a deadpan manner, as though it were perfectly academic. No one laughed or said one word during the performance. At the conclusion of my lecture, or one-woman comedy show, Professor Coburn looked at me as though she had never seen me before and said, "That was extremely entertaining, and it included all of Coleridge on Shakespeare, and what was most laudable is it was done in the true spirit of Coleridge."

In my mind, there was one person in the class who was most suited to take over the notebooks. It was the Indian woman, Deepti Mukherjee. She had obviously had a broad education and was as conversant in philosophy as she was in literature. She reminded me of many of the students I'd met at Oxford who knew how to tie ideas together from several disciplines and create a textured intellectual landscape. She could command a room with her intellectual sophistication and her magnificent saris and kohl-outlined eyes. The other amazing thing about her was she had a small child in India whom she'd left with her husband and his family. I had never heard of anyone doing that and getting away with it. She was a Commonwealth Scholar who clearly was not fooling around.

I thought it was obvious she was next in line to get the professorship. She had given up her husband, country and child for it. However, she had one flaw, which was in her case fatal. She thought she could offer a serious criticism of Coleridge and get away with it. In her presentation, she pointed out Coleridge had misunderstood Kant and that Coleridge's theory of the creative imagination was built on that misunderstanding. Toady was thrilled when she'd criticized Coleridge. During the class break, he leaned over to me and whispered, "Poor Deepti. Stick a fork in her. She's done like dinner."

When she'd finished her talk, Professor Coburn didn't look at her but beyond her out the window into Queen's Park, where the pigeons were despoiling a historical statue, and said as she packed up her papers, "Mrs. Mukherjee, thank you for your occasional nuggets of clarity."

——

In October Professor Coburn had our entire class of Coleridgean wannabes up to her farm in Uxbridge, a rural community outside of Toronto. Seeing that farm for the first time left an indelible imprint on my mind. I had never known a woman who lived alone, who'd never been married, who was a scholar and self-supporting. She had a working farm with animals and hay and tractor-driving farmers who followed her detailed instructions. She'd made a huge library and office with a view of all the horses, wheat fields and trees then fiery with fall colours. I saw for the first time what my life could be like if I were a scholar living alone. It looked marvellous to control my own destiny, ride horses, have my own home that I designed but that was historically tied to the landscape, and have a life's project that I could create and enjoy.

The majority of men in the class were not outdoorsy, and the two other women didn't even go outside of the farmhouse. Professor Coburn and I took long walks, as we were both early risers. It was during these long walks that I realized what she'd been through and what a tough bird she was on so many levels.

She was from a poor vicar's family and she never once thought of being anything other than an academic. She was one of the few women in her undergraduate classes and, as valedictorian, got herself to Oxford. She was wise enough to make the right social connections with the Coleridge family and had the chutzpah to ask the wealthy family if she could go through their closets. Professor Coburn devoted her life to the notebooks and letters she unearthed and began a race against time to get them edited and published. She dashed all around the world collecting and verifying information. Coleridge's handwriting was nearly indecipherable, and she told me she had to stand where Coleridge had stood when he was describing the landscape in order to make sense of his screed.

There is no doubt she had guts and dedication. She was desperate for the money to buy the papers and had to go up against the Ivy League schools and their deep-pocketed donors. She had to ward off the villainous and frightening men who traded in these papers, marking up the prices and then selling them to private holders around the world. Wanting the papers for Victoria College at the University of Toronto, she was undaunted by the competition and borrowed the money from a former prime minister to buy the papers until finding a private donor. Professor Coburn was threatened, followed, intimidated and offered huge bribes for the material. She worked in secret at an island cottage on Georgian Bay so she could not be found. Only two Ojibway guides who led her through rough waters knew where she was. I loved hearing these suspenseful stories and always made her repeat all the fine details. Of course this is about as exciting as academia ever gets and Kathleen Coburn, a Canadian scholar, made it happen.

I was not the only one who found this an exciting tale. The novelist A.S. Byatt used to talk to Kathleen Coburn in the British Library where they were both researching. Eventually Byatt modelled *Possession*, her novel about twentieth-century research into a nineteenth-century poet, on Kathleen Coburn's search for Coleridge. Even the name of one of the characters in the book, Christabel, is the same as Coleridge's poem of the same name. When I ran into Deepti Mukherjee years later, she said that she believed that A.S. Byatt named the novel *Possession* because she was aware of how possessed Professor Coburn was by the dead Coleridge, and also how possessive she was of his works. Professor Coburn was not only the researcher in the novel, but also the lover.

—

After a long winter, Professor Coburn invited us again to her farm. Only this time, she only invited Deepti, Toady and me. I'd made

it to the semifinals. Then in the spring, I *alone* was invited to the
farm. When Toady found out I was selected, he said over a beer
in the graduate pub, "You're it, Miss McClure. You've made it. I
only hope you don't marry and throw it all away. You should think
long and hard about that before you take the job from a man who
would use it to support his family."

"Is this a proposal?" I asked, and the bartender and I killed
ourselves laughing.

On my visit alone with Professor Coburn at the beloved farm,
we talked about nature. We collected wildflowers and made bou-
quets for each room. The day before I was to leave, she said to
me, "Miss McClure, I would like to go for a long walk and discuss
your future." My heart was pounding, and as I put on my hiking
boots, I pictured telling my mother that today I had a prestigious
fellowship, doctorate, and post-doc lined up.

Once we reached the highest point of the property and could
look down at a view that resembled a stark Wyeth painting with
a brick house, a red barn and a stone milking shed, she said, "It
may be none of my business, but I have some advice that I hope
you will heed. In terms of a career, I think you should become a
comedy writer."

*A comedy writer?* Was she serious? Did she mean comedy on the
side? As a hobby while I am editing the Coleridge letters?

I was stunned into silence as she blathered on, unaware that
she was shattering my dreams and making me look like an idiot
to all of Victoria College, which was abuzz with my new appoint-
ment. "It wouldn't be easy but I really believe you have the tenacity required for performance with that miraculous timing of yours
and your gift for the written form."

She was having me up to her farm to suggest the most plebe-ian, non-academic job in the world. I was mortified. How could I have been so grandiose? I could hear Roy quoting Yogi Berra: "It ain't the heat, it's the humility."

Now when I look back on this incident, I realize that I had done what I often do in life — fantasize myself at the hub. I was never a poet, a critic or remotely suited for the job. I got to Oxford based on one poem written while on some strange amphetamine. I got to the University of Toronto more legitimately, but I was never cut out for bibliographic research.

Professor Coburn had simply lanced my delusional boil. What I had taken as an insult was, in fact, kind and flattering. At that time, I still felt like the Catholic schoolgirl who had been told all her childhood years to *stop* being a comedian. The nuns said, "Catherine, you will soon learn that life is no joke." As Mother Agnese used to say to me, "Many souls were laughing until their smiles were licked away by the flames of hell."

My father and Roy used to say that I should be a comedian, but I didn't pay either of them any heed. Traits that come naturally are rarely valued. I wanted to be important, which meant being what I wasn't.

The man who had always encouraged my inner comedian was now, after years of pain that he never once complained of, dying. My mother called me in Toronto to say that he had nothing left but was still breathing. She said he'd forgotten how to walk so he was stuck in a bed, and then he forgot how to breathe and was placed on a respirator. He had lost his ability to swallow and was fed by a tube.

As I waited in my car to cross the bridge from Canada into

the U.S., I thought of the fun my father and I had had playing practical jokes, laughing at my imitations of people, especially when I was Cassius Clay and he was Howard Cosell. Our hijinks were our bond. All of it was done while working hard — many times until midnight.

When I reached the hospital in Buffalo where he now lived, or I should say was "plugged in," I saw the six-foot-one former tennis champion of Buffalo, who now weighed ninety-seven pounds. His porcelain-thin white skin, so much like my own, appeared like a finely woven translucent cocoon and the veins looked like caterpillars writhing underneath. Aside from a brain tumour and lung cancer, he had thrush, an impacted bowel, skin cancer, bedsores and innumerable thrombosed veins. Yet his heart continued to beat. The doctors said his brain was an empty honeycomb.

I suggested we call the fight, as he'd gone way past the ninth round and was taking an unnecessary beating. My devoutly Catholic mother said that she was not going head to head with God in deciding when to end my father's life. I said I would take the responsibility for the decision to end his life, and she could stay at home. All she said on her way out of his hospital room was she hoped God knew my voice from hers.

I was alone with my dad when they unplugged the respirator. As the air left his body, his cheeks slackened and it looked exactly as though he was smiling — the same warm smile he reserved for me when we'd worked side by side at the drugstore. I could almost hear him say, "Great work, Peaches."

CHAPTER 17

# ginger crab

*Humpty Dumpty sat on a wall.*
*Humpty Dumpty had a great fall.*

I'd had little to do with Rochdale during the school year. With courses to finish and papers to write, I had scant free time since I was determined to finish my M.A. in one year. Rochdale was ideally located a block from the library where I had a carrel, so I usually left early in the morning and didn't get home until near midnight. I had the reverse schedule from the other Rochdale residents, which gave me the run of the place in the daytime. I never had to photocopy at the library; I could just nip home in five minutes and use the general office at Rochdale. Spencer left it open and anyone could use whatever he or she wanted. Since I was the only one who needed office supplies, I was usually alone except for the occasional stoner that came in to photocopy his face or his rear end for posterity.

Not surprisingly, Ginger turned out to be one of Canada's biggest dope dealers. He said his rule was to never leave the apartment. Actually, he said what my father had said years earlier, "If you want to have a successful business, you have to be on the premises and have the respect of your employees." Ginger sold only *large* quantities of dope and acid, as he said, "to avoid the dime-bag riff-raff."

My friend Leora came to visit me from Chicago, where she was in graduate school. She was fairly shocked by Ginger with his mountains of dope, the security system of bikers, the flunkies, the dogs and his tattoos. (This was back when tattoos were mostly seen in circus sideshows and on sailors.) She studied the cherries up and down his arm and the tattoo across his chest, which read, *I am a cherry picker*, complete with a large cherry picker truck done in three colours. It was easy to study all of his tattoos because on laundry day Ginger stripped to his underwear and put his clothes in the washing machine on the eighteenth floor and sauntered around in his briefs until they came out of the dryer. He changed his T-shirt every day; however, on top he always wore the same bright orange flannel shirt littered with burn holes from cascading spliff sparks. He referred to that shirt as his "work uniform." Leora marvelled that Ginger had work clothing and had to stay inside to avoid the "riff-raff."

When I would see him in the gargantuan ashram apartment, he was usually sorting through a bundle of dope that was as large as a bale of hay. It was brought in by truck, unloaded in the underground parking garage, brought up the freight elevator and then rolled to our ashram right beside the elevator. When the police caught onto the basement gig, the dope started to come in food crates that were delivered to Etherea, the connecting restaurant. Then it was sent over to Rochdale through the dumbwaiter.

When there was a police raid, the "security" set off the fire alarms, then froze the elevators, giving the dealers enough time to relocate the dope to another unrented apartment. Over time I learned that I had been placed into Ginger's ashram as a cover. Ginger paid for the whole unit; however, he had fake names on all of the dope storage rooms so that if there was a raid, he could say he didn't rent the rooms where the dope was and the "management" would produce rental agreements for fake people. Ginger wanted a real student with books instead of dope, so that the place would look like a student co-op apartment instead of "the largest drug supermarket in North America," as it was later labelled in the *Toronto Star*. I came along at just the right moment to get free rent.

I learned a bit more about Ginger as the year wore on. He hated surprises of any sort. (He said he'd never had a good one.) He also didn't like people he didn't know. Meanwhile, I had something that Ginger longed for more than anything in the world: a vacuum cleaner. Ginger and I were both highly allergic to cats. When Sara and I lived together in Cleveland, she had left an amazing small vacuum that you could wear on your back. Whenever I started sneezing, which was often since the whole building was overrun with cats, I vacuumed and that usually did the trick. This vacuum had disposable bags, which allowed us to get rid of all of the cat hair. If it stayed in the vacuum, it would make me sneeze, but it would make the tall, muscular Ginger turn into an asthmatic wreck and he had to resort to an inhaler.

I witnessed Ginger's feelings about cats one evening when I was in the living room using the communal phone. I never had any idea who paid the phone bill; Ginger said it was "on Ma Bell." Ginger was busy with his flunkies, weighing dope on a large stainless steel scale, when his quasi-girlfriend — a sort of dope dealer–groupie, appropriately named Crystal, who had been pregnant for the entire duration of my M.A. (Leora said she must be giving birth to an elephant) — came in with a tiny tabby kitty. She sneaked up behind Ginger, put it on the back of his neck and started giggling. Ginger wheeled around and swatted the cat off his neck with such ferocity that it splatted on the wall and fell to the floor, looking like a miniature bear rug. She sobbed, collapsed to her knees and cradled the dead kitten. He yelled, "Shut up. I'm counting." But she kept sobbing, so he got up and started toward her.

I had to hang up the phone (my mother thought the screaming was from a TV crime show). Intervening, I stood between Crystal and Ginger. He kept advancing toward her with clenched fists, so I sent Crystal out of the apartment and he yelled after her, "That baby is *not* mine. You better take care of it or it's going the way of the cat." Crystal slammed the door. Ginger stood for a minute looking down at his hands, which were in tight fists, and then said, "I need a strong ol' lady like you."

"Yeah, well if I see another scene like that, I'm moving out and taking the vacuum with me." When I thought of what some women had to put out to get free rent — from making dinner, marriage and much more — I was relieved that all I had put out was a vacuum cleaner.

—

One morning I came out to the kitchen to get a coffee. I was in a really expansive mood since I was actually going to finish my M.A. within the next few weeks and I was on the conclusion of my last paper for my course on the Victorians. I had no one to tell, so I told Ginger. He looked up from his scale, smiled and said, "Congratulations."

Later that night, I was quite surprised when Ginger knocked on my door and presented me with a cake-sized box containing a giant cookie that said *Fuckin' A.*

A week later, I'd officially earned the cookie, having just finished the last line of the last paper for my M.A. I emerged from my room at 1:30 a.m. and told Ginger I was on my way to drop it off at Victoria College.

"You shouldn't be walking over to the university so late."

No one as scary looking as Ginger could ever accost me on the street. I replied, "It's a few blocks away. I'll be fine."

"I'll walk with you — if, and only if, you'll have a joint with me." I looked dubious, so he added, in a demanding grouchy tone, "*Come on* . . . for once be a human being instead of an iron maiden."

I *did* need to celebrate my M.A. and I knew that I shouldn't walk alone, so I agreed. I packed up my paper on Browning's poem "Fra Lippo Lippi" and parked myself beside Ginger on the couch in front of his huge fish tank. (He'd had his piranhas for twelve years — his longest relationship to date.) We smoked our joint, something I hadn't done for the duration of my M.A., and had a cigarette chaser. Then we began laughing and imitating the piranhas that had actually taken on human qualities. They showed their tiny rows of teeth when they saw the Fuckin' A cookie, so we shared with the fish, who were rather tragically named Mom and Dad.

It was spring, and we cut through Philosopher's Walk, a winding path that went through greenery behind the university. We smelled the lilacs at the law school and watched the butterscotch forsythia glow in the dark night.

Ginger asked me what the paper was about and I said it was an explication of Robert Browning's poem about a fifteenth-century Florentine monk, Fra Lippo Lippi, who didn't believe in the laws of the Church anymore; although he'd lost his faith and had relations with women, he felt guilty when he "sinned" against the Church. The laws he no longer believed in, as Browning said, fettered the monk.

"I know how that Fra Lipshit guy felt," Ginger said. "My father took me by surprise, burned the back of my neck with cigarettes, beat the hell out of me every chance he got, even broke bones in my body, but I still feel guilty when it's Father's Day and I don't visit him in Millhaven."

When I told Ginger that I had really liked Professor Enright because he was passionate about ideas and could jump out of his chair over a new interpretation, he suggested we leave a big joint rolled up for him in the manila envelope that contained my paper. I told Ginger that Professor Enright, who always wore a tweed jacket, once had our class come to his house. His wife showed us her Hummel collection, which consisted of shelf after shelf of strange little statues of Bavarian children in lederhosen and little green felt hats with feathers in them.

After I explained in detail that the ancient professor and Mrs. Enright were clearly not the countercultural dope-smoking types, Ginger said, "Hey, this stuff is Colombian. No one turns that down." I explained that the professor called me "Miss McClure" and his wife wore sensible wool skirts and boiled-wool jackets bought at Petra Karthaus: Maker of Fine Bavarian Clothing.

I slipped the paper into Professor Enright's mailbox and confiscated the joint Ginger had rolled on the spot. I realized at that point how out of touch Ginger was and how addled his brain must have become. He lived in Rochdale, a place where everyone smoked dope, and there he was the big cheese. He had no idea how little cachet dope dealers held with Victorian literature professors and their Hummel-collecting wives.

On our way back to Rochdale, Ginger said we got along so well because we were both workaholics. Then Ginger explained that he had the busiest workweek of his life ahead of him. Next Saturday there was a Maharishi coming in the afternoon to pray and bless us and do whatever Mararishis did, followed by a music festival of sorts with oodles of bands booked to play during the day and into the night. Thousands of American attendees couldn't clear customs with dope, so it was all coming from Ginger and associates: "We're selling it from a gas station in Fort Erie and all the way up the Queen Elizabeth Way." Everyone would be dropping acid because, after all, it was acid rock music; he had a lot of work to do. He said, "You know, I never thought I'd be the type of guy to have employees. But hey, I've got fifteen guys working for me. If my ol' man heard that, he wouldn't believe it." I realized that Ginger thought of himself as a success and, in his world, he was.

The following Saturday, Rochdale was jumping and the concert had begun. It was still light outside around dinnertime and there were about five live performances planned through until midnight. I was in my apartment on the fourteenth floor, and the concert was below me on a large cement patio off the mezzanine floor that stretched the length of the building. The hundreds of people milling below me looked like ants wearing colourful Mexican shirts. Even though the terrace was huge, it was still far too crowded so people were hanging out of their windows watching or lowering dope down on a rope to the party (that way if plainclothes cops caught them, they could always run to another room within the building).

I sat at my desk, with a Canada Council grant proposal spread in front of me; I hoped to get funded for my Ph.D. However, I was procrastinating and reading *The Sound and the Fury*.

I remember the exact spot I was at in the novel — Caddy was up a tree and her brothers were looking up her skirt at her muddy underwear — when it happened. Suddenly I saw a shadow fall across my book or maybe I heard a scream. Possibly I saw a tiny bit of orange out of the corner of my eye. I looked out my window and saw a body plummet past. Then I heard a thud on the pavement, and then another. I ran to the window. One body had hit the pavement while the other had landed on a canvas awning or a tent set up for the day, and then rolled off and dropped one or maybe two floors to the cement patio. The bodies below me looked like Humpty Dumpty twins splayed on the pavement. One looked like a ginger crab you order in Chinese restaurants, his claws closed in front of him. It was wearing an orange flannel shirt.

Someone grabbed the mike and told the audience it was Ginger and another guy named Neuter, who was well known in the building for his uncanny ability to "smell narcs." Neuter died on impact. Ginger, luckier than the cat he'd killed, had nine lives. He was still alive; the awning had broken his fall. That day the local news reported fifty drug overdoses had been delivered to local hospitals. Three were dead on arrival.

I later learned Neuter and Ginger had taken acid and were convinced they could fly so they jumped off the roof of the eighteen-floor high-rise. Ginger had snapped and he spent two years, on and off, physically crumpled in the hospital and had more than fourteen surgeries. I went to visit him once, and he said he was lucky to have remained loose when he took his dive and even luckier to have fallen on the awning, which, the doctor said, saved his life. He had to drink through a tiny straw since his jaw was mostly wired shut. I had to lean close to his mouth to hear him as he whispered that after I'd confiscated that joint from him, he'd slipped another one in the manila envelope that held Professor Enright's paper. Even in his pathetic situation, I yelled, "You idiot!"

He couldn't smile, but I could see his eyes dance with merriment. At that moment, Crystal came into his hospital room and said that Ginger could only visit with me for five minutes. His eyes clouded with rage, but he was stuck. He had to count on her now. I waved goodbye.

CHAPTER 18

# german influences

*A person often meets his destiny on the road he took to avoid it.*

— Jean de La Fontaine

After I got my M.A. in fall 1971, I was at a crossroads. I could leave

the university with an M.A. and get a job, or do a Ph.D., albeit not

as the Coleridge notebook scholar. Several other professors had

asked me to go on and work with them. The Ph.D. option had

three drawbacks. First, I would have to teach. Second, I would have to go where the jobs were, like the Canadian prairies. Third, I was beginning to realize that academia was as much a closed shop as Rochdale, and nearly as deluded. Each discipline subdivided into fiefdoms that looked after their own. Just as Professor Coburn was a star in her world, Ginger had been a star in his. All you had to do was surround yourself with people who wanted what you were peddling.

Before signing up for the academic long haul, I decided that I should work for a year and not run the risk of knowing only academia. Besides I didn't feel like academia was an exact fit for me.

A few months after I finished my last paper, I opened the mail and there was my Master's degree all rolled up in a tube. An attached letter stated that I had missed graduation and therefore my degree had been shipped. Just as I was wondering when the hell graduation had been, I heard CRUD, the Rochdale radio station, switch on overhead and crackle to life. The voice blared, "Emergency, emergency, not a bust but a cultural must. Tonight at 7:30 at University College at the University of Toronto begins the great film festival on German influence on John Ford. A double bill followed by a speaker. This is heavy stuff and I would suggest hopping a stagecoach and getting on over there. Giddy up!" The usual ear piercing static followed this and CRUD signed off.

I needed to celebrate getting my Master's so I decided to go to the films. I was actually excited to attend since I had seen all of John Ford's films as well as all of Fritz Lang's and did, in fact, notice that Ford, the ultimate Irish American director, adopted some German Expressionist influences in some of his later films. I wanted to see them together to pinpoint the influences.

Rochdale had helped with my film education, since the powers that be showed a movie every Sunday night. It cost a dollar, but if you went naked you could get in for free. I saw some of the greatest films in my life there, albeit fully clothed. (I didn't relish sitting nude on cold chairs in a Canadian winter to prove a point about my personal freedom.) I saw all of Bergman, all of Truffaut, the most important German directors and almost every other important foreign film. However, I was sick of seeing all the naked bodies in the elevator. I felt like giving some of the bodies a dollar just to cover up.

I threw on my multicoloured toque (the French-Canadian name for a wool-knitted hat) since it was starting to get chilly in the fall and dashed over to University College. In my first winter in Canada when Mr. Toady Henchman said he needed a toque to warm up, I thought he meant "toke" and I told him I didn't have any. He asked, "What is that red, green, yellow and orange thing on your head?"

When I walked into University College, I was knocked out by its beautiful architecture. It reminded me of the University Museum in Oxford with its medieval revival styles — Gothic and Romanesque. It was built in the nineteenth century and you could see that the style and shape were influenced by Ruskin's ideas.

I entered a huge lecture hall and faced hundreds of empty chairs lined up in forlorn rows. I was a bit late and out of breath. There were only two people sitting near the front. When I got up close, I could see they were two guys about my age. I figured I might as well join them; it was stupid to sit alone in a huge lecture hall, especially since there was a speaker.

I should have a sociological sidebar here to say that I was relatively new to Canada — I was only beginning my second year.

Now that I have been here for over forty years, I have finally figured out that it is a very different place from America. It is not
that weird in America to join others in a lecture hall and introduce
yourself. It is a little forward but not over the top. In Canada, it
is definitely over the top. I didn't know that then. I would never
have joined others when uninvited in England because there the
rules are clear: never address a stranger unless there are bombs
falling and you need shelter. Otherwise you look disturbed, in a
manic state or, worse, *American.*

I came to learn that this form of friendliness is what Canadians
dislike most about Americans. They see this friendliness as phony
because you are not their "real" friend. My father, who was a typical American, used to say, "What does it cost to be friendly? You
only go around once."

I had my multicoloured toque atop my waist-length blond hair
and wore my Oxford favourite, the long, hairy sheepskin fur vest
that curled and smelled like mutton in the damp weather. I also
had on my blue suede short boots, which I had bought because of
the song Elvis made famous called "Blue Suede Shoes." I plopped
down panting next to the two guys and said, "Hi, I can't believe that
I just heard about this festival ten minutes ago and dashed over."
They nodded as though I were a bag lady begging for popcorn.
I introduced myself and actually had to say, "And you are . . . ?"
One said his name was Carl. He was about my height and weight
and had delicate features and a tentative smile. The other smiled
my way and I felt that smile down to my blue suede soles. He had
one of those grins that could never be mistaken for a smirk or a
snicker. It filled his whole face. He was easily six-and-a-half feet
tall. He wasn't big in that vulgar, fleshy football kind of way, but in

a lithe, lanky way. He sort of looked like Abe Lincoln with edge. He had shoulder-length black curly hair and large features, the kind you would have if you were drawing a caricature of someone. Even his teeth were large, like Chiclets. But I thought he was really gobsmackingly gorgeous, not in a traditional leading-man kind of way, but more like a character actor. From the side, his face looked elongated, like the figures in an El Greco painting.

He said his name was Michael. When I said I had just finished my Master's and was out to celebrate, he lit up with another smile that could brighten the gothic gargoyles in the corners of the room and said, "Congratulations," and he shook my hand like I had done something really great. (My mother, on the other hand, hadn't even forwarded me the letter about graduation. She said she assumed it would be too hot to attend.)

I could tell by the way he pronounced the letter R in congratulations that he was American. He was either from the Bronx or Brooklyn — somewhere funky near Manhattan.

As it turned out, this was only *one* of the things I was wrong about. I said, "Hey, man, you just came here from the States, right?"

"Right," he said.

"Where were you?"

"Grad school."

"Where?"

"Cornell."

"In what?"

"Engineering."

"Building bridges or theoretical?"

"Theoretical — games theory." When I still looked quizzical, he added, "A kind of applied math."

It turned out he and Carl shared a house in Toronto. Michael had taken a leave of absence from Cornell and Carl was doing a Ph.D. in philosophy on Heidegger.

The lights dimmed and some academic who'd been flown in for the evening began speaking about the influence of German expressionism on John Ford. Basically all he said was that Ford was influenced by German Expressionism, went to Germany, came back and then did some of his best work. I leaned over and said to the guys next to me, "Wonder how much they paid that guy to come and tell the three of us *that*." They just looked at me blankly, as though I was being rude while Mr. Academic was droning on.

We were to see *Nosferatu*, made in 1922 by the German Expressionist Murnau, followed by John Ford's *Four Sons*, made in 1928.

While we were watching *Nosferatu*, I kept telling the guys to watch the use of long shadows and static shots.

Carl said, "I know," and Michael just nodded.

During Ford's *Four Sons*, there is a great scene when the mailman comes to the door but is preceded by his elongated shadow. I said, "Guys, look. That is the same shadow as in *Nosferatu*, foreshadowing that the sons have died in the war."

"We see it," Carl said.

I had no idea that Ford had so many German influences and kept up a running commentary on all of them for Carl and Michael. Over the next four hours, we saw Fritz Lang's *M* and then John Ford's *The Informer*. I said, "Wow, this time Ford tried to use Lang's idea of making the villain pardonable, allowing us to get into the mind of the informer. You know what I mean?" Not pausing, I said, "It isn't working. Lang knew how to make people appear ill and not evil, but Ford hasn't managed it here. The soliloquy doesn't work as Peter Lorre's did in *M*."

Carl said, "Actually I can't hear it."

"Nor can I," said Michael.

"That's weird because I can hear it," I said, shaking my head. What were these guys, deaf?

——

After the movies, it was past midnight, and I was still spouting forth all the German influences I'd seen. They just nodded. As we walked out of the hall, I was bubbling over with enthusiasm. "Guys, isn't it amazing that out of the whole city, of millions of people in Toronto, there are only three of us interested in the German influence in Ford's work? Wow, now we're together! We have to go somewhere to discuss the films."

Neither of them jumped on this idea.

"Where do you live?" Carl asked.

"Rochdale."

"*Rochdale?*" Carl glanced at Michael.

"Yeah, let's get a burger at Zumburger's."

"Zumburger? I haven't been there in years. Speed freaks eat there. It's fast food," Carl said.

I'd never heard the term "fast food" before. I thought it meant something good, as in fast service. What did he want — *slow* food? Confused, I said, "Well, that's what we need right now, isn't it?"

Anyway, we were walking right by Rochdale after the movie, so I said, "We could go to Etherea and get cosmic sandwiches and take them to my ashram. There's actually a living room and kitchen. I used to share it with a dope dealer, but he jumped off the roof in the summer, believing he could fly. He was unfortunately mistaken. He's alive, but probably won't be back. So now the huge place is mine."

Carl and Michael exchanged wary glances and finally nodded in agreement. We got our cosmics and walked into the elevator. Carl stepped on my foot by mistake since I had not moved very far back in the elevator. (I never stood very far back because sometimes you had to pry the doors open on your floor. Plus pets went out on their own and sometimes didn't make it.) When he stepped on my foot, I broke into my rendition of "Blue Suede Shoes." The taller of the two, Michael, broke into the second verse: "You can burn my house, Steal my car, / Drink my liquor from an old fruit jar." And we laughed all the way to the fourteenth floor. His bursting into song had that kind of American insouciance that made me feel at home.

I thought I had better warn them about the mounds of dope and the scales and the biker bodyguards but, then again, they weren't born yesterday.

We sat eating our cosmics in the living room at the long dope table, and when I had finally run dry of German influences, I asked Michael about Cornell. He said he lived in a large co-op house with eleven people and everyone had to take a turn at cooking, shopping and cleaning up for one-week stints. He explained you were run off your feet for one week, but then you had a ten-week rest in a clean house with great meals every night. (Some of the people from that co-op moved on to cook at the Moosewood Restaurant, which was the test kitchen for what would become the famous *Moosewood Cookbook*.)

I said, "Yeah, I never got involved with that kind of thing because it was always the women who wound up doing it and I had no idea how to do it, so I just ate on my own."

He said, "Well, the people in this house were active politically and in the feminist movement."

"What's the feminist movement?" I asked.

He looked at me as though I was from an Annette Funicello movie. Was this something I should know? I had been only reading nineteenth-century texts for a year and had been living in Toronto, where bars still had a "Ladies and Escorts" entrance and another for "Gentlemen Only." Nothing was ever open on Sunday in Ontario. And before that, I was in England and Ohio. I had been in spots that were clearly the last link in the information food chain.

"Haven't you heard of Germaine Greer's new book, *The Female Eunuch*? It just came out last year. I think it is still in hardcover. I have a copy I'll lend to you if I ever run into you again," Michael said.

—

The next morning, I called long distance to my friend Leora and said I had finally met some interesting guys to go to film festivals with. I said I liked the tall guy.

"You have never liked any man under six-five. Small appendages are not your thing," she reminded me.

"He is a weird combination of things. He is an engineering-math guy from Cornell grad school; he had read the Faulkner that he saw lying around in my room and, *get this*, he knew the lyrics, the second verse I might add, to 'Blue Suede Shoes.'"

Leora took in all the information and then agreed that the blue suede shoes bit augured well.

"And he started talking about a thing called feminism. Ever

hear of it?"

She said, "Of course. Remember that book you gave me called *The Feminine Mystique*? The one you got from that woman who was in the audience you read to in Buffalo?"

"Oh, yeah that."

"Well, that was the kickoff."

"What are they fighting — men?"

"Patriarchy. Read up on it."

"Oh," I said. "I don't think that movement will affect my life much. If I recall, that book said you didn't have to be a caregiver, take care of others and cook and give up your life for your family. I never was a caregiver or a cook, and I never plan on having a husband or family. So neither my mother nor I have any bad habits to kick. Still it was nice of that Michael guy to offer me that eunuch book. Have you read it?"

"Are you kidding? That book was so powerful I hid it from my mother. I was worried she'd get a divorce or think her life was meaningless if she read it."

"Really?" How had I missed all of this?

"Yeah, it's shaking stuff up in Chicago and it is huge in Boston and New York. It's going to spread. I'm thinking of joining a consciousness-raising group."

"What's that?"

"It's about realizing that women have been brainwashed into believing that they need to have a certain role in society. It's heavy stuff. You have to rethink how you act all the time."

"Jeepers."

"Truthfully, for once you are in the vanguard, and you don't even know it. You might just have had feminist genes or something. You don't have a lot of work to do. No wonder you haven't paid attention to it. I have always liked to make everyone happy. I thought it was my job, just like it was my mother's. You never bought into that."

"I have always liked to cause human misery," I said proudly.

—–—

Years later, I found out what transpired between Carl and Michael after they'd left Rochdale on the night I met them. As they walked home, Carl said, "Well, she was nuts."

"Completely gone," Michael agreed.

"I can't believe she talked through the whole movie — and didn't even get the hint when we said we couldn't hear a thing."

"It went right over her head," Michael agreed.

"Christ. Is she going to join us for the whole series?" Carl asked.

"Oh, she'll join us for sure. It's not like we can get lost in the crowds."

—–—

The night after I'd met Michael and Carl, I was sitting on my bed reading Faulkner's *As I Lay Dying*. (I always read all the works by one author before I go on to another.) Someone yelled from down the hall, "Cathy, gentleman caller."

A man? To see me? That was a Canadian first. Carl appeared holding a crumpled yellow film schedule and simply said, "Hi."

He said he'd brought a copy of the OISE (Ontario Institute for Studies in Education) film series. We were discussing which movies were worth seeing when the motorcycle gang called on the phone from downstairs and said, "Cathy, some other tall dude is here for you. Doesn't look like a killer. Should I send him up?"

The door opened and it was Michael. He had a copy of *The*

*Female Eunuch* with him. Carl and Michael looked a bit sheepishly at one another. Neither had told the other where they were going. I guess there was something about me that wasn't as nuts as they'd let on to each another.

CHAPTER 19

# a surprise party

*If we listened to our intellect, we'd never have a love affair.*
*We'd never have a friendship . . . You've got to jump off cliffs all the*
*time and build your wings on the way down.*

— Ray Bradbury

Michael, Carl and I went to all kinds of movies, including an amazing four-month Japanese film festival. It was before the era when movies could be rented, so we had to travel all over the city to see retrospectives. We also went to the Friday midnight screening at Cinecity, which showed avant-garde movies, reverentially called "films." I remember the night we saw *Blow-Up* by Antonioni. We were enthralled by the scene where the actors played a tennis match with no ball.

We emptied out of the theatre on Yonge Street at 2:00 a.m., and since there were no restaurants open, we went instead to Queen's Park, flopped on a bench, covered ourselves with our coats and chattered like magpies until dawn about what that tennis match meant: that we all make up our own reality — we don't really need the tennis ball, it is the same game; that reality has to comprise individual perception, social consensus and art; that ultimate reality is something unknowable; that if some creature landed from Mars, it would watch the mimed tennis game not knowing there was a ball "missing"; etc.

Although it was December in Canada, and below freezing, none of us noticed the cold. Every intellectual idea was new and had to be explored. Nothing was more wonderful than these talks with people of like mind who had read what I read, or who had read far more than me and from other perspectives. We pooled our ideas: Michael from physics and math, Carl from philosophy, and me from literature. I remember being so excited that I climbed the park's enormous cast iron horse, riding double with King Edward VII, and recited Dylan Thomas's "Fern Hill": "Time let me hail and climb, / Golden in the heydays of his eyes . . ."

As our twenties wore on, the three of us felt the inexorable pace of time shadowing us and we all opted for more hands-on professions: Michael chose medicine, Carl law and I studied psychology. For sure we opted for practical careers where there were jobs at the end of the voyage, but we had a marvellous time on the journey, docking at every port that interested us.

The worst thing about the best time of your life is that when you are living it, you have no idea how precious it is. I was unaware that later, when the responsibilities of life had swallowed me whole, I would look back with pure joy on the night I sat with my friends in the cold until dawn. These were the days when you'd left your parents, made it through the university slog and now there was that small window of time when you could try to understand the world before you actually had to become a cog within it. When you are part of what makes the world go round, you can never really see it with any perspective. The precious years between freedom from home and "settling down" are so short in the fullness of time, yet so vivid in memory.

Michael had all kinds of politically "heavy" friends visit from Cornell. The college had been a hotbed of discontent in the late '60s. Cornell even made the cover of *Time*, with an angry black radical wearing crossed bandoliers upon his chest, shooting daggers at all who viewed him. Next to the activities at Columbia and Berkeley, Cornell was roiling. The worst thing you could be labelled in those days was "bourgeois." I'd rather have been a labelled a bank robber.

Michael's old housemates, six men and four women, came to visit from Ithaca, and we all went together to a film festival. We saw *Jules et Jim* by Truffaut and then went out for dinner to a Tibetan restaurant where they served a "hot pot." This culinary mishap was a dinner where each patron was served their own raw food, which you, the customer, then threw into a large black Macbeth-type boiling cauldron in the centre of the table and watched it cook. Then you lifted it out with your own little individual strainer, popped it in your mouth and scalded your tongue. Finally, at the end of this boiled meal, you drank the soup, which was basically your own garbage. Everyone talked about how this was such a "real" dining experience. I kept quiet and didn't want to embarrass Michael in front of his friends, but it seemed stupid to pay a restaurant to give you a pot to cook your own food and then for dessert you could drink the dregs. I had spent lots of time in restaurants in my life, and I never had to sweat making my own meal over a boiling pot — and then pay for the experience. I think there are better ways to feel virtuous.

As we all stirred the pot, the group began to wax eloquent about *Jules et Jim*. Everyone loved the Truffaut film, saying it was a masterpiece, a breakthrough. They admired the characters, saying they were brave for having a *ménage à trois*. As my spices slipped through my strainer and I wilted along with my Chinese broccoli, I realized I'd had enough toadying up to this group of Marxists. I said, "I loathed those characters. That woman couldn't give up her youth and being adored." I took a deep breath and continued, "*Ménage à trois* was one thing, but the fact is the woman was a liar and a cheat. She wasn't worth the heartbreak the two chronically depressed men put themselves through. I think those men wanted to be miserable, and they found the perfect woman to blame their despair on."

There was a silence among the group. The pot hissed and smoked. Finally one guy who had done a thesis on Marx said, "Don't you think monogamy is part of a capitalist plot?"

A woman with a thick New York accent said, "Cathy, I felt that way too once. You will feel differently when you read more Marx and some of what the new feminists are saying about marriage."

"Wasn't Truffaut trying to say that there are other options?" another ventured.

I realized I was not as hip or as left as these avant-garde Ivy League intellectuals. However, call me the dreaded "bourgeois," but I didn't think Marx was the answer to anything. If Michael didn't like me as a liberal capitalist, then so be it. Let him move to a collective farm in Ithaca. Forging ahead, I said, "I am not saying there are not other options, but watching a narcissistic airhead bounce around the screen while two malcontents moon over her is not my idea of a political statement. In fact, their threesome was so bad, it almost made monogamy look good. It was hours of boring pathology that the French love to call 'the drama of relationship.'"

The table was silent. We all watched the skim rise to the surface in the cauldron. Finally, Michael said, "I feel the same way as Cathy about the film."

Everyone looked at him as though he had just jumped into the pot. We would forever after be shrunken heads to this group. After drinking the dregs of our hard-earned meal, we walked home somewhat subdued on a cold winter night. Forever after I felt a chill from the Cornell cadré.

—-—

A few months later, more left-wing pilgrims made the journey from Cornell to Toronto for a jazz festival. It was freezing in March as we trudged to various bars around Toronto. This time it was three women and a man. One woman named Polly had long blond braids and wore "working-class chic" clothes: bib denim overalls (the kind that had a loop for a hammer), a blue denim shirt and Kodiak steel-toed work boots. For a winter jacket, she wore long underwear topped by layers of corduroy shirts, a checked wool lumber jacket and a quilted black vest. She didn't own makeup.

She'd had trouble getting across the border because there was a warrant out for her arrest. She'd stolen an American mail truck. (What was she going to do — commandeer the mail? To where?) Apparently after hijacking the truck, she just drove it around Cornell and dropped off leaflets about a demonstration. She became a local celebrity and the event had made it into all the papers with a picture of her behind the giant wheel of the mail truck. She returned the truck to the post-office parking lot the same day, hoping to have been undetected. Oddly enough, she *had* been spotted driving up and down the hills of Ithaca, beeping her horn in a red and white truck that had *U.S. Mail* blazoned on it, and she was arrested that evening.

This Cornell faction plus Michael, Carl, our other Toronto friend Stanley and I went out to hear jazz at George's Spaghetti House. We sat down near the stage, and Stanley lit a joint. Everyone seemed cool with this gesture; however, I suggested that it was a really bad idea to toke up in a public restaurant, albeit a jazz bar. Stanley, a man who eventually helped start a hostel in British Columbia called Cool Aid, said in all seriousness that if anyone questioned him, he would just point out the long-standing tradition of black musicians using marijuana.

I said, "Are you nuts? I think jails are full of men for whom that 'long-standing tradition' may have been missed by the police and courts. I mean Ray Charles's lawyer must have forgotten that defence." I said if he wanted to smoke dope, he should go elsewhere, as I had no intention of being arrested. Stanley was always completely agreeable and went backstage with the others to visit with Honeyboy Edwards, the performer. (I guess Stanley was going to enlighten good ol' Honeyboy, the aged blues guitarist, about this "long-standing tradition.")

Only Polly remained at the table with me. To me, Polly was an intimidating leftist. She had established her credentials by being a union organizer. When she'd told us of her organizing work in factories throughout New York State, Stanley held up his glass and said, "To Polly, a comrade who walks the walk." I had heard that she had been involved in some clandestine way with the SDS Weathermen bombing in Greenwich Village. She knew one of the guys who was killed and said that the CIA had set the bombs. No one could ever have called this poster girl for the '60s bourgeois. She was, as Michael said in an admiring tone, "hard core."

As we sat alone at the table, she silently removed a blue bag of pouch tobacco and a small metal device from her black quilted vest pocket and rolled her own cigarette. After she licked the end of her cigarette paper, sealing her creation shut, she leaned over the table, looked into my eyes and said, "I know no one owns anyone. I just wondered if you knew that Michael and I were 'doing a thing' at Cornell." She held up her fingers to make air quotes when she said "doing a thing." "Look, 'things'" — again the hand quotations — "can happen anywhere and I'm not trying to express possession. I just thought you should know the history and you should know why I came to Toronto." I wondered why she was telling me this, so I just looked at her blankly. She continued, "I mean we have jazz in Ithaca and in Manhattan, where I'm from. I didn't have to come to Toronto. I'm just putting my cards on the table."

I said, "Well, I can tell you one thing. I am not in any way involved with Michael. Carl, Stanley, Michael and I are friends.

Three or four of us go to movies together."

"It doesn't look that way to me. You make every effort to sit next to him when we go out. Women are attuned to the sexual politic. I'm honestly not trying to do a monogamous possession thing here. I am just being no bullshit. I want you to know the facts. You can do with them what you will." As she lit her tightly rolled cigarette, she gave her summary statement: "Michael and I have a history that is probably ongoing."

I just nodded as the guys came back to the table and the set began. I sat next to Stanley and only half listened as he told me that Walter Cronkite was a plant for the FBI and that the fake news was fed through him. I could not get it out of my mind that Polly thought Michael and I were "doing a thing." I had a strange feeling about the whole conversation. For some reason, I was embarrassed that everyone knew Michael and Polly were together and I was in the dark. I tried to rein in my emotions. Michael had been a friend for five months and I had never even touched his hand, so I had no right to go head to head with Polly. When everyone went back to Michael's place after the concert, I said I was tired and went home.

As the snow fell and slush from Bloor Street splashed and then froze in layers on the huge statue called *The Unknown Student* in front of my building, I realized I had to get out of Rochdale. Once Ginger had gone to the rehab hospital, there was no one to watch my back. We'd had a strange kind of bond, but it served as occasional companionship. Now I rattled around in that huge place alone with strange scary men coming to the door every now and then looking for Ginger. Plus I needed a rest from weirdness and edge. I needed to move where dogs didn't take the elevator alone, where no one lived in the washing machines and where you were expected to wear clothes to the movies. I was even willing to pay rent for the privilege of normalcy. I went to the office and told Spencer that I would be moving and wanted to give him notice. He said, "Okay, I noticed," and then went back to talking to some runaway teenage girl.

I'd decided to rent in an unhip house in the west end with three men who'd placed an advertisement in *Guerilla* that said *Room in house available, must be reliable with rent.*

As I was carrying a load of belongings down the stairs at Rochdale, I heard CRUD snap on. "Hey, CRUD heads or, as they say in France, crudités, listen up. You better be at Cathy McClure's surprise going away party on Saturday. Ginger is springing for the dope and chips. Bring your own beer. The Ginger Snap is hoping to make it his first outing in his wheelchair. It is at Bob Miller's penthouse, so wear clothes. Signing off."

I froze in the stairwell, holding a heavy box of books. Were they having a going-away party for *me* at Bob Miller's? Bob was an interesting older intellectual and one of the founders of Rochdale. He'd hung on too long and the place had fallen from intellectual experiment to drug warren, which saddened him. However, he still had his great bookstore, the SCM Book Room, on the first floor of the building and maintained his apartment in the penthouse. I liked Bob but had no idea he'd thought highly enough of me to host my party. He was one of those older English gentlemen (probably only thirty-five), who knew every intellectual in the city because he ordered the books they needed. He seemed to know everything about everything, like so many of the Brits I'd met in

England. In its heyday, England had been overrun with Renaissance men.

It was typical of Rochdale to host a party for me and forget to invite me. Details like that fall through the cracks when you neglect to delegate. I assumed it had been Ginger's job since he'd arranged it all, but clearly he'd forgotten. He was on enough pain medication to quiet a nation. I was shocked and touched that anyone thought to have a party for me. I could count on my right hand the number of interactions I'd had with others in Rochdale. When I expressed shock to one of Ginger's flunkies as I was carrying out boxes, he said, "Yeah, well, you never made enemies and you weren't a freeloading stoner." If only the rest of the world had such basic rules to define social success, I could have been Miss America.

I woke up on the morning of my Rochdale departure at 5:00 a.m. and heard CRUD jabbering. If they were playing *Tommy* again, I'd kill them. However, when I listened closely, I heard the words of James Joyce. About a year earlier, I had told Ginger that someday I'd love to wake up to Molly's soliloquy in Joyce's *Ulysses*. Ginger, a surprising character in lots of ways, had arranged it for my last day in Rochdale.

Suddenly, I felt nostalgic for Rochdale, which was a bit silly for a number of reasons. The first and most important was I hadn't left yet, and the second was all I'd ever done while living there was complain about it.

Living in a commune was a lesson for me in human nature. Some of the ideologues remained and tried to talk Russian political theory to the parasitic, psychopathic and power hungry. They weren't listening. Parasites only *look* lazy. Have you ever tried to pull them off the guest host? They are tenacious little buggers who can put tremendous energy into clamping onto a free lunch. Everyone should have to live in a "Marxist" or "egalitarian" commune sometime, and then they would see that a democratic society may have its faults, but even if you get a total lunatic running the asylum, it will only be for four years.

—

The Saturday of my going-away party finally rolled around. Ginger had organized all party arrangements from his bed at the rehab centre. He was doing physiotherapy that would eventually allow him to walk again. (Although he was never pain-free and he needed a walker, a brace or canes.) He had the flunkies whipped into a frenzy of preparation. CRUD had actually contacted me at my boring new rooming house and had put together a list of my favourite tunes for the party. To my horror, Ginger had invited my professors. He left a note in Professor Enright's mailbox, inviting him to my surprise party and then told him, *like it was his job*, to make sure he told all my other professors about the party. Once I heard *that*, I decided to invite all the people from my classes that I'd ever spoken to. I even invited the ones who wore plaid drop-pleated skirts and nylon stockings. I figured none of them would come, but at least if any of the professors showed up they would have someone to feel appalled with. I also invited my new best friends: Michael, Carl and Stanley.

I arrived at Bob Miller's place before the party was in full swing. The door opened to a gorgeous penthouse, which had a wall of patio doors opening up to a wraparound balcony. There were views all the way through the city to Lake Ontario. In every room the walls that weren't windows were covered with floor-to-ceiling bookshelves packed with classics. The furniture was black Scandinavian leather and the floor had bright coloured kilim rugs scattered everywhere. Bob had invited all of the old guard who'd started Rochdale when it was in its experimental stage. (Several went on to become part of Toronto's intelligentsia: some became poet laureates, others opened elite presses and theatre companies.) The music started, and CRUD had touchingly followed my suggestions to the letter. We started out with Richie Havens and moved on to Procol Harum, followed by some Dylan. At the door, everyone was given a joint that was rolled with American flag rolling papers in honour of my origins. As Ginger said from his wheelchair, "This is the big send-off; no sharing joints. You want to bogart that joint, you go right ahead." To my shock, every one of my professors came. It was really funny to see Professor Enright and Professor Coburn walking around with an American flag joint. (Professor Enright's wife left hers unlit but seemed to admire it.) Northrop Frye, one of my favourite professors, came and was his usual cordial self. To my surprise, he knew Bob and several others. He was one of the last to leave. I loved when his wife called him Norrie. I never made any explanation to anyone about Rochdale. As the night wore on, I chatted with everyone, and Ginger and I formed a duet to imitate Janis Joplin, as Big Brother and the Holding Company's *Cheap Thrills* album blared on the loudspeaker.

Then my favourite music came on. I have always separated the world into two groups: the Beatles acolytes and the Stones celebrants. I am in the latter group. I'd played *Let It Bleed* with that gooey pink cake on the cover so much that it actually bled and died. I would eventually also wear the threads off *Sticky Fingers*, the album with the zipper fly you could actually unzip.

I can remember that party as though it were yesterday. When I heard "Jumpin' Jack Flash," I grabbed Michael, who was wearing a black turtleneck sweater and jeans. As we danced, he had to take off his sweater because it was crowded and hot. He was wearing one of those Stanley Kowalski undershirts. We continued dancing to "Gimme Shelter" and then swung into "Satisfaction." To my shock and infinite admiration, he was a fabulous dancer — just like Roy. His six-five body rocked with the music and he was clapping and smiling that huge, unmistakable smile. He lifted me up and we rocked across the floor. Suddenly I looked at him and realized that a mathematician with rhythm should not be passed by. Plus I never forgot the lightning that went through me the second I'd met him.

Everyone was dancing, drinking and partying. Professor Coburn danced with everyone and even gave Ginger a spin in his wheelchair. Michael and I danced all night until our hair was dripping on the red rugs. All the balcony doors were open and some idiots actually danced on the railing. Toady Henchman took a break from sucking up to Northrop Frye to come and tell me that the rail dancers were in peril. I told him I wasn't a den mother. Professor Frye came out onto the balcony, looked at the idiot balancing on the railing, smiled and quoted Dryden, "A daring pilot in extremity; / Pleas'd with the danger, when the waves went high / He sought the storms."

"Right on, man," said the stoner on the railing.

"Oh, that I could be so bold," Professor Frye said. I loved that guy and was thrilled he came to my party. Harold Bloom was right when he said that *Anatomy of Criticism* established Frye as "the foremost living student of Western literature."

Bob Miller, a theologian by training, gave me a going-away present on behalf of Rochdale, a book by Paul Tillich called *The Courage To Be*. Bob wrote inside, *Cathy, read this sometime in your life when you need "to be."* He was right. Later in my life when I was at a low that book pulled me through.

—

Everyone has moments in his or her life when time stops and everything in the room gets fully recorded. I remember when I won a high-jumping medal, won an essay contest, when Kennedy died, when I had my first romantic feelings in New York, when I got into grad school, the moment my father died and the moment I fell in love — the kind of love where you know in a flash that you have met your life's partner. I guess that our unconscious mind knows more than our conscious mind knows. The unconscious knows what is important and it gives us an Instamatic to record it for safekeeping. That picture comes out on many occasions in hard and trying times. It becomes ragged around the edges, creased and faded, but it never disappears. Darwin says important moments are on file because we are supposed to learn from them. They are so important they are stored in a number of places in our brains so that if we have a brain injury, they are on backup files.

There is a difference between "falling in love" and realizing you have met the man that you will spend your life with. You want a man who doesn't judge you, who knows who you really are, doesn't put you in some weird box or even on a pedestal, for as Gloria Steinem wrote, "A pedestal is as much a prison as any small, confined space." The electric-Kool-Aid-acid-test for landing a good man is to ask yourself the big question: could you see yourself having his children? If the answer is yes, you'd better move on it.

I'd thought I was through with men; they seemed to be more trouble than they were worth. Laurie had lied, been married, made a fool of me and wasted years of my life. Then Clive was one of those English aristocrats who was wonderful and like his father *most* of the time — except when he turned into his mother.

Men and marriage involved all kinds of expectations in terms of cooking, having a home and raising a family; none of which I had *ever* longed for. In fact, my mother had found all of the above onerous and had warned me off them. Why would I want the hassle of "working" on a relationship? Lots of work for a reward I didn't want.

Who knew that a gorgeous smile could change all of that? I had no idea my heart could turn on a dime and that, even more shocking, it could pull my mind along with it. All of your previous beliefs and ideas seem anachronistic and you are left with an abruptly altered life plan.

When you fall in love, most of it is inexplicable chemistry, but with Michael I had a few facts to justify my expanding heart. I knew that I could be with a man that I respected, who was honest, had integrity, was bright and fun, could dance and, most importantly, I didn't want to change him in any way, nor did he want to change me. He was secure with who he was. I didn't have to fit into his fantasy of what a woman was "supposed to be." I could never have passed that test. Michael never tooted his own horn. Stanley told me he was accepted at MIT but he took a full scholarship from Cornell. They'd even paid his living expenses. Michael had never mentioned any of that. I mean, one blowhard per couple was all I could take — and I was already it.

But I had to get him on side. Then there was the thorny Polly issue. Also, what if he only liked me as a friend? Maybe he wanted to be with someone who designed her own recipes, like the Moosewood Cooking Collective, or stole a mail truck for the good of the working class, like Polly.

Since I was the guest of honour, I stayed until the very end of the party and, believe it or not, some of my professors did too. The last person left at 4:00 a.m.

As we left, I realized that I needed the subway to get to my new home in the west end, but it had stopped running at 2:00 a.m. Michael had moved to a new place above a store on Bloor Street only a few blocks from Rochdale. I told Michael I would come in, have a coffee, pull an all-nighter and then go home to sleep at six in the morning when the subway started up.

"Sure," he said.

As we arrived at a dingy door that led to his apartment above the Village Belle Boutique, I began to get nervous and have feelings of dread. Michael was chatting away as though nothing had changed between us. The narrow stairway was shrouded in such darkness that I had to put my hands out to feel the walls.

I heard the irreversible thud of my feet as I climbed the steps. I tried to give myself a pep talk, suggesting that this was *not* the time to be Cathy McClure. I needed to shed my thin skin and emerge as another, bolder woman. The Cathy McClure that was attached to me like a conjoined twin was really getting too heavy and too old to be lugged along wherever I went. In some ways, I knew I had a lot of guts; I would take on anyone or any group over any intellectual issue. I could also get into physical fights over disputed parking spots. Yet the shyest, most quiet girl in the world knew how to flirt or had some vague idea how to nab the man of her dreams; I, however, remained clueless. In some ways, I admired girls who flirted. They were doing the act without a net. It was far more than I had been willing to venture. My inability to gauge romantic phenomena left me with no idea if Michael was interested in me in any way other than as a friend. I was in the wilderness with no compass or even a sun or moon to guide me.

We reached the top of the dark tunnel of stairs. I told myself to go for it, and if it failed, so be it. The time had come to pull out the slogan from my teenage Mary Kay Cosmetic days — *fake it till you make it*. I pushed ahead based on one pathetic hint: while Polly was warning me off Michael, she had inadvertently encouraged me by saying it *looked like* we were "doing a thing." I had never thought along those lines. While Michael was getting his key out, I thanked God there was another long walk up another set of pitch-black stairs so I could summon up my nerve.

A voice in my head warned me not to make an idiot of myself. I was not like other girls. I had cared for a priest who was sleeping with my best friend; I had thought I loved a man who "forgot" to tell me for years that he was married. Why would I set myself up for that kind of pain again? "Jesus Christ, Cathy! Don't listen to this forked-tongued asinine devil within you. *Give it up*," I yelled at myself. "You're in your twenties. Do you want to be Miss Havisham crying over your mouldy wedding cake? *Move on!*" I could hear my mother's words if she had been there. "So every man in the world didn't love you perfectly or disappointed you in some way? Not everyone is perfect — not even you." She was right, of course. If Michael was not perfect, what was lost? It didn't have to be for the rest of my life. Germaine Greer made one point that had hit home: maybe we will only have *fun*. Suddenly I remembered a line from Roy: "A rut is a grave with the ends knocked out."

Michael yawned and said as he hung up his coat, "The couch in the living room folds out. I'll get a blanket."

"I'm not staying there," I heard my quivering voice reply.

"Oh" was all he said.

CHAPTER 20

# <u>falling</u>

*And that's why birds do it, bees do it*
*Even educated fleas do it*
*Let's do it, let's fall in love.*
— Cole Porter, "Let's Do It"

When I hit on something I like, I can be single-minded. This definitive quality has its pros and cons. In the case of Michael, it was a trait that worked for me. I realized that he was the man for me, and I never once looked back or had second thoughts. The good thing about having had intelligent, loving parents is it is easy to recognize a winner when you meet one. It just feels right.

It was 1972 and I was twenty-four years old. At that age, it's easy to split your time between two houses. I lived at my rooming house during the week and at Michael's on the weekend. All you really needed were birth control pills, a small foldable suede miniskirt, jeans, a T-shirt and a toothbrush. It all fit in my purse.

I had a job editing books that never got published. Michael, taking a break from his Ph.D., had a job doing statistical forecasting for an airport that never got built. It was the first time in both of our lives that we were not rushing toward some goal. We had useless jobs but didn't care since our minds were on each other.

I had the luxury of having my life before me. I'd finished university, been to Oxford and received an M.A. Though I may not have made my mark yet, I still had a few years' grace before I'd be labelled a slacker. It was as though my guardian angel landed on my shoulder and gave me that little nudge that I needed, whispering, "Go ahead — have fun; it's time for sex and rock 'n' roll." It was finally my turn.

The *falling* in *falling in love* says so much. It is a time when all else *falls* away in importance and you see only the other. Your head is cleared of all other emotional debris and you luxuriate in one another. The long chats in bed on a Sunday morning, going to a restaurant for the all-day breakfast, reading the *New York Times* together, going out to plays on the pay-what-you-can Sunday matinees, dining in cheap restaurants and only having appetizers and lots of bread because that was all you could afford — these are all the strands of the nest that you are building for the future. You never have that time again to glue all those fibres together. You have no idea that the nest you are building those first few years will have to withstand some mighty strong winds and innumerable predators.

Years later when you are overwhelmed with the endless responsibility of childcare, the squirrelling away of money and the exhausting and sometime dizzying climb up the professional ladder, you need to know that you had this carefree time and that you unconditionally *fell* in love with your mate. You won't have those halcyon days again, but you will always have the memory of them. When you're in your appalling minivan on your way to mini-hockey practice and "Satisfaction" comes on the "oldies" station, you need to be able to rock on together, revive those old memories and pump out the feelings that accompanied them.

We had friends in New York who "shacked up" as it was called at the time; however, no one I knew in Toronto lived "in sin." Yet I decided after several months to move in with Michael.

I remember when I was a little girl, my mother would occasionally mention that a couple in our town who owned the filling station was unhappily married. When I asked her why the woman had married the man who was clearly unsuitable, my mother's answer surprised me. "Well, she didn't really know him very well. In courtship men show their best side; when courtship is over — watch out." I had no intention of having a *courtship*. I wanted a real relationship.

Of course, I had to break the news to Michael that I was moving in, but I was not quite sure how to do it, so I simply didn't say anything. He opened his closet on a Monday morning to get his one suit to wear to work and said, "Why is your wooly vest here?"

"I moved in."

He smiled that huge toothy grin, shook his head in despair and said, "I was afraid that was going to happen."

—

After the first year of our McJobs, we decided that we needed career paths. In retrospect I wish we'd waited a few more years to breathe and simply live. However, we were both used to getting back on the horse — or maybe we were used to being the horse. So we chomped on the bit and giddy-up'd into professions.

Michael announced he really didn't want to finish his Ph.D. He said, "Well I guess I'll sign up for medical school." I thought he was delusional to think of applying way past the deadline. He hadn't even done the necessary paperwork he needed to be considered. He took the MCATs late. We were the Baby Boom. You don't just call the best medical school in the country and say you *might* drop into the party on a whim. I was, as usual, wrong. He was accepted within days.

Since Michael was away on a business trip, it was my job to take all of his information into the medical school office and sign affidavits for him by proxy. We now had lived together for well over a year. The woman at the desk asked me where Michael was born. I said I had no idea. She asked what country he was born in. I said I really wasn't sure. Then she asked his date of birth and I didn't know. Had he had financial assistance in the past? I didn't know. Did his parents live in the province? I didn't know. Did he have relatives in the university? How would I know? What was his religious affiliation? I had no idea. Finally the people in the medical school admissions office refused to believe that I knew Michael. They suggested that I go home and send someone who was at least acquainted with him.

It was then that I realized we didn't have the typical relationship. We'd paid no attention to birthdates, religion or other earthly landmarks. I was overjoyed to have a loving, honest man who had a brain the size of a giant pumpkin. Why would I ask him his birthdate? We'd spent hours reading Russian novels together and discussing the characters and their motivations. We both read Freud and decided to be psychoanalyzed just to find out more about ourselves and the "language of the unconscious." Contrary to the registrar of the medical school, I thought I knew a hell of a lot about what he thought and felt.

When he got home and I told him about my failed medical school interview, he laughed his head off. He said in his usual laconic tone, "Well, for Christ's sake, who knows stuff like *that*?" When I asked him my birthdate, he shrugged, saying, "We look about the same age."

I, like Michael, felt the need to do something more applied. Reading Freud and being psychoanalyzed pushed me in the direction of psychology. Even as a kid, I was interested in behaviour and mostly in the extremes of the bell curve. Roy had said if there was one weirdo in Niagara Falls that I didn't know, then he must have lived under a rock.

When I was a kid, I had been interested in science, and my father gave me all kinds of books on butterflies and lizards. My favourite had been a book called *What Is Oxygen?* In the summers, we'd collected specimens together and glued them to charts labelled *Binomial Nomenclature at Work*. When the teenage schism occurred between me and my father, I also left science behind. Michael revived my interest and began giving me all kinds of science to read. I guess it is true that we return to our first influences and inclinations. I was really riveted by the philosophy of science and how science progressed. Being a therapist didn't look that hard. If you were a psychoanalyst, really all you had to do was sit there and shut up. If you were a child psychiatrist, all you had to do was have a small plastic furnished house and a Fisher-Price plastic farm set, then watch the kid play. As a child, I'd gone to a tiny psychiatrist, incredibly named Dr. Small, for stabbing a bully at school with a compass. All he'd done was show me pictures of a dog named Blacky and asked me how Blacky felt, then charged my parents a fortune.

I found out that to even apply to psychology graduate school I had to have certain prerequisites that I was lacking. It would take me two full years to get them. I decided that was far too long, so I crammed them all into one. I needed to take all kinds of courses on the brain: Neuroanatomy, Perception, Memory, Instinct and Emotions, all kinds of science courses and several maths. The most notable was Univariate and Multivariate Statistics. I found it so stressful that year that once in a statistics exam I got a bloody nose. Michael's medical opinion was that I'd "blown a gasket."

On his first day of medical school, Michael arrived home looking beleaguered, flopped down in a chair and said, "What's for dinner?" (Now that we had almost no income we could no longer go to restaurants.)

I had no idea why he was asking *me* this question. My father had never asked my mother that question in his entire life. I had never asked anyone I had ever lived with that question. I just looked at him, befuddled. "How would I know?"

"Didn't you ever make something — like on a holiday or Thanksgiving?"

"On Thanksgiving I just gave thanks that I wasn't cooking."

He didn't laugh as he usually did. He looked hungry and annoyed. "What kind of food did your mother make?" He'd never mentioned my mother or my family before.

"She never made a meal in my living memory."

"Didn't you have a family?"

"Of course I had a mother and father. He didn't expect her to *cook* for Christ's sake." While he sat silently looking numb, I snarled, "Who made your food?"

"When I was small, it was my grandmother in Poland. Then we moved to a *kibbutz* and I lived in the 'little boys' house' without my parents and we all ate dinner in a big compound and some people were assigned to cooking."

"A *kibbutz*? Where?"

"Israel."

He'd lived on a commune? In Israel? I knew where Israel was and I had read about *kibbutzim* in terms of a social experiment, but what had he been doing there? We'd both had unusual childhoods where neither of us totally depended on our mothers. It is interesting that we found each other and saw things so similarly — that is, until this fractious moment.

Michael made his first criticism of me and I will never forget the words: "I wish that you took more joy in household tasks."

"How much joy do you take in them? I haven't seen you whistling the Israeli national anthem while you clean the toilet," I responded.

"Let's avoid mudslinging here. We have a problem that needs to be solved." He got out a piece of paper and began writing numbers on it. "We each have student loans of $2,300 dollars a year. That is around $5,000. We have to live on it. The scholarships only pay the tuition."

"Okay. So?"

"Well, I have classes from about 9 to 5. I have my Marx study group one night a week and I am supposed to study medicine sometimes."

"I am taking two years of science courses in one. I have to get all As to get into grad school in psychology. What's your point?"

"We have a problem. Firstly there is nothing to make dinner with and secondly there is no one to make dinner." I nodded in agreement, and he continued. "Have you ever opened the oven?"

"Why would I have done that? Who do I look like — the witch in Hansel and Gretel?"

"There is a guy in my cadaver group whose French-Canadian wife makes this amazing food every night of their lives and she even makes dessert. Sometimes he brings in *tortière* or apple pie with cream *and maple syrup* in it."

"God, I wish I was married to her," I said.

He looked out the window into the back alley that was swarming with cats scrounging in the Dumpster for scraps from the meat market. He continued staring out for a long while and then said, "Do you see we have a problem?"

"No, not exactly. I mean I doubt we'll starve." I thought he was pretty fixated on food.

"We can get meat at Elizabeth's Meat Market next door every day. We can buy a vegetable and a potato."

"Don't they have to get cooked?"

"I will cook and buy the food and clean for one whole week and you do the next week. That way we are on one and off one."

We followed the system faithfully and it worked well. Over the

years, it got slightly amended. I didn't mind cleaning as much as cooking so we often traded chores. Also he had branched out and even used the oven. That cavernous thing scared me, so I stayed on the top of the stove. Michael learned how to make great Indian and Greek food. I learned to buy cleaning ingredients and tidy up. It did take me three years to realize that garbage was emptied on a particular night. My family never had garbage. The first year Michael and I were together, neither of us did the dishes in a conventional way. We just used what was there until they were all dirty and then the one who used the last dish had to wash them. It was usually Michael, because I cheated and drank milk from the carton when there were no more dishes left. We were really exacting about the rules, and I was way better at getting around them than he was. I was great at predicting how many glasses were left in the cupboard.

When it was my week, I was run ragged. I could suddenly see what the women had been doing all these years. Is it any wonder that women hadn't advanced the sciences? They had to start worrying about dinner as soon as they ate lunch. You had to plan the meal, shop, carry it home, unpack it, cook it, serve it and then clean up the dishes afterward. The second you opened your eyes in the morning, you not only had to think about what you would eat for breakfast, but what the whole household would eat.

It was better for everyone when we were hunters and gatherers. Just eat a berry as you walked along. If your husband brought home an animal, it was great for the tribe, he was proud of it and most importantly he was tickled pink to roast it.

When I called my mother to say hello, I mentioned I'd had a bloody nose during a statistics exam. She, a former math teacher although she only taught for one day, said that you can't take two statistics courses at one time. You need to know univariate before you can understand multivariate. "For heaven's sake, your whole brain is going to turn into molten lava and float out your ears. Why don't you just take life easier? No one is behind you with a whip." I told her that Michael, "a guy I shared the apartment with," would tutor me in statistics.

"Who's Michael? I never heard his name before."

"I just told you. He lives here — and guess what? He came home from medical school one day and said, 'What's for dinner?'"

She laughed that kind of belly laugh that I have always enjoyed so much, saying, "That's hilarious. For goodness sake, don't get started on that route. There's no exit. Be careful. He might want you to type a paper for him and before you know it, you'll be his medical secretary."

"We're sharing the cooking."

"You mean you are eating off each other's plates?"

"No! I cook one week and he cooks another."

"It sounds terrible to me" was all she said.

⎯⁓⎯

I found myself having similar conversations with my friend Leora, who now lived in Boston and was a researcher at a major Boston hospital connected with Harvard. When Michael and I visited her in 1972, she gave us a copy of a book that a number of her friends had worked on called *Our Bodies, Ourselves*. I was gobsmacked, as they say on the streets of London, by that book, which actually wrote about women's health from a *woman's* perspective. It made the point that a lot of male doctors, and almost all were male at the time, had no idea what caused most females' pain. I was thrilled to realize I wasn't a classic hysteric when it mentioned PMS as though it was a real entity.

The book described how birth control pills worked, giving the reader all the pros and cons. I'd never had any idea there were cons. The second edition included letters from women who had all kinds of advice they had learned by trial and error. There were letters from women across the country who were fed up with women's health information being disseminated by drug companies and researchers from a male perspective to male doctors. Suddenly I felt part of a movement, since I viscerally shared similar sentiments of so many of the disgruntled females. I thought of my gynecologist who had handed me a disk that looked strangely like a child's blue and yellow rattle. "If you don't want children, take these," he said, then his nurse pulled out the white paper sheet from under me as a hint that my time was up.

The book talked about how we needed to see the ways we had been programmed to conform to a submissive role that was not really in *our* best interests. I put this information together with *The Female Eunuch*, which basically said that women had been cut off from their libidos. Germaine Greer said women are like farm animals that are castrated to serve the profit motive of the farmer. Women have become leery of sexuality because it is in the interest of society to make them passive, not only sexually but in life in general. I had felt this to be true for all my life, but had never been able to put it into words. I had just known that my active nature had been universally frowned upon by society at large and would have been extinguished if my parents had not applauded it.

I went to some meetings of the NAC (National Action Committee on the Status of Women), and through them I found that many women were in consciousness-raising groups to attempt to "deprogram" themselves. I decided to go to a feminist group that I saw advertised in *Guerilla*, thinking I would finally find like-minded women and that we could share our histories. When I arrived, I found twenty-five mostly middle-class women sitting on folding chairs in a circle. Half of them were married and one quarter had children. Some of the real movers and shakers of the group were fugitive SDS sympathizers who had come to Canada from New York and Boston hoping for political asylum. None of them shaved their legs or wore a shred of makeup.

The majority of the group said they didn't want to end up like their mothers, who catered to everyone else's needs. They talked about their mothers as though they'd had the most unimaginably terrible lives. They described their mothers as powerless, and how quiet but deadly anger had oozed out of their every pore. The more educated the mother, the angrier she was. I had no idea what they were talking about.

Each week they made pacts to work at not always taking responsibility for other people's hunger or unhappiness or unpressed clothes. The women in the group seemed to share this preoccupation. I had never taken on any of these issues as my responsibility, nor had my mother. Again I had no idea what they were talking about. My mother said when she got an iron as a wedding gift she threw it out, saying she was afraid she'd use it. She said God invented dry cleaners for a reason.

I would sporadically jump into the fray and say things like, "Just don't make dinner." They would reply in an exasperated tone, "Then who will do it?" or "You just don't get it, do you?" I had no idea why they thought all this was *their* job.

Everyone in the group was born the late '40s or early '50s and it seemed that they were rewarded for being quiet and nurturing and they were sick of it. I had never been rewarded for that, so I felt I was another species — a duck in a room of fish. I was in the right pond but the wrong animal.

I would come home each week and tell Michael the group's resolution for the week. We always found them hilarious. One week, I tore in blasting, "I refuse to cook day and night any longer, and listen, buster, there are no more casseroles in the fridge when I'm away. It's over, done, finished!"

As I sat in "the women's circle," as it was reverentially called, drinking inka — a barley, rye, chicory and sugar beet drink (coffee was an artificial stimulant) — I was surprised and sadly alienated by the domestic concerns of the group. They talked about how they would stop pleasing men. I asked one striking woman who had jumbo hair knotted on top of her head with a stick going through it like an African queen, "What do you mean exactly by 'pleasing men'?" I honestly had no idea.

"Are you a lesbian?" she asked.

"No." Why would she ask *that*?

After that, I decided to listen instead of talk. Most of the women had their first sexual experiences far younger than I had. The majority of the group had been pleasing men sexually since they'd become sexually active, which for most of them was around the age of sixteen. There seemed to be two sexual themes in the group: the married ones wanted to have *less* sex, and the ones who were dating wanted to have *better* sex. Almost everyone complained that sex was only good for the male.

I wondered why women didn't just ask for what would give

them sexual pleasure. As I said to the group, it was like going to a restaurant, looking a menu and telling the waiter, "Surprise me." The response of the group was interesting. The married ones said that their husbands would feel inadequate if they said anything other than "Wow, that was great." Some other women, who I thought were brave for speaking up, said they had no idea what to ask *for*.

Myrna, from Brooklyn, said, "Ya have to know what you want, before ya ask for it, right?" Then she suggested that we should pass around a magnifying mirror and all learn the sexual parts of our bodies and identify parts that are responsible for sexual arousal. I had read about this in *Our Bodies, Ourselves* and thought it was a great idea. At least it had some biological validity. It was informative and devoid of rhetoric. At the end of the evening, we'd actually *know* something. So we all took turns looking at our vaginas in the mirror. When we each looked at our clitoris, most of the women in the group were amazed that we had a sexual organ and were shocked that it really looked like a miniature penis.

When I came home and told Michael we all looked at our sexual organs in a magnifying mirror, he said, "Stop making up crap," and went back to reading his *Gray's Anatomy*.

Clearly I felt like I was from another planet when it came to personal development; however, on a societal level I related to a lot of what was said. More than two-thirds of the group had had a sexual attack of some sort in their lifetime, and several of the group members were incest survivors, which shocked me at the time. As we each told our stories, I began to realize that I, like the rest of the group, had blamed myself for my attempted rape. It was remarkable to me how the majority of us had been subtly blamed by the authorities at the time of the crime. When I told the group that the police officer had asked if I had been naked in the shower, they all laughed. But the story was no longer funny. I began to cry. I sobbed, and I realized how much I'd absorbed that officer's disdain.

As the years went on, I saw that many of those women who'd been in my consciousness-raising group had moved into government and become big players in the Women's Bureau, Ontario Women's Directorate and the National Action Committee on the Status of Women. Some became lawyers and started feminist law firms and later became judges. As a psychologist, I was an expert witness in a lawsuit and before I gave my testimony, the judge, a woman, leaned down, laughed and whispered to me, "Didn't I meet your sexual organs in 1973?"

After thirty years, our group had a reunion at a resort up north. Some women now had their own grown children. The ones that had daughters were telling those of us who didn't that these young women now think feminism is passé. They had no idea why women were angry. One woman quoted her teenage daughter as saying, "Mom, those feminist battles are such ancient history." In fact it was two generations ago. It *was* another era. It is hard to explain that without those battles fought and without those laws in place, our daughters would not be sitting in law and medical schools that are now almost fifty percent female. The problem with having rights is you have no idea how precious or how precarious they are unless you've struggled for them. I guess that's the nature of historical change. The hard-fought battles won by one generation are only boring history to the next — but I suppose that's what we were fighting for.

CHAPTER 21

# always there

*The real religion of the world comes from women much more than*
*from men — from mothers most of all, who carry the key of our*
*souls in their bosoms.*
— Oliver Wendell Holmes, "The Professor at the Breakfast-Table"

After I read *Our Bodies, Ourselves*, I called my mother, who had had

a bladder infection called chronic cystitis almost all of her adult life.

She had been on antibiotics for decades. I called her and said that

women talked about the illness and together they had found a way

to prevent its recurrence. I said drink cranberry juice, wear cotton underwear and when home wear no underwear with a skirt. That way no germs build up in a moist area. Never take a bath, only shower. I said, "If you are having sex, get out of bed the second you finish and empty your bladder."

She said, "Sex? Are you kidding? I'm Catholic."

She took these suggestions and within two weeks her cystitis was gone and never returned.

Since her doctor never once told her any of these tips over a thirty-year period, I decided to call him and tell him so he could pass on the information to his other patients. Isn't it our job to spread the word, especially to those who can actually help others? I doubted he was reading *Our Bodies, Ourselves* on the weekend. Not many seventy-year-old men pick up books whose covers have women holding up a huge *Women Unite* banner.

Over the phone, I gave him the information about preventing cystitis recurrence. When I was finished, he said, "Cathy, I took this call because I *thought* this was an emergency. Everyone has his own folklore. You needn't have spread it long distance during work hours."

I said, "You know, I hoped you might be grateful. Clearly you have never had cystitis or vaginitis and have no idea what pain it can cause. I guess it's doctors like you who inspired a group of women to write a book called *Our Bodies, Ourselves*. Note they didn't call it *Our Bodies, Our Doctor*."

"I don't think we have to worry about your mother's cystitis when she has leukemia. Or have you called me with a cure for that too?" After a long silence on my end, he said, "Now, if you don't mind, I'll get back to my patients, who, however prosaic this may sound to you, need me."

"Wait a minute. Leukemia? I had no idea she was even sick."

He hesitated for a few seconds. "I assumed she'd told you — especially since your dad is gone and you are all she has."

After a few seconds, I asked, "How long does she have?"

"That depends, doesn't it?"

"I don't know. You're the doctor."

"She has turned down platelets, saying she's lived long enough. It is a form of chronic leukemia, not acute. So she may have years ahead of her, or she could go soon."

"Why didn't she tell me?"

"That is between you and your mother. I assumed you knew."

"Thank you for the information. I'll contact her right away," I said with a formality that masked my shock and pain.

I was about to hang up when he said, "She is not in immediate danger." Then he added what must have passed for comforting words to him, but to me were a non sequitur, "Cathy, she is still one of Buffalo's greatest bridge players."

I sat in the hallway, looking blankly at the black phone. The first thing I thought of was how short her life had been and how little she had participated in it. Yet, I told myself, she never expressed unhappiness. I had always felt it was my job to make her happy, to draw her into life at home and tell her of the fun and adventures we'd had at the store. I had always taken care of her, and now I could not protect her any longer, no matter how hard I tried.

—

I borrowed a car and returned to Buffalo immediately. While waiting at the border, I thought about how little I'd seen my mother since I'd met Michael. I had hardly been home at all and I was only ninety miles away.

When I entered the house, she was, as usual, lying on the couch. She was reading her bible, *Championship Bridge with Charles Goren*. On the coffee table lay a library copy of *Tinker, Tailor, Soldier, Spy* by John le Carré.

"How are you doing?" I asked.

"Fine. Why are *you* here?"

"I came to visit. You're lying down. Are you feeling well?"

"I always lie down."

"Feeling all right?"

"Sure. Why, don't I look all right?"

"I spoke to Dr. Clark." Hearing those words, she closed her book and sat up. "He told me you have leukemia."

"What a blabberpuss," she said.

"I've never liked that guy. Anyway why didn't you tell me?"

"What's the point? It's not like you can do anything about it."

"I am your daughter and only living relative."

"Gee, that's scary," she said with her usual dry wit. Then she looked blasé and said, "Why cry over spilt milk? So I have leukemia. There is nothing to be done about it."

"Leukemia isn't the common cold, you know," I said, attempting to insert some perspective into the conversation.

"Well, everything has an up side. Now when I get up at noon, no one will think I'm being lazy. I don't have to do volunteer work. No one will ever expect a meal." She smiled the conspiratorial smile we shared when we were being sarcastic. When I was a little girl, we used to watch *Queen for a Day* together. Whenever bad things happened to someone on the show, I would imitate Mother Agnese, the long-suffering nun who taught me for eight long years, and said things like "God gives those with strong backs the heaviest crosses." When a contestant would lose her home to creditors, I would say, "No more to clean" and my mother would say, "No beds to make." I would add, "No guests to entertain," and on we would go, jauntily mocking blind stoicism.

I wasn't willing to go that route with my mother, although she'd started it and clearly wanted to handle it that way. I said, "Dr. Clark told me you didn't want any platelets."

"Have you seen those homes for the aged and infirm? I'd rather die right here, thank you very much."

"Most people want to live."

"Well, they haven't seen the table manners of the people in those places."

"Mom, did you hear me? *Most people want to live.*"

"I have lived."

"I could take care of you," I said as my eyes filled with tears.

"Don't be ridiculous. I would absolutely hate that. This could go on for ages. So far I'm fine. I want you to do your psychology graduate degree. Then you can psychoanalyze me on my deathbed. Oh, speaking of deathbeds," she said, almost leaping off the couch, "come in and see the outfits I've chosen for my open casket. I like to refer to the collection as my shrouds for all seasons."

She proceeded to show me four garment bags labelled *summer*, *fall*, *winter* and *spring*. Each one contained a seasonally appropriate outfit, complete with gloves, matching shoes and purse.

I said, "Purse? Where are you going?"

"You should never travel without a compact."

I couldn't help but laugh.

She looked relieved and said, "Glad you are home. Let's go and get a beef on weck. Wait, I just remembered it's Friday! We'll have to have fish."

"The Catholic Church rescinded that rule years ago."

"I never have followed anything post Vatican II and I hope you don't either. I never believed that Pope Paul XXIII had the ear of Our Lord."

"Why not go pre–Martin Luther?" I picked up the car keys. "Let's go."

⁓

That night I stayed at my mother's house. At three in the morning, I awoke with a start. I remembered the chemicals that Hooker Chemical dumped into the water. We all knew it was there because the water smelled exactly like the plant and made our eyes run. It took another decade for it to come to light that Hooker had dumped 950 pounds of toxic chemicals in the river *every day*.

I am a researcher at heart, and when I feel overwhelmed I dig for information like a ferret down a rat hole. I got up, got dressed and was ready to go at dawn. I went to every library and every archive in the city to research the chemical dumping in the area. I searched for days but found inconclusive evidence.

On the last day of my visit, while we were eating wings at the Anchor Bar, I told my mother that I believed there was a connection between her illness and the chemicals that festered in the Niagara River. I said eventually the truth, just like the toxic chemicals, would bubble to the surface.

"Oh, you're always railing about something," she replied, dipping her wing into her spicy blue cheese sauce. "People have to die of something, you know."

I couldn't get over the fact that she was so blasé about the Hookers, who had been our neighbours in Lewiston, slowly poisoning us. "Mom, as you were playing bridge with the Hookers in their magnificent historic home, you were slowly being poisoned by waste their chemical company dumped in the area."

"To say nothing of their stale bridge mix."

A few years later, state officials discovered toxic chemicals had leaked from Hooker Chemical's Love Canal dump site, and two decades later when the epidemiological studies were completed, I read that benzene, the most toxic chemical found in the dump site, was associated with several health hazards. In the New York State Department of Health Archives, I read in black and white, *Benzene at Love Canal caused chronic lymphatic leukemia.*

———

When I got back to Toronto and told Michael of my mother's illness, he commented that my matter-of-fact tone surprised him. I had to admit that, however strange, I wasn't devastated by my mother's leukemia and impending death. I suppose I'd internalized the Irish Catholic view of death, which is "well, you've had a good run at it," or "it's all in God's hands now" or "she'll meet her reward." More importantly, my mother said she'd rather quit while she was ahead. She wanted to die in her own home with all of her marbles. Other than that, she was happy to go.

I felt sadness but also a kind of peace in knowing that I had had the best mother-daughter relationship possible. I had never once in my life been seriously angry with her and I had always been happy that she was my mother. I don't think a lot of people can say that. On the other hand, when my father got his brain tumour when I was a teenager, we'd had a bad few years and he lost his mind before I could ever repair the damage I'd done. You can't take back awful things you've said if someone has lost his mind.

I also knew that even if my mother wasn't with me, I would always have her in my mind. When I was in grade school, I would run home from school and tell her an amusing story about something that had happened that day. I always gave it the slant that I knew she would enjoy. To this day, when something funny happens, I file it in my "mother file" and tell her about it when I am alone in my car. I can hear her laugh and imagine her wry comments. I think that's one of the reasons I became a writer: to keep telling the stories I know she'd love. When I write, she, like Long John Silver's parrot, is always sitting on my shoulder. You can't feel the loss of someone who is with you.

CHAPTER 22

# the catacombs

*If you talk to God, you are praying.*
*If God talks to you, you have schizophrenia.*
— Thomas Szasz, *The Second Sin*

It was 1973, and I was about to embark on my second Master's

program, this time in psychology. I learned all the testing proce-

dures and knew how to run statistically significant studies. I was

heading into the life as a researcher and even had my own white

lab coat with my initials in red to prove it.

Although I had a research stipend and a scholarship for my tuition, I needed money to live on while at school. Making a living can be distracting from a person's life goals at the best of times, but it was especially vexing at this point in my life when I needed to devote nearly all my time to my research. I solved the problem by taking a job working the night shift at a psychiatric hospital. I also took day shifts when I didn't have classes. When I look back on it now, I have no idea how I ever managed to work all night and go to school all day. Oddly enough I never felt tired.

When I went to the child and adolescent ward for the job interview with the chief of psychiatry, Dr. Dekker, an eastern European with a Bela Lugosi accent, asked for my qualifications. I said, "None really." He asked if I had a degree in psychology and I said I'd just started grad school a week ago. He asked if I liked children and I said, "No, not at all."

He said, "I think you will be perfect. Start immediately."

Lakeshore Psychiatric Hospital opened in 1889 on the rocky shores of Lake Ontario. The grounds and placement of the buildings were inspired by the work of Frederick Law Olmsted, the father of American landscape who built Central Park in New York City. It was structured according to the European model of making the "inmate" healthy and productive. The hospital was built like a small town on sixty of the most picturesque acres in Ontario. The grounds led down to the lake with tree-lined walkways, and there were vegetable gardens for the patients to till, a small farm for meat, a church and a town hall. There was a beautiful gazebo down by the crashing waves. Originally, the hospital had its own blacksmith shop, pumping station, fire brigade, cemetery and supply of natural gas. It was designed to offer the utmost in therapeutic landscaping, and maintenance of all of the facilities was to be done by the patients. There would be medical care available, but the idea was that the more people controlled their own lives and lands, the healthier and literally more grounded they became.

The tragedy, and there is always tragedy in the way the mentally ill have been treated, is that in the early 1970s, when I was there, the patients were so heavily drugged that they never wanted to go outside. Although the medication often prevented florid psychosis, it also prevented engaging with the world in any meaningful way. The patients preferred to sit and look out the window or to read donated *Time* magazines from 1958. Huge weeds had choked the vegetable gardens, the town hall was used for electric shock therapy, and the pigeons and seagulls used the gazebo as a dumping ground. The myriad of old red brick buildings making up the Lakeshore Asylum looked like an abandoned Hollywood set that had once been used for filming *Bedlam*.

Nowhere in the literature of the original plans does it mention that there is a whole city of underground tunnels that connects the buildings. These miles of subterranean passageways had not been repaired since the nineteenth century. There remained a decrepit underground metropolis, where there were no cars but rolling stretchers, and the pedestrians were little white moles scurrying around with hypodermics filled with cocktail sedatives.

The night shift ran on a skeleton staff. There were two workers in each of the nine ward buildings. I worked with only one other woman. Sandra, a trained childcare worker, was one of those people who was innately bright but didn't care about continuing her education or what my mother called "bettering herself." She

read only Harlequin romances and refused to date or marry anyone who was not a card-carrying member of the working class.
She said if a man didn't have a hockey jacket or know how to play
darts in a bar, then he was a pansy. She had no idea why I found
anything said by the psychiatrists, whom she called "permanent
fuck-ups," of any interest. To a litany of her complaints, I read
aloud all of Freud's cases in the wee hours of the morning just so
I could stay awake.

This hospital was a dumping ground for Canada's Hannibal
Lecters, the dangerous men who'd had lobotomies, electroshock,
medication and still bayed at the moon on a good day. A number
of men had been thrown in Lakeshore after the war, remained in
locked wards and never saw the light of day. If they got out for
even ten minutes, a SWAT team of police had to be called and
every unit had to be on lockdown.

There is something bonding about working all night in a dank
old bastion. We had to depend on each other. Usually our shift
was uneventful and the patients slept, but occasionally, when we
had a pyromaniac start a fire, or a suicide attempt that caused an
hysterical outbreak, or a group contagion, all hell broke loose and
we had to work together like a well-oiled machine. We could call
the goons, as the strong-armed "medication squad" was named,
but it took them ages to get to our building, which was at the end
of a long row of old fortresses. If they were on another call elsewhere, we had to do everything on our own.

—-—

One humid August night in 1974 when even the usually tumul-
tuous Lake Ontario refused to stir, Sandra and I had done our
suicide check on Eddie, a fourteen-year-old boy who had been

with us since he was six. We'd checked on Brad, our nine-year-old feces smearer. When he lived at home, he used to put feces in his mother's purse. Now that he was in the hospital, he smeared the walls with it. The psychiatrist thought this was progress, probably because he didn't have to clean it up.

Having finished all our odious tasks, we took our first break of the day, putting our feet up on the coffee table to watch the 11:00 news and have a cigarette.

As I was rummaging in my purse for a cigarette, Sandra screamed, "Holy shit, look at this, Cath, Nixon is resigning!" There he was on television, reading from a trembling script. We watched mesmerized as he rambled on, his lower jowls quivering. Brad, or as Sandra called him "Master Shit Disturber," crept out in his Batman pyjamas to watch the news with us. He was supposed to be in bed, but we let him watch. I told him not to say a word, emphasizing that this broadcast of President Nixon resigning to avoid impeachment was a historical moment. I still remember at the end of his speech, Nixon said he'd "felt a very personal sense of kinship with each and every American."

A slightly bewildered Brad said, "I didn't feel his kinship. Did you, Cathy? Did you, Sandra?"

We assured him we didn't feel the kinship either.

"That's good," he said. Clearly he didn't want to feel left out of Nixon's kinship just because he was crazy.

While the commentators were droning on about a dark day in America, Sandra was screaming at the TV, "You think you got troubles. It's darker right here in Canada right now because we're in a loony bin with no goddamn cigarettes at midnight."

This was indeed the first time that Sandra and I were both out of cigarettes at the same time, and we had a twelve-hour shift ahead of us. I had smoked since I was nine years old and I was not about to quit now. There was no way we could go out to a store for smokes. First, there wasn't one, and second, it was late. Sandra said there was a cigarette machine in the underground tunnels that connected all of the ten wards. She announced that she'd once made the trip alone, and she said, in her usual offhand tone, she was "alive to tell the tale." We flipped a coin and I lost. As she drew me the map, she said the cigarette machine was in a maze between wards seven and eight. I hesitated at the top of the stairs and she pushed me, saying that all the ward doors were locked at dusk and the tunnels were empty. The map had about ten different turns through the tunnels lit only by a few bare light bulbs at each end. She assured me that the whole trip would take about eight minutes each way. The fact that I was willing to do this tells you everything you need to know about the nature of addiction.

Even so, after what happened that night, I never smoked again. Sometimes fear actually changes your neural configuration: I never had nicotine withdrawal and never thought of having another cigarette.

I descended the old stone stairs, ignoring the thick cobwebs in the corners. Sandra had warned me that it was poorly lit, but she didn't tell me that it was totally black in certain parts. All of the bulbs were in thick cages that obscured much of the light. We had the cages on the wards as well so the patients couldn't steal the bulbs, start fires with the hot filaments or break them and cut themselves. The faint light illuminated rudimentary carvings in the stone walls, which, when I looked closer, were words and phrases such as *help* or *God take me*.

When I was about five minutes into the maze, I heard what sounded like footsteps behind me, but Sandra had warned me there was an echo. I slowed down, knowing that if the steps were only an echo they would also slow down. Then I realized how stupid that was. If I were being followed, the footsteps would also slow down when I slowed down. I was too frightened to turn around.

I had heard from the goon squad that there were some guys who had to stay in locked cells. Once one got a hold of one of the goon's pencils and within seconds had it chewed into matchsticks and spit it out. I tried to repress stories like that one as I trudged on in my wooden Dr. Scholl's exercise sandals, which banged and echoed with each step.

Finally I stopped and heard no footsteps behind me. When I checked my watch, I realized I'd been travelling for only five minutes, but it felt like an hour. According to Sandra's hand-drawn map, the cigarette machine was around the next corner. Sandra, although lackadaisical in certain ways, was exacting if she thought something was important and she *wanted* a cigarette. Suddenly I heard a scrambling sound. *It must be mice*, I thought. Then the scrambling turned into a rhythmical scurrying. An anguished cry and scratching against the wall followed. I decided to ignore it and dash around the corner at breakneck speed. I'd buy my cigarettes as fast as I could, turn tail and run like hell back to the ward. I tried to convince myself I'd made the sounds up. I heard my mother's voice in my head saying I had an overactive imagination.

I rounded the final bend and there, in a corner under a stone stairway, crouched a human figure. He peered out of small black wide-set eyes. All I could see were his eyeballs in the dark, but somehow I knew it was a man. I decided to ignore him and hope that he didn't think I had seen him folded up like a troll. With a thundering heart, I nonchalantly sauntered up to the cigarette machine lit by a single bulb and slipped in my thirty-five cents. I heard it jingle down the metal slot like a warning bell.

When he heard the change ring into the machine, he sprang out from his squatted position under the stairs and into the light. He looked as though he'd been buried alive and someone had just popped open his coffin lid. He began bowing and chanting in an otherworldly voice, "*Sanctus, Sanctus, Sanctus Dominus Deus Sabaoth.*"

Just as I was about to run away, he blocked my path. I had a wall behind me, a wall on my right and a locked staircase to my left. The only way out was down the long hallway and this heavy creature was obstructing it. *I was trapped.* He had an unusually large head with a scar over his right temple and an institutional haircut, which Sandra had labelled "the-chronic-axe-murderer trim." He was overweight and appeared to be about middle age. He had that grey pallor of an inpatient and the large stomach and thin limbs of a psychotic who has taken many years of ineffective antipsychotic medication that has remained lodged in his now-bloated stomach. His trousers were held up to an empire waist position by old-fashioned wide suspenders, and his shirt was drenched in sweat.

When we finally made eye contact, his look changed from fear to rage and he held up a knife, albeit only a regular knife from the dining room, but still it was a knife. Then he screamed, "Octavia, you Jezebel. I am not going to be persecuted by you any longer." The words echoed through the tunnel system until they came back to us. He went up to the cigarette machine and began to pull savagely at the handle of each brand. He methodically pulled each knob twice more, and then fell to his knees and fervently prayed with his hands folded toward the heavens. As I started to back away, he jumped up, grabbed me and cornered me. His face was so close I could smell his institutional breath reeking of undigested medication as he said, "You will not feed me to the lions." I thought of dashing past him and up the stairs, but all the doors were locked — except for one obviously. He held the knife to my throat and said, "You will not leave here until I've finished my services. Kneel in the sarcophagus. I'm praying."

"Who are you?" I asked.

"I am St. Stephen."

"Ah, the martyr?" He didn't answer. "I get it. We're in the catacombs."

He looked pleased for the first time and nodded. He walked up and down in front of the cigarette machine, and about every third time he paced by, he would say, *"Dominus vobiscum."* I joined in the service, saying, *"Et cum spiritu tuo."* (Who says being a Catholic can't save your life?) As long as I participated in the ritual that he had to compulsively perform, he ignored me and continued. Agitated, he pointed to an area under the stairs that was dark and about five feet wide and six feet deep. I looked in as he lit a match and I saw an amazing altar made out of cigarette papers and wrappers. The silver paper was wrapped around stones, coins, bottle tops, old broken crockery and hundreds of other solid small objects. These small objects were artfully layered to create a glittering mound about two feet high that included a tabernacle, which was a Chock full o'Nuts coffee can. (I thought of the *heavenly* coffee jingle.) Some of the other coloured parts of the cigarette wrappers were also twisted in so that all the colours reflected onto the aluminum foil. The walls of the side chapel were covered with religious imagery: the Lamb of God, the fish, and the Stations of the Cross. It looked like he'd dug out the images and then stuffed different coloured paper into the cracks. The Virgin Mary's dress was done in Player's blue. Christ's side bled in Du Maurier red. The pallor of Christ was Craven A white. The crown of thorns was made of tiny twisted twigs with bits of Peter Jackson gold on the tips. You could see that stations thirteen and fourteen, the last two, were not finished. They were carved but had no coloured papers embedded into the crevices.

When I figured I had worshipped long enough, I whispered, "I have to go now."

He looked up at me as though I were a child trying to get out of mass early. "Not until I do this for each year since my death."

"When did you die?" I asked, hoping it had been a fairly recent event.

"I was killed by Nero. I've come down here many nights to meet other Christians but they have all been thrown to the lions." He looked at my white blond hair and said he had to offer up a lamb to Our Lord. "One that is as white as snow." I noticed for the first time that when he said the word *white* he had a slight European accent.

As soon as I made a movement away from participating in the ritual, he immediately became agitated, pointing the knife in front of him and frantically yanking the cigarette knobs. I thought for sure the machine would fall forward, but true to government form, it had been nailed to the wall and the floor. Then he held up his own cigarette package as though it were a Eucharist, went into his little side chapel under the stairs and lit a cigarette. He swung the smoking cigarette back and forth in the air as though it were a thurible, the container for burning incense that the priest swings on a chain in religious rituals.

If I edged away even slightly, he started the whole thing again. We had a long time to go, since he had to do this for every year since 64 AD, and we were in 1974. I decided to sit down. When I defied him or questioned his obsession, he began to sweat so profusely that even his hair dripped. He smelled like a caged animal that needed his pen swept out.

He pointed to his sparkling altar, which must have taken years for him to assemble, and said that he was leaving it to his "fellow man." He began rattling off some more Latin, and I answered with words from a Christmas carol: "*Adeste Fideles.*" He seemed to relax at my continued participation, and he told me that it was time for communion. He lit up another cigarette and gave me one, saying it was the body and blood of Our Lord. He said we were going to make a sacrificial offering. Wanting to avoid the idea that I was the sacrificial lamb, I said, "Christ sacrificed a lamb."

He looked at me sadly, as though he had bad news. "You must be the blood of our Lord." He walked toward me. He had no socks or shoes on and his feet were filthy with yellow-brown thickened nails that had not been trimmed and had begun to grow under. They looked like pig's trotters as they scratched the floor. Thus the scurrying sound I'd heard earlier. Once I saw his feet, I lost all hope that his ward staff would miss him at head count. No one even gave him a bath.

He came toward me and grabbed my hand. I recoiled in terror but thought it best not to resist. Suddenly I heard the door open at the top of the stairs and I yelled, "Help!" A man darted down the stairs and grabbed a hold of the early Christian and pinned back his arms as though he'd done it many times. He was a handsome blond man who was only slightly older than me and wearing a blue cotton shirt and chino pants.

"Zekas, that's enough." Zekas struggled and the blond man said in a low, calming voice, "Let go of the lady. Follow me right now or I'll have to call the goons." Zekas looked like a large ape weighing his options. The blond said, "The goons will do more than give you a shot. They'll take the key so you can't get any cigarette wrappers. The doctor will have to tell everyone not to give you their empty cigarette packs." The blond hesitated and then added, "They might even move the cigarette machine." With that, Zekas ran to the cigarette machine, fell to his knees and hugged it and wept. "I'm . . . I'm . . ." He kept trying to talk between sobs.

"You're a martyr. I know that. All of your sacrifices go up in smoke," the blond man said. Zekas nodded, pleased to be understood. The blond man patted him gently on the back and told him he had to go back to the ward.

"He is really harmless," the blond man said to me as Zekas lumbered up the stairs.

"Well, he mentioned making me a sacrificial lamb," I said, begging to differ.

"Oh really. *That* is a new twist to the ritual."

"I put the money in once already but the machine went crazy when Zekas pulled all the knobs. Before leaving, can you wait a minute while I quickly drop thirty pieces of silver in here and get a pack of Du Mauriers?" The aggrieved Zekas stood panting at the top of the stairs, but I knew Sandra would never forgive me for not getting the cigarettes, and I never wanted to come back here. The attendant said he would take Zekas back to the ward and lock him in and then walk me back to the adolescent unit.

When he returned, he introduced himself as Dennis and we set off for my building. He said he did troubleshooting all over the hospital.

"Interesting ritual that Zekas has going on here," I offered.

"I know. His parents were deaf Lithuanians who were killed during the war. He heard no speech for the first three years of his life and then he was sent to Canada as a war orphan. He only went to grade school but seems to know several ancient languages."

"Is it language or gibberish?"

"Who knows? Wouldn't you think they'd get a linguist to check it out?"

I thought it strange that this night watchman would be talking about a linguist and not just saying Zekas was crazy like most ward attendants would have said. Hearing that Dennis was interested in the content of psychotic hallucinations, I ventured, "Rituals are interesting. They are so often religious. Zekas looked crazy but his behaviour was no crazier than anything else in theory. I mean Saint Francis wore a hair shirt and ropes and Saint Thérèse of Lisieux, one of the most popular saints, practised self-inflicted corporal mortification. For these feats, they became saints. In fact, eating a host or smoking a cigarette is really not that different. They are both oral experiences of ingestion. This is a man who knows ritual. Fire is used in most cultures for worship. Cigarette smoke is a kind of incense." As we turned a corner and I could see that I was almost back to the ward, I added, "You know Jung or Freud would have made the most of this event. It would have been one of their cases in defence of a collective unconscious. Are ancient memories stored somewhere? Here is a man who is actually enacting an ancient ritual in a compulsive way. Why a ritual in the catacombs?"

"Obsessive behaviour is when your brain is a very long playing record and the needle gets stuck in a groove," Dennis replied. "As the years go by, the groove gets deeper and deeper. You have to keep enacting the same behaviour because you are programmed to do it. The thinking in the '50s was to excise the groove directly in front of the problem groove. That's what happened to Zekas."

"A lobotomy?" I asked.

Dennis nodded. "Almost all the lobotomies are in building nine. Up the stairs from where you saw Zekas. The problem is that the brain is not as precise as a record. The operation was crude and it wound up cutting huge sections on either side of the obsessive groove. There was hardly anything left of the record. Like you're listening to a symphony and then suddenly there are huge gaps until you can't make heads or tails of the music."

Shaking my head, I said, "It must be hard to find a place to house all of the mistakes they made in the '50s."

"Most of the lobotomies are dying off now. In building nine they use medication for obsessive behaviour. That's like spraying the record with WD-40 and hoping that the needle slid over the sticky groove. The problem is the needle slides over the whole record and no grooves are penetrated. Those patients don't hear any of the music of life, or else it is a one-note song."

"That medication hasn't worked at all? Why do they still use it?" I asked.

"It has worked for some people. Just not the people stuck in here — they have ruts so deep that when a synapse fires a spark it just keeps shorting out. No amount of medication can work."

We'd made it back to the ward without incident and I thanked Dennis for rescuing me. When I knocked on the ward door, Sandra opened it and bellowed, "Where have you been? I am *dying* for a cigarette." She pulled me in and slammed the door on Dennis. As I sank into a chair, relieved to be alive, she continued. "I gave you up for dead and I was really worried since I'd given you money for a *large* pack."

Sandra tore into the cigarettes as I told her what I'd seen. When I finished, she shook her head and said, "Christ, what the hell does someone have to go through for a frickin' cigarette around here? We should get time-and-a-half for that kind of shit."

I said that the only decent part of the tunnel tale was that I had met Dennis and he was an interesting ward attendant and we'd agreed to exchange books. I said, "At least we'll have someone stimulating to talk to in the staff cafeteria."

Sandra sat in her plastic-coated easy chair with her feet up on the coffee table and took a deep drag on her cigarette. She slowly blew out the smoke, then said, "Dennis is so *stimulating* that he is in his own locked ward — or is supposed to be. He is an obsessive-compulsive who *has* to lock all of the doors every night. He's fine as long as you let him perform his ritual. If you don't, he'll peck your eyes out. That's why he usually lives behind fine-mesh screening."

"Seriously? He seemed so smart and normal."

"He's about as normal as you are. Next time you meet him check out the primary-coloured Fisher-Price plastic keys that hang from his belt."

# different people
# have different customs

*You don't choose your family.*
*They are God's gift to you, as you are to them.*
— Desmond Tutu

1974 was the happiest year of my life to date and, now that I look

back on it, probably the happiest in my entire life. Something had

happened in the tilt of the world. Feisty women who didn't put up

with crap, the ones who came fully loaded with their own brand

of testosterone, were suddenly in vogue. For the first time in my life, I *belonged*. Although I was popular in high school in Buffalo, I, like my mother, had for the most part learned how to look and *act* normal. I also knew how to be amusing and quickly learned that any group will put up with a lot of personal differences if they are entertained. I was like a really good spy; I had learned how to fit into an alien society without detection. The only place my normal veneer failed miserably was in Ohio, where I never got close to mimicking the others. It was the only place I have ever lived where even the girls were from Pluto. Maybe I was isolated because I'd dated a black man, but the upshot was I felt as alone as the boy with no immune system who lived in the glass bubble in Texas.

Then in England, although many of the people were intelligent and interesting, they'd been through the meat grinder of the boarding school system and were emotionally stunted. They may have *wanted* to leave the class system behind, but they couldn't; it had done too much to mould them. We found one another mutually amusing and had respect for one another, but we were nothing alike. We were always looking at each other curiously as one looks at the orangutans at the zoo who bear an uncanny resemblance to us, until they do something revolting.

Finally I'd come to Toronto and found a man who saw the human panoply as I did. On the rare occasions when we didn't buy into the same version, he, at least, found mine interesting or entertaining. The result was we rarely disagreed or quarrelled. I couldn't believe my luck! I made friends who didn't think I was eccentric, or if they did, it was the era when "eccentric" had taken on a more positive connotation.

I'd found an intellectual discipline for which I was suited and was feverishly working on my Ph.D. thesis on Darwin's influence on Freud. What could be better than locking yourself away all day in a carrel with two of the greatest geniuses of the last century? How many people got to spend the day with Darwin and Freud with no interruptions? Michael thought medical school was boring, so I would regale him with all I'd learned during the day and we would talk into the night.

One chilly Saturday in late March, when everyone in Canada couldn't take one more day of the cold, sun-deprived winter, we were preparing to go to the north end of the city to hike in a provincial park when Michael said, "I have to go to my parents' apartment to do their income taxes on the way up."

"Don't they have an accountant?" I asked.

"Yeah, me."

I'd never heard of a child doing their parents' taxes. We drove for miles and miles up Bathurst Street in the Valiant, the car we'd bought for fifty dollars then covered the hole near the gas pedal with a cookie sheet. I felt we must have been north of the tree line. I'd never travelled from the core of downtown Toronto, and I had no idea the city and its suburbs sprawled into the near tundra.

As we entered his parents' neighborhood, nearly all the men we passed were wearing small skullcaps with bobby pins holding them on. (The bobby pins on men seemed weirder to me than the skullcaps.) Then we passed men who looked like they were extras in *Fiddler on the Roof* and a parade of men in long coats and hats like the man on *Laugh-In* used to wear — the one who fell off the park bench every week. These men had long curls on the sides of their faces as though they had set one piece of hair in a pin curl and it had unfurled.

"Wow, get that," I said, staring in amazement out the car window.

Michael gazed out at the men who were streaming down the sidewalk in nineteenth-century costumes accompanied by sons who dressed just like their fathers. The boys dressed more like midget men than children. Looking unfazed, he asked, "What?"

"Did we just drive into a pioneer village or what?" I asked.

"They're Orthodox Jews." Then looking across the street, he added, "Those guys there," pointing to the long-coated parade that wore black wide-brimmed hats, "are Lubavitchers."

People were spilling off the crowded sidewalk and into the street. "Why are the sidewalks so packed? Did a game just let out?" I asked.

"None of them can drive on Saturday so they are walking to *shul*."

"What's *shul*?"

"It's Yiddish for synagogue."

"Do you speak Yiddish?"

"It's my first language."

Was he kidding? His first language was something I've never heard of. Was there a Yiddishland? I'd honestly never met anyone whose first language wasn't English. I decided to file that on the back burner because the large families crowding the sidewalks were fascinating. Glued to the window, I said, "I wonder why they have such large families? Hey, wait a cotton-pickin' minute here; I think all of those women are wearing wigs? Look, I'm not kidding!" He looked out and seemed unfazed by this klatch of women in wigs or else hats much like the ones worn on the trolley in *Meet Me in St. Louis*.

"Jewish law says that a married woman should keep her hair covered. A number of them live in my parents' building."

"Do your parents think they're weird?"

"No. Why would they?"

"Well, they kind of look like Mennonites — only Jewish."

"My parents are Jews who grew up in a *shtetl* in Poland. They lived through the war. They lived through starvation in Leningrad. Believe me, this scene does *not* look odd to them." After a brief silence, he added, "I'm a Jew from Poland. I came here after the war, when I was already a teenager, in 1956. We lived with my grandparents, who looked *exactly like these people*."

I was confused. When I first met him, he said he was Jewish, but he also said that he and his parents were atheists. If a Catholic is an atheist, then they are no longer a Catholic. They are mutually exclusive. I was confused so I asked, "You said you were an *atheist*. How can an atheist be a Jew?" He looked straight ahead with a set jaw. I guessed from this lack of response that I'd asked a dumb question.

After a few minutes of silence, he asked with an edge to his voice, "Haven't you ever seen a Jew before?"

"One third of my high school was Jewish but they didn't wear period costumes."

"People in this area are mostly Orthodox and most are from Russia or Poland. They are first-generation immigrants who lived through the war."

I stared out the window again, getting my bearings. No one I grew up with ever mentioned the war other than as an historical fact. To me it seemed so long ago. I had never met anyone who had actually lived *through* it or even *fought* in it. Befuddled, I looked at Michael. He looked back at me and, noting my confusion, said, using a low guttural tone that I'd never heard from him before, "You know the war where they killed six million Jews or, as you say, *people in costumes*."

"Look, you're being unfair. Every Jew I've ever known has looked just like me and many had Christmas trees."

"I would *never* have a Christmas tree in my house."

*Uh oh.*

At that moment, Michael turned off Bathurst Street onto another major artery called Wilson Avenue. As far as the eye could see, I saw only cement in several of its incarnations: road, sidewalk and cinderblock low-rise apartments. Even the grey snow on the curbs matched the cement. It was the only place I'd ever been where you couldn't see any vegetation on the horizon even if you did a 360-degree turn. *Michael grew up here?* I'd never met anyone who'd grown up in an apartment. I'd only read about it in *A Tree Grows in Brooklyn* when I was young girl.

I'd assumed (clearly, I'd made a number of wrong assumptions that day) that since Michael's parents had two sons in medical school, they were wealthy. Everyone I knew in Buffalo who'd gone into medicine had fathers who were either doctors themselves or were on all kinds of boards. It was hard to get into medicine and you needed some clout, as well as tutors for the medical boards that only upper-middle-class parents knew how to orchestrate. Over the years, Michael had made comments about his father, indicating he spoke many languages, read all the time and loved political theory and history. I'd never met a working-class family in Lewiston or Buffalo who had those interests. To my narrow middle-American mind, people who had these lofty interests were cultured, and culture spelled wealthy; who else had time or the energy for culture?

We parked the car and walked down the dreary main artery of Wilson Avenue. We were flanked by small six-plex apartment buildings in dingy cement block with aqua chipped metal railings. This was where Michael's parents lived. Sandwiched between the apartment buildings were kosher delis and laundromats, and many of the signs were in Yiddish. On the streets, nearly everyone was speaking either Yiddish or some language that sounded like they were constantly arguing with one another.

We walked into the tiny lobby and I looked for the elevator, but there wasn't one. As we walked down the narrow hall of the second floor toward Michael's parents' apartment, a woman, leaving the chain on the door, opened it a crack and her frightened dark eye peered out at us. Michael smiled and said, "Hello, Mrs. Jacobson," as we passed; she didn't say a word, just closed and bolted the door. All the doorjambs had small, crookedly placed caskets on them. (I later found out that the boxes contained *mezuzahs* that signify that you are entering an observant Jewish home.)

We knocked on the door, heard footsteps and then nothing, so clearly someone was looking at us through the peephole in the door. Michael said, *"Czesc, tat. To jestem ja. A to jest moj kolega."*

Were we in the Tower of Babel? I knew he was from Poland but I'd never heard him *speak* Polish. I had never known anyone who spoke another language to his or her parents. I assumed he said that it was Michael and a friend. Although judging by his father's stricken expression when he opened the door, he may have said, "Hi, Dad, it's your doomed son. I have brought the grim reaper with me today. She is the blond standing next to me."

The father looked exactly like Michael. He had the same wide mouth and exactly the same long face. He looked at me gravely, bowed slightly and said formally in an accent that was hard to decipher, "Mary, we open our home to you." He gestured expansively to their tiny one-bedroom apartment. I would have felt very at home if my name had been Mary. When I got inside I heard, but did not see, Michael's mother, who chastised her husband from the bedroom, saying, "That is not Mary. That was his *old* girlfriend. I guess she's gone now."

*Mary? An old girlfriend?*

There was a tiny galley kitchen and a small table in a corner to dine on. The living room had a couch and one chair and all kinds of paraphernalia around the apartment about Israel: maps of the country; Jewish calendars, which had no bearing on the Gregorian one; and a sculpture, or actually a doll, that was two feet high and dressed as a Russian Hassidic rabbi in a flat fur hat. On the rabbi's nineteenth-century long black fitted waistcoat was pinned the math award Michael had won for all of Canada when he was in high school.

Michael's mother now made an entrance from the bedroom. She shuffled in wearing pink terrycloth mules that dragged on the wooden floor as she walked. She was a tiny woman with legs like kindling, matchstick arms and a larger middle. Clearly she had once been a real beauty. Her face still had a beautiful bone structure. His mother sat on the couch and leaned her head back on a cushion, looking as though someone had just told her that her son had died.

The father asked me about myself and we talked a bit about my studies. His English was halting, but he tried; he hadn't come to Canada until he was over forty. His mother just sat looking at a fixed spot on the wall and audibly sighed. Once in a while, she mumbled in Yiddish. She was whispering *"Oy"* and then *"Oy gevalt."* She wore a housedress (*schlafrock* in Yiddish) that zipped up the front and is used as a full body apron for house cleaning. Finally Michael's father said to his wife, in a pleading voice, "Ida, please make Mike and his friend," he hesitated, then haltingly said, "Ca-thy, something from which to eat."

The mother said, "What? I run a restaurant?"

"Ida, they need a nosh. The children, they are hungry."

She didn't look up at any of us but addressed the ceiling as she remained on the couch. She threw her hands up and said, "What? What should I make?"

"Ida, what do you want from me?" Michael's father asked, splaying his palms in front of him. "Make a tea."

"How should I know *how* she wants it or *where* she wants it?"

I remember what happened next so well because I had never heard Michael's voice sound so harsh as he retorted, "What? Where do you think she wants it — on the floor?"

She shrugged and said, "Different people have different customs."

Both Michael's father and Michael glared at her, and she finally shambled into the galley kitchen and made tea with lemon squashed into it with a fork and served it in glasses with small handles. She put a cube of sugar on everyone's saucer and then placed her cube between her teeth and began drinking the tea through the sugar cube. It seemed a cumbersome method for sweetening tea and made it impossible to converse without a speech impediment, so I just left mine on my plate. Not that anyone was conversing.

I had no idea why she was so hostile and clearly depressed. Strange as this may seem, it had never occurred to me at the time that she didn't like *me*. I mean, she didn't know me. How could she dislike me? I assumed something bad had happened and we had come at an inopportune moment.

I can make conversation with a doorknob so I tried to chat. However, by this time the father had settled into silent despondency. Michael, following suit, set his jaw and his eyes seemed to pull back closer to his ears, an expression I had never seen before. The mother answered me in shrugs.

After about fifteen minutes of this oppressive silence, Michael stood up suddenly and said we were leaving. His father said, "Mike, *please* stay."

Michael said, "What's the point?" He looked at his mother, a vein pulsating down the length of his long brow. "Thank you for the hospitality." She didn't get off the couch and we left. I could tell he was upset and we walked back to the car in silence. We were too emotionally spent to go on a hike, so we went home. I now understood why he'd waited almost four years to introduce me.

A few weeks later, when Michael and I were out to dinner at a Hungarian restaurant across the street from our apartment, we ran into Barry, a high school friend of Michael. His family was from the same town in Poland as Michael's parents and they had maintained their friendship in Canada. Barry said, "So your mother's sitting *shiva* now that you're dating a *shiksa*."

Michael shrugged, laughed and said, "Of course."

Later when I asked Michael what Barry was talking about, he said, "Let's not get into it," and then he started another conversation.

I went to the university library and found a Yiddish dictionary and looked up the word *shiksa*. It said *Gentile girl, a detested thing. Offensive. Used as a disparaging term for a non-Jewish girl or woman.* I quickly looked up *shiva*. It said *Mourning period of seven days observed by family and friends of deceased.* So, in effect, Barry had said, "You are going out with a detested thing and your mother will mourn your death. You are now dead to her."

*Holy shit.* This was serious.

I had gone to school with Jews and my best friend Leora was Jewish. How could I not have recognized this attitude before? I had never even noticed if people were Jewish or not. In high school, no one made much mention of it. I was from an assimilated American suburb where the goal was to be alike, not different. I had noticed that many Jews were in advanced classes (the classes were nearly empty on Jewish holidays) and had parents who were really on top of the schoolwork. My father had said that the reason my mother's master's bridge club was mostly Jewish was because "Jews used their heads for more than a hat rack." That was his full explanation of religious and cultural differences.

I decided I had better learn a bit more because I could tell that Jews who lived through the war in Europe and had come here after the war were nothing like the Jews who'd lived in the U.S. for generations. In fact, this was the first time I'd ever met an immigrant other than the Puerto Ricans I'd worked with at the doughnut shop, and they'd liked me.

I remember when I used to complain about customers that I didn't like, my father used to say that we had a business to run and we had to find a way to get along with people. He said the best way was to walk a mile in someone else's shoes. When I complained that someone had been rude to me or attacked me, he never defended me, even when I was little. He taught me how to defend myself. He also said that before you attack anyone, always know more about them than they know about you. Or as Roy said, "You best know shit from Shinola before you shine your shoes."

I decided at that point to read everything I could get my hands on about the Holocaust, and I would read *all* of modern Jewish literature. By the end of the year, I was on a first-name basis with every librarian at the Jewish public library. As Roy used to say, "When Cathy's got somethin' cookin', stay away from the stove."

One day when I was reading *The Pawnbroker*, Alina, Michael's younger sister, and her giggling wild friend Yael dropped in. Alina, then sixteen, was tall and thin. She had the exact wide, sensual mouth as Michael; however, she'd inherited her mother's beautiful bone structure, and was, as my mother would say, "an arresting beauty." She'd moved out of her family home when she was fifteen years old and never lived there again. When I didn't look surprised by this fact, Alina said, "That wasn't exactly a Jewish thing to do."

When she visited her parents without Michael, it was her job to drop off a care package of food to our apartment on the way home. The food was always the same: *kreplach*, a stuffed dumpling; chopped liver homemade by his father; chicken soup; a strange tube of derma called *kishka* — intestine stuffed with potato and bread and unfailingly accompanied by a side of gravy. Then the chaser was always *cholent*, a bean and barley concoction that in my opinion could have been packaged and sold for window caulking. Upon opening a care package, Michael always said, "Oh

Christ, I don't want any of this," and then sat down and ate every bite in one sitting.

While Alina and I watched him eat, she said, "Mom said that you were probably starving." Then she commented on how much bigger his care package was compared to hers. When Michael left the room, Alina said that Michael was the cherished eldest son who could do no wrong. I looked at her in amazement. How did they treat their least favourite?

Alina noticed my pile of Jewish literature on the coffee table and said that she could see that I was struggling to understand what it was to be a "shiksa in a foreign land." She offered, with her teenage optimism, to explain the whole thing to me in about two minutes. She spoke in short, precise phrases as though she were quoting sociological data. "Jews who came to America before the war have no idea what Jews suffered during the war. They are totally different people. They didn't have gentile neighbours turn on them. They didn't lose all of their relatives and friends. The ones who lived feel guilty for being alive when their relatives died. In order to keep the Jewish race from becoming extinct, Jews have to marry Jews. If they assimilate by marrying goyim, then eventually the Jewish people will only be a quaint sect who were wiped out during the war. Hitler will have won."

"Is this your view? Is it your parents'?" I asked.

"During the war, my parents fled Poland hidden in trains to Russia. There wasn't a scrap of food, and they lost a child to starvation in Leningrad. That does something to you. Then they moved back to Poland after the war where my father was a party official. Ultimately they settled in Israel and lived on a kibbutz, but they were six million short. I am not saying that I agree with my parents' position. I'm just giving you the drill." Before I could say anything, she was off down the hall to borrow our typewriter to fill out a summer job application.

Alina had returned with the typewriter and was busy pecking away when Yael said, "Actually Alina didn't tell you the bottom line about so-called *goyim*; she skipped the most important part." I looked at her with rapt attention. Finally I was getting the key. One thing I'd learned about Yael, she was a teenager with no censor. "Jews think *goys* are stupid, drink too much and that *shiksas* give blowjobs. They don't know that *everyone* gives blowjobs. Guess what? Guys like it." She began giggling that uncontrollable high-pitched cackle that can only come out of teenage girls, particularly when they are talking about sex. After Yael's treatise on "cultural differences," I was shocked into silence: Alina looked askance at her, which suggested to me that she might have thought Yael had contributed a tad too many tribal secrets to the Global Village.

Well, at least I didn't drink.

CHAPTER 24

# passover

*Tradition is a guide and not a jailer.*
— William Somerset Maugham, *The Summing Up*

Shortly after the "different people have different customs " disastrous meeting at Michael's parents', Michael's aunt called one day and said, "Hello, I'm Aunt Clara." She paused as though I was supposed to know her. I asked if she was calling for Michael and she told me she was inviting him to Passover. I assumed I was being passed over. Just as I was hanging up, she said, "I'm Michael's father's sister. I came from Poland when I was fifteen years old. I brought my brother, his family and our parents over when Mike was a teenager and they lived with us until they learned the language and were on their feet." After a lull in the conversation, she added, "I'm surprised he never mentioned me."

"That doesn't mean much. I haven't had a lot of contact with his family but I'm sure you're in his thoughts."

"What a lovely thing to say. *In his thoughts* — I like that." Then there was a silence and she said with a soft accent, "Would you like to come to Passover dinner as well?"

I'd had enough rejection so I said, "Only if I would be welcome."

"I wouldn't have asked otherwise. I don't ask someone and then put my nose in the air."

There was something I liked about Aunt Clara right away.

—

Michael, his sister and I arrived on a freezing evening in April for Passover at Aunt Clara's. As I walked up the gigantic driveway that had been professionally ploughed, I saw one of those sprawling split-level homes that defined the '60s. There was a double front door with matching knockers shaped like lions with their tongues out. When I tried to lift the tongue to knock on the lower jaw, I realized it didn't move. Alina was onto this and she found the lighted doorbell connected to an intercom. Suddenly we heard the echoing chimes of Beethoven's Fifth. A male voice blasted out of the intercom: "I'm coming, I'm coming! Where's the fire?" The voice was attached to a handsome, jovial man who answered the door. *"Gut Yontiff."*

Assuming he was inquiring about the hazardous driving, I assured him I was used to snow. He shook my hand, saying, "I'm Uncle Jack." Strange that the house was called Aunt Clara's when she had a husband of thirty years called Uncle Jack. I'd assumed she was a widow. He was nattily dressed in a pinstriped suit, complete with a tailor-made shirt, tiepin and cufflinks. When someone said he looked good, he opened his arms expansively, shrugged and said, "Why shouldn't I look good? I'm in the *schmatte* business. Otherwise I'd be a bad advertisement."

Aunt Clara yelled out from the kitchen, "Jack, off with the boots!" in the same tone that the queen in *Alice's Adventures in Wonderland* said, "Off with their heads!" Jack handed us each a pair of paper slippers that were exactly like hospital slippers. I had never taken my shoes off at anyone's house before. While we were all attempting to stay on the tiny mat as we removed our footwear, Uncle Jack pulled Michael aside and began telling him a joke — something about two gynecologists in Miami. Michael was laughing hysterically, which surprised me, as I had never heard him say an off-colour word. Clara, yet to be seen, yelled again from the kitchen, "I can hear you, Jack! Enough with the jokes."

I held my breath in embarrassment, wondering how Jack would handle being reprimanded in public by an angry wife. I couldn't imagine my mother ever raising her voice to my father or vice versa, let alone in front of guests. I assumed he would be either profoundly furious or humiliated. However, he didn't seem to be either. He just laughed and said, "Uh-oh, I thought she had the tap on." Then he whispered, "I'll tell you another one later — heard the one about the tailor from Minsk?"

Then Uncle Jack looked over at me, and Michael said, "This is my friend Cathy."

Jack smiled, shook my hand and said his first word directly to me: "Converting?"

Shocked, I just stood there. Clara whipped into action. She whirled out of the kitchen with a knife in her apron pocket. She had dyed red hair, a shade I later learned was called Hungarian bar mitzvah red, and wore Marilyn Monroe–red lipstick. Already a grandmother, Clara was still a beautiful woman with the same warm smile of her brother, Michael's father. "Jack, mind your own business." She put her arms around me, hugged me and said, "You better be hungry. Jack, take the kids downstairs and get them a drink."

Jack looked at me and said to Aunt Clara, "Look at that blond hair on Mike's girlfriend. She's going to put Izzy out of business." (Uncle Izzy owned a company that sold lines of hair dye wholesale to beauty shops.)

The home was an ode to square footage with a Tara-goes-to-Toronto foyer complete with marble floors, winding stairway and flocked wallpaper. It was one of those split-level deals where you were always walking up three steps or down four. Paper slippers crinkling, we shuffled like wardmates down to the recreation room and stood behind a black leatherette bar. Jack lined up our options on top of the bar. I had never seen no-name pop before and I had been in the business for years in the drugstore. The bottles were all the same strange size with pot-bellied middles and labelled *The Pop Shoppe*. There was even pretend Coke called Cott Cola. Michael had a no-name vodka. It was strange living in a huge home and having no-name pop and alcohol. I thought they only drank these poor substitutes in third-world countries.

When we walked to the living room, we had to shuffle on narrow plastic runners that were laid on top of the white shag carpet. We had to make sharp turns to stay on the runners when entering another room and, since the slippers were too large and had no grip, we had to drag our feet. This combination of sliding and making sharp sudden turns made us look like a parade of Frankensteins. When I saw our robotic gait in the gilded mirror on the wall, I started laughing. Once I started, I couldn't stop. Uncle Jack said to Michael, "You've got a real live wire there, Mike. I haven't even told her a joke yet."

We arrived in a living room that was so huge that it had twin seating arrangements at either end. There were white brocade French provincial couches with matching chairs and curtains in the same fabric as the couches, with huge tassels holding them open. Everything was cocooned in plastic. The chandelier lit up the room like an operating theatre and light glared off the plastic — even the lampshades — and light from the chandelier glared off all the shiny surfaces. When I sat down on the couch, I nearly slid to the floor. I had never seen plastic covering on furniture before, and I had no idea if this was a regular occurrence. My research told me that while sitting *shiva*, all mirrors were covered with black cloth. Maybe during Passover all furniture was covered in plastic? Even the pictures, dot-to-dot needlepoint of biblical figures from the Old Testament, were covered in plastic. I whispered to Alina, "When does the plastic come off?"

"Never."

No one else was there yet except for one couple sitting in the corner of this cavernous room. The man was reading *The Canadian*

*Jewish News* and the woman was sitting primly, clutching her purse on her lap. They were clearly the relatives who dressed in an old-world style, while the others wore the latest in fashion. The room was so large I didn't recognize them at first. As I walked toward them, I realized they were Michael's parents. I smiled at them and Michael's father returned the huge Michael-smile I'd come to love and the mother nodded almost subliminally while uttering the forlorn greeting, "Next year let's hope for better things." What had gone wrong with this year?

Wanting to avoid that subject, I detoured into the dining room. Every square inch of the table was covered with food piled high on platters. Several tables had been joined together, and the seating stretched out into the hallway. There must have been seating for thirty to forty people. Oddly we were the only ones there. I asked Uncle Jack, "Where is everybody? Is this the right night?"

"They're on Jewish time," Uncle Jack announced, as though it were Daylight Saving Time or a newfound Greenwich Mean Time. Finally a half an hour later, the doorbell rang and Uncle Jack said, laughing, "Ah they're early," and trotted upstairs, leaving Michael with his nuclear family.

Michael's father grasped his son, throwing his arms around him. "I'm so glad to see you, *synu*," he said, hugging him as though they were two men who had found one another after the siege of Leningrad.

Michael's mother, who had remained on the plush chair, squinted my way and asked, "Who is *that*?" She took her husband's glasses off his face to further assess me. When she put those huge glasses on her delicate face, she looked like a giant grasshopper.

"It's Cathy, obviously," Alina said.

Michael's mother didn't say anything when I came into focus but looked as though she'd seen a *dybbuk* and Satan rolled into one blond *goy*.

"Mom," Alina said, "why don't you get your own glasses instead of using Dad's?"

She shook her head. "What? I need glasses? Believe me, I see too much already."

Alina let out a long breath as though there was no point in saying any more about the glasses. Then she leaned over, placing both hands on the arms of her mother's chair, and looked straight into her eyes. Just like Michael, Alina had a vein in her forehead that pulsated when she got angry. She hissed in her mother's face, "Do not utter one word about finding a man for me." She leaned forward and spat, "*Un-der-stand?*"

I was shocked that a daughter would speak to her mother with such ire. Michael's father, who had returned to reading his paper, didn't look up, even as the mother grabbed her chest and said as though wounded, "Listen to how your daughter speaks to her mother. What? I *need* to ask relatives for a man for my daughter?"

Michael, sitting in a chair across from his parents, interrupted her and said in a tone I had never heard from him before, "*Enough already . . . Just don't do it.*" Everyone was silent. His voice dropped an angry octave and I was as shocked by his tone as I was by Linda Blair's voice change in *The Exorcist*. His ire terrified me — my parents had never expressed a harsh word to me or to each other. If I had spoken to my mother that way, she would have been crushed and gone home immediately, and my father would have been furious with me or anyone who dared to speak rudely to her.

Michael's father said to his wife over the newspaper, "Do you hear Mike?"

His mother theatrically grabbed my hand with both of hers, saying in a stage whisper, "You want someday to marry a man who speaks to his mother in such a way? You'll be next, believe me."

I kept looking over at Michael for clues — anything that would give me a context for this behaviour. He never acknowledged one thing his mother said, but, to my amazement, she continued undaunted. The doorbell rang, thank God, and within a few minutes an agitated older European man entered, wearing a large black coat and old-fashioned boots with metal buckles that crawled up them like ladders. He was panting from either exertion or anxiety. "I can't find my wife," he said, gesticulating wildly. "She was supposed to pick me up at the bus stop on my way home from work. She never showed. A wife of forty years and she's missing. With my luck, she had an accident."

Uncle Jack patted him on the back and said, "Come in, Leo. With *your* luck, you'll find her."

Uncle Leo tried to tell everyone who would listen how worried he was, but no one even answered him, except for Aunt Clara, who came out the kitchen, yelling at Uncle Jack, "You had one job, *one job* — get the boots!" Then she turned to Leo, saying, "You have to drag in salt to ruin my floors? What kind of *schlepper* stomps in wearing dripping boots? Both of you mop this up with paper towels."

Eventually, other families with scads of children dressed up in little suits and party dresses arrived and everyone kissed and hugged everyone else. I don't mean little kisses; I am talking about bear hugs with screamed greetings. It looked like those extended families at the airport, except these people had all seen each other the night before because this was the *second* night of Passover. No one kissed in *my* house unless it was to kiss someone goodbye after extreme unction — the ultimate kiss off. Uncle Jack introduced me as "the perfect sample size" to his sons-in-law who shared the *schmatte* business with him.

Finally Uncle Max arrived. He was the uncle who Clara said thought he was a "big *macher*": "He thinks he made it rich with his stretch limo company." Everyone said he was crazy twenty years ago, but he *knew* that people wanted stretch limos for proms and birthday parties. Clara pulled back the curtain an inch and peered out the front window. When he got out of the limo, she bellowed, "To your seats and pretend we're saying the prayers and eating." Everyone ran to their chairs and crumpled matzo on their plates. She said, "Why should Mr. Big Shot think we waited for him? Close the curtains. He wants to make a grand entrance. Of course he has a limo — it's his *business*."

He came in and said, "You couldn't wait?"

Aunt Clara said, "What, you're the *rabbi*?"

Uncle Jack said in a conciliatory tone, "Who's eaten? Who's eaten?" and Uncle Max condescended to stay after pointing out that he had helped everyone in the room get a job. "When you're hungry — how soon you forget."

"Who is *that*?" he asked, pointing to me as though I were a wolf in a chicken coop.

"That is Cathy. You didn't get her a job so she ate," Aunt Clara said, laughing. She covered my hand and whispered into my ear, "So *prust*. In-law by marriage. What can you do?"

To him she said, "Have some *maror* on *matzo*, Mr. Big Macher."

We'd arrived at the religious portion of the festivities. I felt more comfortable with this because at *least* I knew how to be devout and religious. I'd spent my whole childhood in Catholic school and I also knew the Old Testament. The Haggadahs, paperback prayer books, were passed out and to my shock, the swarms of kids said to each other, "Read fast, skip lines. *Zeida* Jack won't notice. Just keep up the rhythm."

One teenager said, "*Zeida* Jack, it's the Stanley Cup playoffs. God heard all these prayers for hundreds of years already." Other males at the table made loud affirmative noises.

Jack implored, "People, people, it's *once* a year." Aunt Clara called Uncle Jack "Sholem Aleichem" and told him to hurry it up. There was an uncle next to me named Ira who lowered his head toward his book and was praying. As he moved his head up and down to his book, I admired how he could *daven* in all of this chaos.

Aunt Clara tore over to his chair and said to this devotee, "Every year we tell you," and she grabbed the book. When she opened it, there, in the hollowed out centre, in this pre-Walkman era, lay a transistor radio no bigger than a playing card and the Stanley Cup played on.

Uncle Jack said, "Okay, okay let's have Uncle Isaac do the *bracha*." Uncle Isaac was blind and had been since the war. I never asked what happened to him. He had a white cane but was mostly led around by his rotund wife. Her feet were folded into her tiny high heels and large chunks of flesh gushed over the sides of her pumps as she lumbered to her chair. (She was the only one who didn't have to wear paper slippers for, as people said, "She has her own burdens.") She sat her blind husband down and hit his hand when he reached for the kosher wine that tasted as though it could put a diabetic into insulin shock.

One of the nephews said, "Do the blessing, Uncle Isaac." At this point, he leaned over the table, took a piece of *matzo* and ran his fingers over the top of its rough edges, pretending to read Braille. Then he asked, "Why is this night different from all other nights?" He smiled as though he were still reading the *matzo* with his finger. "Tonight is different because your Aunt Clara is going to let us watch the Stanley Cup playoffs." All the nephews laughed wholeheartedly at what was obviously the annual blind Passover joke.

After a long Passover tale with the little kids acting out *all* ten plagues, an overwhelming mountain of food was passed around and Alina leaned over and provided some advice that I have used for forty years. "Hints on Jewish dining. Rule number one: always say you're *not* hungry and only want one *kreplach* in your soup. If you ask for two, you get four. Rule number two: go heavy on the appetizers and desserts. The main course is seven meats cooked at 500 degrees for eight hours — skip it."

When it was time to eat, Uncle Jack gave a toast to "next year in Jerusalem" and Michael's mother stood up and said, "What's wrong with this year? Let's hope Uncle Max can find some nice man for my daughter." As her husband glared at her, she said, "What, what? Max doesn't drive rich people around all day? He can't find one for my Alina?"

# coming ashore

*Time let me hail and climb*
*Golden in the heydays of his eyes*
— Dylan Thomas, "Fern Hill"

After four years of living with Michael, I was getting furtive

inklings that it was time to get married. I had always remembered

with trepidation what my friend Sara had said about courtship: it

is the brief time when the man pleases you, and then marriage is

the rest of your life when you please him. I figured five years was long enough to figure out if a person was the real deal or a snake charmer.

However, what eventually forced my hand in the nuptial department had nothing to do with feelings, but ambition. My professor said that I should really be in graduate school at Columbia University in New York City since there was a large history-of-science department and some world-class Freud historians as well as Darwinians. He knew people there and offered to write a referral letter for me to a few of his colleagues. I'd learned with my Oxford letter that when a heavy-hitting professor goes to bat for you, it pretty well means you're a shoo-in. What could be better than being in New York in your twenties doing a Ph.D.? I remembered with awe the colossal New York Public Library I'd gone to with Laurie so many years previous. My mother would be thrilled for me, as she had loved New York as a young woman.

I had one problem — Michael. He was in medical school in Toronto and could not transfer to another country for licensing and financial reasons. I had to make some decisions. I was willing to stay in Toronto for him because, although New York loomed large, I was at a stage when I knew that loving and being loved was more important than all other accomplishments. I just had to make sure Michael was on the same page.

I told him I was willing to stay in Toronto, and give up a great opportunity to work with a famous psychologist, but I wanted to know that I had placed my eggs in the right basket. If he didn't want to marry after five years of living together, it was time for me to move on. Lots of women give up all kinds of career options for love, but I wasn't the type to do it with no tangible assurances. Love is one thing, the real world another.

Michael gave all the reasons men give for not marrying: "What's the point?" "Aren't we happy now?" "Why do we need society's approval?" I wasn't buying it. I told him to let me know in a week or I'd apply to Columbia. It was a big deal to apply to an American university. The application itself cost more than one month of my living expenses. Many American grad schools wanted you to write essays about your life experiences and take all kinds of costly achievement tests. The whole application was as much work as at least one course. Plus, my professor had to write to his colleague. You can ask for that kind of favour from a professor only once. After all it was work for him as well as me. I had to proceed with caution. I told Michael to think carefully, as it was a big decision.

The Day of Judgment was upon us. It was a Sunday evening and we were eating *aloo gobi* at the Rajput Restaurant. I can still smell the curry in the air and see the scene as though I had a camera in my frontal lobe. I was sitting in a booth opposite Michael and wearing a black turtleneck, jeans and Clarks Wallabees. Michael had not said a word about my proposal or even acted as though he'd been preoccupied with any decision-making during the week. I'd hoped he would bring it up at some point. This whole "engagement" was not turning out to be the stuff dreams are made of. I was not expecting roses and a man on his knees begging, but I had not expected to be on my knees either.

Finally while sipping my chai, I said, "Well, the week is up and I guess you have thought of the" — I held up my fingers to make a quotation signs — "'marriage question.'"

His face clouded. He exhaled loudly and looked pained. He was never unkind or said mean things in a fit of temper. Even with his mother, he tried his hardest not to blow up, and believe me, Job could not have passed that test. I had seen him angry about twice and then he just rationally expressed his position. He hated hurting people's feelings. I could tell by his face that this wasn't going well. Finally, he swallowed, his Adam's apple climbing his neck, and said, "The only way we can work this through is by being painfully honest, no matter how brutal." Whenever anyone prefaces a statement with having to tell the *unvarnished truth*, you know that the guillotine is about to shear off your head and it isn't going to be a clean cut. Finally, the blunt blade fell with him saying, "Honestly, I feel railroaded."

The first thing I felt was fear, then profound disappointment. Since those two emotions were too unbearable, I let anger swirl into my brain like dry ice, and it forced the other feelings out of my mind. I sat there for a full minute with my heart racing. I got hot and my neck began to itch under my turtleneck. I wrapped both of my hands around my warm teacup so they wouldn't shake. Eventually I said, "Let me get this straight. After *five* years of living together, you feel railroaded?" I thought a note of clarification was in order.

"I am just trying to express how I feel. I am not guaranteeing it will be rational. One should marry when one wants to."

"Let's cut to the chase and minimize the psychobabble," I replied. "Most men don't want to marry. They do it because they have to for sex or pressure from the little wife to be. Sexual liberation did away with the first, and we are left with the latter," I used the most business-like tone a spurned lover could manage.

With a set jaw, he looked right into my eyes and said, "Okay, then the answer is no."

I was shaken. Involuntary voices entered my brain. The first was Michael's cousin's vile wife who'd come from Israel the previous year and told me in her thick Israeli accent that no one in Michael's family in Europe or in North America had ever married a *shiksa* and no one ever would. Her summary was "No Jewish girl would ever live with him without being married, so he is living with you and when it is time to marry you'll be," and then she motioned to the alley off the kitchen, "tossed in that alley with the other *curvehs*." I responded by throwing her suitcase off the balcony into the lane and told her if she wanted it she'd have to scrounge for it with the other alley cats.

A cacophony of derision thundered through my brain — all the warnings those women of my mother's generation had given me. Aunt Clara's voice led the brigade with "So you are *living* with Mike in the same house? *What?* You think men buy the eggs when they can get the hen for free?"

Wow, had I screwed up *yet again*? Why is it that people who fantasize that they are in the avant-garde are really the last to know what every schmo on the street knows? I was rocked and held on to the table for dear life. I figured that it was best to simply smile and move on. I am the queen of bravado so I simply broke into an off-key rendition of "New York, New York."

---

I had no time to mourn my thwarted proposal. I worked feverishly on the Columbia application since I only had one week to send it in, plus the application was expensive and I didn't want to blow it. I had to get all kinds of legal documents, transcripts and certified cheques plus write an "intellectual autobiography from 500 to 700 words." I also had to write in what ways I was unique — that part was a breeze.

I couldn't move out that night or anything that satisfyingly dramatic. Melodrama like that is only for the rich. We shared the cheap rent and I couldn't afford to live alone. I would have to wait until I got in Columbia and then move to New York with whatever money they gave me. We solved the problem by not mentioning it again. We were both too busy with labs, work and studying to sit around crying in our soup. Fortunately civilization offered superficial politeness to hide a broken heart.

My application was due on April 1, so three hours before the deadline, I had to ride my bike at breakneck speed to the one all-night post office in order to get a March 31 postmark. I made it with ten minutes to spare. I got back on my bike and leisurely rode home. I remember thinking on that cold night that the die had been cast and a new chapter of my life was about to begin. I tried to ignore the tears that were falling down my cheeks, chaffing my skin and running into my wool jacket collar.

As I climbed up the apartment stairs at about one in the morning, Michael was sitting at the kitchen table, studying *Gray's Anatomy*. He had his cadaver skull out of his carrying case. He often brought home a skull or some human bone in a square wooden box in order to study it. The skull was shellacked and smelled like a gravedigger had just unearthed it. It had a round trap door on the cranium with rusted latches so you could flip it open and see its brainless interior. He was looking inside the skull and feeling for certain bumps. Never one to lose graciously, I said, "Well, Hamlet, enjoy your skull, because that's all you'll have come September 1."

"You mailed it?" He looked simultaneously surprised and disgusted, as though someone had just hit him in the face with a rotting fish from Lake Ontario. I found his response perplexing. What did he think I had been frantically doing over the last week? He'd even helped with the autobiography. "I can't believe this," he said. He honestly did look pale and taken aback. He knew if I mailed it I was serious and the money was gone.

There was no point in saying any more. It's bad enough we had to have the *aloo gobi* showdown. I was going to New York. He had his chance and he'd declined. By this point in our relationship, I'd come to realize he was from a family that chronically complained but never did anything to alter their lives. Perhaps he'd had no idea that I was not bluffing or just whining. Did he think I was going to perpetually moan and act wounded but stay by his side on *his* terms? That would be the definition of neurotic dependence.

He closed the lid of his skull and gently placed it back in its wooden box. He flopped back into the kitchen chair and stuck out his long legs, flung his palms in the air and said, "All right already, so when are we getting married?"

By this time I was sick of the whole thing. Who wants to marry someone when they feel backed into a corner? I thought about it for about thirty seconds.

"This week."

"Tell me we are not having some kind of a formal wedding?" he said.

"No. Your mother doesn't even like me. She will sit *shiva* and my mother is not the type to get into wedding planning; besides she is dying of leukemia. Let's just go to city hall and call it a wrap."

"Will you regret not having a wedding do?" he asked.

"No. Will you?"

"*God no*," he said. "Are you *ever* even once going to say that if it weren't for me, you could have gone to Columbia and lived in New York?"

"Nope. Never." The real reason I never mentioned it again was not emotional restraint, but because I wasn't accepted. Several weeks after our marriage, I received the rejection letter saying the professor was on sabbatical and I should reapply in a year. When I read it aloud to Michael, he hit himself in the head and wailed, "I can't believe I married you for nothing!"

—

Our parents had more in common than I thought. When I told my mother I was getting married, she said, "Oh how nice — to whom?" Michael's parents said the same thing. Did they think we were living together, but hiding our true loved ones in the basement? Since neither of them seemed to care in the least, I was freed up to plan whatever I wanted — which wasn't much.

Michael was in his internship year and had to be in the hospital all day, so I had to get things organized for the wedding. I had the blood test at city hall and then crossed the street to Eaton's department store to get the rings. I bought both of them and then the sales lady said they are always engraved with a statement. When I asked what kind of statement, she said one of "enduring love." I had Michael paged at the hospital. He said he was in the middle of a procedure and I could inscribe whatever I wanted, and then he had to hang up. I chose *love, forever, Michael* for mine, and soon after we got married at a crowded city hall. We had no money for a honeymoon and no time off so we went back to school the next day.

—

A week after we were married, there was a long weekend so we tacked on a day or two and went to Ithaca to visit Michael's friends at Cornell. They lived in a huge old American colonial clapboard home, near the top of a steep hill. The house was like the white colonial I'd grown up in. Ithaca resembled my hometown of Lewiston, a small sleepy New York town in the snowbelt. We arrived late and in a snowstorm — the windshield wipers actually got stuck in the wet snow on the centre of the windshield. The snowflakes were so enormous I swear I saw Queen Anne's lace in their structure as they fell.

Since everyone was asleep when we arrived, we made ourselves hot chocolate, which was all we could find. Smelling my cup of cocoa made me feel like I did as a kid when the hot drink warmed me up after playing in the snow. I remembered those early mornings at the drugstore when my hands were so frozen from selling newspapers at dawn that I could hardly grip the cup of hot chocolate with mini marshmallows that Roy would always have picked up for me on his way into work. The storm had added five hours to an already long trip, so we flopped into bed.

We had both loved *The George Burns and Gracie Allen Show* when we were younger and we often quoted gags from it. Our relationship somewhat resembled George and Gracie's: Michael played George, the put-upon male, while I was the outrageous and often silly Gracie. When we crawled into bed that night, Michael mimicked George Burns, shaking the ashes off his pretend cigar and saying, "Say goodnight, Mrs. Gildiner."

In Gracie's ditzy voice I responded, "Goodnight, Mrs. Gildiner." It was at that moment that I realized that I really *was* married. I actually heard my new name for the first time. I was no longer Cathy McClure. I was starting a life with no tracks, no paths, nothing to tell me what to do. That didn't worry me. I was always good at blazing a new trail. Besides security was mostly a myth. My future didn't feel empty or frightening; it felt pristine, like skiing on new powder.

That night I had a dream that was basically a rehash of a memory from 1960. I was twelve years old and standing right against the fence of the Horseshoe Falls. It was hot and the mist was cooling my face as I sucked on an orange Popsicle. Out of the corner of my eye, I saw a young boy go over the Falls. We spectators on shore all watched helplessly as his orange lifejacket bobbed in the whirlpool at the bottom. The *Maid of the Mist* tourist boat sped over to him and threw him a life preserver. Several times he missed it as the current spun him away. Finally, just as he was going under, he reached out as far as could and grabbed the ring and was hauled in. We all watched with relief as the blue-eyed blond seven-year-old came ashore bruised, but alive.

Everything until this point had been true to life, but in the dream, Roy, who in reality had departed years earlier, stood next to me at the fence, just inches from the Falls. He put his arm around me and leaned down and said to me over the roar of the Falls, "That youngster musta knowed he was too close to the Falls and jumped ship just in time. He beat the odds in comin' ashore alive and in one piece."

The next morning when we woke up it was freezing, since our second-floor guest room was in reality an uninsulated glassed-in sun porch. From our bed, we could see out the window, and we looked down the hill to a town blanketed by well over two feet of sparkling snow. The snow buried all landmarks like streets, signs and sidewalks; even the telephone line sagged under the weight of several feet of snow. There were no car tracks. Not even pedestrians had wandered out. The blue sky blazed in the pure sunshine, and it was so quiet that, as Roy used to say, "you could hear a mouse piss on cotton."

The moment was right out of my childhood. I loved the days when the world stopped for heavy snowfalls and here I was back in New York State in another immobilizing snowstorm — the kind that knocked you out of your regular life and closed the schools. The combination of the perfect childhood memory and the perfect adult moment next to the man I loved gave me the first instant in my life that I was *sure* I would always remember.

That day I did something I had never done before: I lived in the moment. I savoured Michael's long arms around me, the warmth of his body next to mine as we both looked at a red cardinal on a snow-covered fence. I didn't speak, but I knew that it was the most cherished moment of my life — and it has remained so.

It was the first time in my life that I knew what contentment meant. I had no desire to move on or plan the future. I realized that I had come full circle. One of the conundrums of life is that it takes so long to figure out what it is *supposed* to be about. I thought the goal was getting as far away from my childhood as possible, seeing the world and finding the right career. I had done all of these things. They were all great adventures, but they didn't add up to what life was about.

As I lay there, I realized what I had been looking for. Really, the first experience of childhood love is what we look for until we have replicated it as adults. I thought of the cold days when Roy, my dad and I worked in the store, all doing our jobs with quiet affection for one another. We marched through the snow, united and undaunted. It was our faith in each other that got those deliveries out on time, even in six-foot snowdrifts.

I thought of my mother, so much like Michael, who loved to talk about ideas and share information no matter how esoteric. That was our bond. My father's unfailing kindness and generosity were also reflected in Michael. I was able to resuscitate the deeply buried joy of unconditional love. Once I'd found that dormant inchoate feeling, the search was over.

Roy used to say when we were planning deliveries that you had to plan for the round trip. Never get so far out on the road that you can't find your way home, and plan deliveries on the way out and on the way back. He was right. It was far easier to get out than it was to get home. Finally I'd gotten there.

## ACKNOWLEDGEMENTS

I would like to thank my first readers, Jon Redfern, Janet Somerville and Linda Kahn. They have an unerring nose and hopefully have saved you from a snorefest of four hundred pages.

My thanks to my husband's extended family, notably the three Hilf sisters and their families, for allowing me to write my impression of my first Passover over forty years ago. It takes a secure and generous group to say whatever was my reality at the time is fine with them. I don't know if I could have done the same thing. I perceived them as so different from me almost half a century ago, but now I see them as the siblings I never had.

My admiration goes out to Alina and Karol Gildiner for letting me use their family in my memoires. Alina, special thanks for letting me describe your teenage years. I would also like to pay a tribute to my recently deceased father-in-law, Chaim Gildiner, who helped me with some of the details of the book, and who was the most admirable man I have ever met.

Speaking of admirable men, I want to thank Michael Gildiner, my husband of forty years, for allowing me to interpret his past, his family, our meeting and engagement (using the term loosely) and marriage. What was surprising to me was how similar our memories were given that it was so long ago. However, I've decided not to push my luck, so relax, big guy, this is the last volume.

I would be remiss if I didn't acknowledge David, Sam and James, the progeny of the McClure-Gildiner union. Boys, you were always encouraging, and Sam, thanks for telling me to just "let it rip."

I would also like to thank Jack David, my publisher at ECW

Press, who has always been there for me since I published my first book, *Too Close to the Falls*, in 1999. He picked me out of the slush pile and will forever be my friend. Jen Knoch did a meticulous editing job in record time and smoothed my historical timeline with a hot iron. Tania Craan has done all three of my memoir covers and interior designs. She has done a remarkable job making all three covers relate to one another, yet each is so evocative of its own era. Thank you to Rachel Ironstone for the typesetting, Crissy Calhoun for the proofread, and publicist Sarah Dunn for spreading the word.

# Get the eBook FREE!